# Britain's International Development Policies

# Britain's International Development Policies

## A History of DFID and Overseas Aid

Barrie Ireton
*Senior Fellow, Commonwealth Studies Institute, UK*

First published 2013 by
PALGRAVE MACMILLAN

Palgrave Macmillan in the UK is an imprint of Macmillan Publishers Limited, registered in England, company number 785998, of Houndmills, Basingstoke, Hampshire RG21 6XS.

Palgrave Macmillan in the US is a division of St Martin's Press LLC, 175 Fifth Avenue, New York, NY 10010.

Palgrave Macmillan is the global academic imprint of the above companies and has companies and representatives throughout the world.

Palgrave® and Macmillan® are registered trademarks in the United States, the United Kingdom, Europe and other countries.

ISBN 978–1–137–27232–4

This book is printed on paper suitable for recycling and made from fully managed and sustained forest sources. Logging, pulping and manufacturing processes are expected to conform to the environmental regulations of the country of origin.

A catalogue record for this book is available from the British Library.

A catalog record for this book is available from the Library of Congress.

Typeset by MPS Limited, Chennai, India.

# Contents

# Preface and Acknowledgements

I retired as Director General at Britain's Department for International Development in 2003 but continued to work for it for a further year or so. The idea for the book came from Suma Chakrabarti, then Permanent Secretary, who suggested that I write a history of the Department since its creation in 1964. Partly because of other distractions, it has taken me longer to complete than I had envisaged.

The advantage of my writing this history is that I served in the Department for over thirty years in a variety of capacities with therefore a long, if imperfect, memory. I also knew what archival material to look for, though the Department's archives are both poor and difficult to access.

The main disadvantage in my undertaking this project is that I was paid by the Department in part or in whole since I left Cambridge for Africa in 1965. For some, that will make me partisan and a less than impartial observer of what has happened in the last forty-plus years.

In writing the book I have tried to distinguish between my memory and interpretation of events, and archival and published material listed in the endnotes. It has not been easy to bring out the difference of views within the Department at any one time: it certainly did not consist of a homogeneous group of people, given their different backgrounds and experience. But that, I believe, has been one of its strengths over the years. However, what mattered at the end of the day were the policies agreed by successive Ministers.

I would like to record my thanks to my ex-colleagues, including Ministers, for taking time to talk to me, and to my family for their patience. Finally, I wish to thank Adrienne Lee who, as my Personal Assistant, has helped in my research and who has typed and edited the manuscript. Without her I could not have done it.

# Tables and Figure

## Tables

## Figure

# 1
# Introduction

The Ministry of Overseas Development was created by the late Harold Wilson when he became Prime Minister in 1964. Until 1997 it was either a separate Ministry for Overseas Development (ODM) under Labour governments (1964–70 and 1974–79) or a distinct part of the Foreign and Commonwealth Office under Conservative governments but with its own Minister and Permanent Secretary, known as the Overseas Development Administration (ODA) (1970–74 and 1979–97). In 1997 the Labour government again created a separate ministry called the Department for International Development (DFID) and this has continued under the current Conservative/Lib Dem Coalition government. In what follows the author will refer simply to each of them as 'the Department' to cover the period from 1964 to the present time.

In order to set the work of the Department in its historical context, the next two chapters pre-date the work of the Department. Chapter Two provides a brief account of the British government's policies towards, and official development assistance to, its colonies. Chapter Three seeks to explore both the changing international context after the Second World War and how the government responded to it in terms of aid policy, and the machinery of government changes that led up to the creation of the Department.

In subsequent chapters, the history of the Department from 1964 has not been recounted in chronological terms but rather by particular themes. Thus, Chapter Four focuses on the stated mission of the Department, arguing that, not withstanding some important deviations, most notably in the 1980s, the underlying mission throughout has been, to a greater extent than often suggested by some external observers, the reduction of poverty in the poorest countries.

A more contemporary account of the work of the Department might have combined Chapter Five (Development Policy) and Chapter Six (Humanitarian Aid), but the author decided to keep them separate. Chapter Five also provides an account of the Department's role in debt relief and, in recent years, its role in wider development issues beyond aid, such as trade and the global environment.

Chapter Seven seeks to analyse the rationale behind the choices made between the various forms of aid, and setting them in an historical context. This leads on to an account of the main bodies for which the Department has had full or partial responsibility for. It explains why the Department shed its responsibilities for these bodies in the 1990s, with the exception of CDC PLC's investment portfolio (Chapter Eight).

The commercial motives for aid have aroused considerable passion and controversy on both sides of the aid debate over the years, and particularly the Aid and Trade Provision scheme, designed to subsidise the financing terms for British exports in the context of the international credit race to subsidise export finance to developing countries. These issues are explored in Chapter Nine.

For many the touchstone of the government's commitment to international development is the volume of aid it has been prepared to provide, particularly against the UN aid target of 0.7 per cent of Gross National Income (GNI) established in the 1960s. Although at the time it was held to be some reflection of the needs of developing countries, today it is essentially a burden-sharing issue for donors and a stick for developing countries to beat them with. Britain's performance against the UN aid target is explored in some detail in Chapter Ten in a wider international context. It also tries to explain the intricacies of defining official development assistance internationally and how it has changed over time. Official assistance counts towards the UN aid target if it is sufficiently concessional and is for the purposes of development of the recipient country.

Chapter Eleven seeks to explain the changes in the way the Department managed itself, both in response to wider civil service reform and the challenges it faced in responding to a changing development agenda and aid programme management.

Chapter Twelve offers some insights into the way the Department's impact on development might be judged, though it does not offer a detailed definitive judgement on the impact of Britain's aid programmes over nearly half a century, which it is better for others to assess and in greater depth. I have left to this chapter a brief comment on the public debate on aid, which has not materially changed over recent decades, but which in recent years has had a growing significance.

I have tried to keep the book up to date during its gestation. It reflects the changing political and economic relationships between the West and the emerging BRIC countries (Brazil, Russia, India and China) and importantly what is likely to be the impact of the recent financial crisis and the fiscal deficits and debt problems of donor countries and their dialogue with developing countries on macro-economic management issues. In particular it reflects the 2010 General Election manifestos regarding aid and the Coalition government aid policies and, importantly, public presentation in the context of its re-affirmation of achieving the UN aid target of 0.7 per cent of Gross National Income (GNI) by 2013, despite the substantial reductions in other areas of public spending over the period of the present government.

I have written this book mainly for those academics and students, and professional development practitioners, interested in contemporary political history and international development and aid, in particular Britain's official contribution towards the latter. However, I hope it is also written in a way that would make it of interest to the more general reader concerned with international development and aid issues, both in Britain and abroad.

# 2
# Britain's Colonial Development Effort

## Introduction

This chapter seeks to provide a brief account of Britain's development policies and assistance in relation to its colonies. It is not intended to be an authoritative and detailed account of colonial development. Nor does it seek to assess the impact of colonialism more generally on the future development of the countries concerned. For these purposes, and also for Chapter Three, I have drawn on the substantial resource material available from official records and other works, including the five-volume study of the period 1921–65 by D. J. Morgan which was commissioned under the Peacetime Series of Official Histories initiated by Prime Minister Harold Wilson in 1969.[1]

The so-called White Commonwealth (Australia, New Zealand and Canada) became independent between 1867 and 1901 and together with the Union of South Africa (1931) became Dominions within the British Empire. On partition, India and Pakistan became independent members of the Commonwealth in 1947. Ghana and Malaysia became independent in 1957.

When Harold Macmillan visited Africa in 1960 he made his memorable 'Wind of Change' speech to the South African Parliament in which he said 'the wind of change is blowing through this continent and whether we like it or not this growth of national consciousness is a political fact. We must all accept it as a fact and our national policies must take account of it'.[2] Much of Africa became independent in the early 1960s – for example, Nigeria (1960), Kenya (1963), Tanzania (1964), (Tanganyika and Zanzibar, having already become independent separately, formed a Union in 1964) and Zambia (1964). Southern Rhodesia (now Zimbabwe) made a unilateral declaration of independence in 1965 under white minority rule until formal independence in 1980.

Apart from Southern Rhodesia, over which it had no control, by the end of the 1960s Britain was left with only a small number of colonies. They consisted of Hong Kong, Gibraltar and the Falkland Islands which did not wish to become independent because of their regional political situations. Hong Kong was returned to China under the terms of the 99-year lease in 1997. There were otherwise a number of small territories in the Indian Ocean, the Atlantic and the Pacific and Caribbean. By 1970 it was the clearly stated policy of the British government that any remaining territory wishing to become independent should be allowed to do so, but any who wished to remain what were then still termed Dependent Territories could do so. In the event the Seychelles in the Indian Ocean, the Solomon Islands, the Gilbert and Ellice Islands (now Kirabati and Tuvalu respectively) and the New Hebrides (now Vanuatu) – a condominium jointly administered by Britain and France – in the Pacific, opted for independence in the early 1970s. Thus, Britain entered the 21st century with the following overseas territories, as they are now known: Gibraltar in Europe; Anguilla, British Virgin Islands, Cayman Islands, Montserrat and Turks and Caicos Islands in the Caribbean; Bermuda, the Falkland Islands, St Helena and Tristan da Cunha in the Atlantic; and Pitcairn in the Pacific. Thus, some might say, not least the UN Committee on Decolonisation, Britain's colonial period has yet to come finally to an end.

By the 19th century Britain had acquired an empire of almost unprecedented proportions, perhaps epitomised by Queen Victoria being crowned Empress of India in 1876. The end of empire could be said to have occurred effectively at the end of the Second World War when Britain's political and economic position in the world was greatly diminished. If not then, the Suez Crisis of 1956 demonstrated that Britain could no longer act independently of the United States.[3] The Falklands War of 1982 showed a determination to defend the interests of one of its colonial peoples but that cannot be said to be part of Empire.[4]

Against this background the chapter sets out Britain's efforts to help develop its colonies in the period from the end of the First World War to 1964, when the Department was established. There were two fundamental policies adopted by Britain in the 19th century that impacted on its colonies. The first was a belief in international free trade which can be traced back to the repeal of the Corn Laws in 1846. It lasted while Britain was the dominant industrial power and until it faced serious competitors who were seen as fostering their industries by domestic market protection. The Great Depression of the 1930s finally brought this era to an end, though the Ottawa Imperial Economic Conference of 1932 re-affirmed a policy of imperial preference. The second important policy framework for the colonies was that set down by Prime Minister Gladstone in the 1860s, namely that colonial governments should so far as possible be financially self-supporting. They should each be able to finance their recurrent expenditures and their capital investments either by a local recurrent revenue surplus or by way of domestic or overseas loan finance from the market which they would be expected to service out of future revenues.

## Development assistance

For the purposes of this chapter we distinguish between three broad categories of colonies which Britain recognised for the purpose of deciding whether or not to provide development assistance, as the Gladstonian principle of financial self-sufficiency gave way over time to the political and economic realities of the 20th century.

Certain colonies, because of their economic condition, required some measure of assistance (grants-in-aid) to balance their recurrent budgets in order to provide a minimum level of public administration and phys-ical and social infrastructure. Those that were either in active receipt of grants-in-aid or were thought to be in 'danger' of requiring such help were known as Treasury-controlled colonies. This meant that the British government retained a much closer oversight of their budgets both to justify the level of grants-in-aid which were already being voted annually by Parliament under the Colonial and Middle Eastern Vote, and to avoid other territories pursuing policies that might result in them needing this form of assistance in the future.

At the other end of the spectrum were colonies that already had what was termed responsible government (that is, a measure of self-government) such that Britain did not then think it appropriate to provide development assistance. This excluded from such assis-tance most notably the Indian sub-continent. The irony of the term 'responsible government' will not be lost on today's reader familiar with debates about aid and responsible economic management and good governance. *A fortiori*, Britain did not expect, at that stage, to provide development assistance to countries after they became independent.

The third category comprised the remaining colonies not in receipt of grants-in-aid and still having constitutional arrangements which gave the Colonial Office, not full control over their policies and budgets, but a substantial measure of influence over their affairs.

Following the First World War Britain experienced a substantial and persistent level of unemployment. It was reasoned that if the colonies were to undertake additional capital projects requiring imports from Britain the unemployment situation at home would be ameliorated. Thus the Trade Facilities Act of 1924 contained provision for the Colonial Secretary to support loans through interest subsidies for agreed investments taken out by the territories for which he was responsible; £2 million over five years was envisaged for projects in the field of public utilities. There were two conditions: first, the projects should be those which would have been implemented anyway at a later date but which could now, with support, be brought forward; and, second, that they should promote employment in Britain. Its take-up, however, was limited because of the terms of the assistance and the two conditions imposed. The Palestine and East Africa Loans Act of 1926 provided up to £10 million to guarantee loans to the colonies. Again the take-up was limited partly because law officers concluded that loans under this scheme could not also benefit from interest subsidies under the earlier Act.

With the experience of the above Acts the debate continued about the economic problems of Britain and the role the colonies might play in alleviating them. There was also a growing official and political consensus that a longer-term and more systematic approach was required for the development of the colonies. On the other hand the Gladstonian principle continued to caution against actions that would result in a long-term financial commitment to improving the social welfare of the colonial peoples beyond which the colonies themselves could sustain. The grants-in-aid to the weaker colonies were now running at about £250,000 per annum and there was no enthusiasm for this help either to widen or deepen.

The 1929 Colonial Development Fund Act provided for the establishment of a Fund (the CDF) for ten years of up to £1 million per annum. It was to be used for approved capital schemes that would promote the economic development of the colonies narrowly defined (for example, it excluded support for general education). It was available to all the colonies save those already with 'responsible government'. Thus, from the outset, colonial development assistance was to focus mainly, though not entirely, upon the West Indies and Africa. In presenting the Bill to Parliament the interests of Britain in colonial development rather than the interests of the colonies themselves was again the dominant theme.

By the end of the CDF in 1940 nearly 600 separate schemes had been approved with a total value of £19.3 million and a contribution from the CDF of £8.9 million. Of the latter £5.7 million was provided in the form of grants and the balance by way of loans.

There were no formal rules for the tying of funds to British goods and services. But colonial administrations had been made aware of the link between the use of the CDF and the objective of promoting British trade and reducing unemployment. Indeed the 1931 White Paper on Public Expenditure[5] stated that wherever possible the Colonial Office should concentrate on schemes which would give 'the greatest and speediest benefit to this country'.

The 1940 Colonial Development and Welfare (CD&W) Act potentially marked a new phase in Britain's policy towards colonial development. But it came at an extremely difficult time. On the positive side the new Act allowed for a wider definition of development: the Secretary of State could finance schemes 'likely to promote the development of the resources of any colony or the welfare of its peoples'. The 1940 White Paper[6] set out the government's new approach and concluded (paragraph 6) that it was time to revise the principle 'that a colony shall have only those services which it can afford to maintain out of its own resources'. Thus funds could be provided for certain recurrent expenditures over a substantial number of years, for services such as agriculture, education, health and housing. The new Act also had a ten-year timeframe and the Treasury were still concerned to avoid a situation of perpetual financial dependency. It was envisaged that while funds would be provided for individual schemes they should be in the context of development programmes prepared for a period of years ahead. The reason for this was reflected in the guidance to colonial governments, consistent with paragraph 11 of the White Paper, that such programmes should focus on improving their economic situation so that they might increasingly finance their own social and other services.

The Colonial Office sought an annual provision of £10 million plus £0.5 million a year to be earmarked for research programmes increasingly seen as crucial to the long-term development of the colonies. With the outbreak of war a compromise was eventually agreed for up to £5 million a year for a period of ten years, including £0.5 million for research, with the prospect of a review after five years.

By the time the Bill reached Parliament circumstances could hardly have been less propitious. Although the concepts behind the Bill were largely accepted, there was criticism about its realism. Indeed one backbencher commented, when the Bill was introduced at its Second

Reading in the House of Commons, that they had listened to a pre-war Minister making a pre-war speech on a pre-war Bill.[7] In a statement to Parliament at its Second Reading in the House of Lords the Colonial Secretary acknowledged that with the intensification of the war 'much we had hoped to do under the Bill when it became law must wait for happier times'.[8] The guidance that then issued to colonial governments in late 1940 made it clear that schemes would only be considered if they were sufficiently urgent and important as to justify the use of British funds in present circumstances; if they would not detract from the war effort; and did not involve expenditure outside the sterling area.

The initial regional allocations for the financial year 1940/41 had little to do with relative poverty and population size and more to do with political considerations, including the pre-war disturbances in the Gold Coast (Ghana) and the West Indies. Thus, West Africa, East and Central Africa, and the West Indies were allocated rather more than £1 million each, and the Middle East, Pacific and Mediterranean £0.75 million. No subsequent allocations for the later war years appear to have been made. In 1940/41 actual commitments and disbursements were £41,000 and £12,000 respectively! By the end of 1943/44 cumulative actual and prospective commitments amounted to £2.75 million out of a total potential sum of £20 million.

With the prospect of the war coming to an end, discussions began about a new CD&W Act for 1945. After a good deal of haggling a total provision for the ten years, 1946/47 to 1955/56, of £120 million was agreed, subject to an annual ceiling of £17.5 million, which meant that unspent balances for any one year would not automatically be lost. The 1949 CD&W Act raised the annual maximum spend from £17.5 million to £20 million, and expenditure on research within that to £2.5 million. Given past underspends this did not require an increase in the £120 million total provided for in the 1945 Act.

In view of the larger commitments envisaged the Treasury were subsequently persuaded to accept an increase of £20 million in the total provision for the ten years to 1955/56 and an annual expenditure maximum of £25 million. This was enshrined in the 1950 CD&W Act which also dropped the provision that colonies having 'responsible government' could not receive CD&W funds, reflecting the constitutional advances taking place in a number of colonies which would otherwise become ineligible for development assistance, though by this time India, Pakistan and Sri Lanka (Ceylon) were already independent and ineligible for such assistance. Over the next fifteen years a number of further Acts were passed which provided for a continuation of

CD&W funding. The annual amounts provided for did not increase substantially and they represented for most territories only a small part of their financing needs.

Whereas CD&W funds were seen as the positive, and in a sense voluntary, aspect of Britain's assistance, grants-in-aid were often presented as undesirable necessities, to be kept to a minimum and eliminated as soon as possible. However, from small beginnings annual grants-in-aid had grown to some £0.75 million in 1940 and to some £13 million in 1960. During the Second World War years grants-in-aid exceeded CD&W expenditure, and in the early 1960s they represented about 40 per cent of all British government financial assistance to the colonies, and for those in receipt of grants-in-aid often considerably more. This arguably reflected a growing political recognition of the needs of the economically weaker colonies to provide for a minimal level of social and administrative infrastructure, which outstripped their own financial capabilities.

## The Statutory Corporations

The 1948 Overseas Resources Development Act (ORD) brought into being two statutory corporations, each with distinct and different objectives. The Overseas Food Corporation (OFC) was given the task of increasing the supply of foodstuffs to the UK market (in particular oils and fats) by the production of such commodities within the colonial empire, and potentially beyond. The Colonial Development Corporation (CDC) was given the objective of assisting the economic development of the colonies.

Given the originally stated objective of the OFC it does not need to be discussed at length here, not least because it became confined to one scheme and was wound-up after a relatively short life in 1955. The East Africa Groundnut Scheme is a cause célèbre for being, in terms of its original objective, a spectacular failure. The scheme was the brainchild of the United Africa Company (UAC) which in 1946 persuaded the British government to back its proposal to clear one million acres of bush, said to be largely unpopulated, for the production of 400,000 tons annually of decorticated groundnuts – three quarters of it in Tanganyika (Tanzania), 15 per cent in Northern Rhodesia (Zambia), and 10 per cent in Nyasaland (Malawi).

Well before the OFC was formed in early 1948 to take responsibility for the scheme things were going seriously wrong and costs were escalating: the original capital cost estimate of £8 million had tripled before the OFC took over, and a review in 1949/50 put the estimated cost of the original scheme at £48 million, £32 million of which would have been spent by the end of that financial year. The scheme was scaled down, and eventually in 1951 it was described as a scheme of large-scale experimental development to establish the economics of clearing land and of mechanised agriculture under tropical conditions. The ORD Act 1951 was passed to reflect the OFC's changed objective of developing food and non-food products in East African colonies and responsibility for which was passed to the Colonial Secretary. This second phase was relatively successful and was taken over by the Tanganyikan Agriculture Corporation in 1955. The only final, and by now obvious, point to make is that, contrary to a widely held belief, the groundnut scheme was not one of CDC's early failures, though it did colour Whitehall's attitude towards CDC's own future operations.

Under the original ORD Act the CDC was charged with 'the duty of securing the investigation, formulation and carrying out of projects for developing resources of colonial territories with a view to the expansion of production therein of food stuffs and raw materials, or for other agricultural, industrial and trade development therein'. Its initial capital was to be provided by way of Exchequer advances (that is, loans from the Treasury) at the government's gilt-edged rate, repayable over periods of up to 40 years, with a borrowing limit of £100 million, plus temporary working capital borrowing facilities of up to £10 million. The corporation had the financial objective of breaking even on its revenue (profit and loss) account 'taking one year with another'. It was allowed to operate in any colony eligible for CD&W funds, subject to the agreement of the colonial government.

The rationale for the establishment of the CDC bears some comment in order to understand the subsequent debate within government, and with the corporation, over the next half-century. There was considered to be a gap to be filled between those activities which were clearly profitable, and would be taken up by private enterprise (local or foreign), and those activities which were not expected to be profitable and were the responsibility of governments. In between there were certain commercial-like activities which, while being of value developmentally to the colony concerned, could not be expected to yield a financial return sufficient to attract private risk capital. The financial objective set for the corporation required it only to make a return equivalent to the interest rate on virtually risk-free gilts plus the overhead costs of CDC itself.

Unfortunately the corporation got off to a poor start in that a number of early investments proved ill-conceived and had to be abandoned. These early losses highlighted the issue of the capital structure for CDC which was to be the source of friction between the corporation and government over many decades. The corporation argued for an element of equity in its balance sheet if it was to undertake relatively risky commercial ventures in difficult environments and spend money on necessarily speculative investigations into potential tropical agricultural developments. It wanted to see the risk capital it invested reflected in its own capital structure. However, the Treasury saw the request for equity as a hidden subsidy, whereas it expected equity to yield a return at least as good as the gilt rate. Nor was the Treasury prepared to write off advances in respect of abandoned projects unless absolutely necessary: CDC's financial objective was for its portfolio overall, not in relation to individual investments.

In later years Treasury ministers questioned whether there really was (any longer) a gap in the market between what private enterprise would do and what governments should do: if not the corporation should be wound down and its assets realised over time. However the early chairmen had succeeded in mobilising a formidable array of support within Parliament for the work of the corporation, so that such a course of action was not thought to be politically possible. In any event it was argued that in place of old style 'gap' projects the CDC was playing an important role in encouraging direct foreign investment by their participation in joint ventures – partly by providing some 'political' comfort and local knowledge, and partly by providing equity and loan finance in excess of the financial exposure private enterprise was prepared to accept.

However, 'finance house' activities, depending upon the precise definition, in 1956/57 accounted for more than 40 per cent of its total portfolio. The central point was that contrary to the spirit of what was intended in 1948, CDC was now lending directly to colonial governments or to entities such as statutory bodies, usually with a colonial government guarantee. This was thought to be either CD&W territory or for the London capital market. The CDC view was that they wished to do more risk capital business in the private or public sector but for which they needed a change in their capital structure.

Meanwhile the corporation had served notice that it expected to run out of commitment authority within its existing long-term borrowing limit of £100 million by 1958. The Chairman asked for the limit to be doubled. The government's response was to agree an increase in the long-term borrowing limit to £150 million, of which up to £130 million could come from Exchequer Advances. These measures were given effect in the ORD Act 1958. The government had two considerations in mind in not being more accommodating. It had decided not to allow CDC to make new investments in a newly independent country on the grounds that such countries should not be a call on public funds for financial assistance. Secondly, Treasury agreement to make Exchequer loans available to the colonies under Section II of the 1959 CD&W Act was expected to reduce demand for CDC's finance house business.

In terms of total investment resources for the colonies CDC's contribution was relatively small, though it did provide more than a quarter of all Britain's official assistance. Its demonstration effect, in encouraging additional foreign direct investment, might have been greater if it had stuck to its original remit and not felt the need to become so involved in finance house business. As regards its private sector commercial investments, it is not readily known how much private investment was associated directly with CDC activity or, still less, what degree of additionality there was. After its initial losses, and together with some interest waiver, CDC did meet its financial objectives, though these were modest and unlikely to impress the private sector.

## Other sources of development finance

Another potential source of development finance was the London capital market. However, as constitutional advance progressed and the prospects for independence grew, the market's willingness to subscribe to new loan issues diminished and yields increased. This led to discussions about whether the government should itself provide loans to the colonies on quasi-market terms separate from, and in addition to, what it would otherwise be doing under existing CD&W arrangements. This was given added impetus when the then Chancellor of the Exchequer decided to announce at the 1958 Commonwealth Trade and Economic Conference that Britain would provide Commonwealth Assistance Loans under Section 3 of the Export Credit and Guarantees Act to independent members of the Commonwealth. With colonial issues on the London market amounting to only some £10 million annually, it was eventually agreed that the new CD&W Act of 1959, under a new Section 2, should provide for up to £100 million of 'Exchequer loans' over a five-year period, at an interest rate only a little above what the government itself could borrow at. The Commonwealth Development Act 1963 extended the amount of Exchequer loans to £105 million up to the end of 1964/65. The Overseas Development and Service Act 1965 further extended the total loans available up to £125 million to the end of 1967/68.

The creation of the International Bank for Reconstruction and Development (IBRD) in 1944 provided another potential source of development finance for the colonies. This required Britain to provide a loan guarantee for which it obtained general authority from Parliament with the Colonial Loans Act 1948. However, loans were denominated in dollars at an interest rate then of about 4.5 per cent. This was more expensive than the London market, at least nominally, and was therefore not seen as an attractive source of borrowing except as a last resort. One early IBRD loan to Northern Rhodesia for railway development ($14 million) was made in 1953 and another was made later in the 1950s to the Federation of Rhodesia and Nyasaland for the construction of the Kariba Hydro-Electric Scheme. In the latter case, following the break-up of the Federation and subsequently Rhodesia's Unilateral Declaration of Independence (UDI) in 1965, the British government's guarantee was called by IBRD on the Southern Rhodesian portion of the loan and became a charge on the Department's aid budget for several years.

## The Colonial Office and the Colonial Service

The Colonial Office in London was originally primarily a set of geographical departments responsible for one or more colonies. With the growing post-war international policy agenda potentially impacting on the colonies, the Colonial Office found its workload becoming more complex: it needed to represent the interest and views of the colonies both internationally and within Whitehall. This led to more functional departments. The move towards self-governance and independence added further to the volume and complexity of its work.

The Colonial Service also evolved considerably between the 1920s and the 1960s. Expatriate officers were recruited for service in individual colonies and their costs were borne fully by the colonial government concerned. In the early days the bulk of expatriate officers were administrators. As time went by and the development challenges became more demanding, the proportion of professional staff (such as agriculturalists, engineers, medical staff and teachers) increased. While members of the Colonial Service were servants of the Crown, and their conditions of employment embodied in Colonial Regulations, they were employees of, and paid by, their territorial governments.

As the pace of constitutional change gathered momentum colonial officers were asking what their position would be once Britain was no longer able to exercise effective control over their tenure and conditions of employment. The government was conscious of the need both to treat colonial officers fairly and to try to ensure continuity in public services. On the one hand it was important for the future of most territories that expatriate officers were encouraged to remain in service after self-government and in the lead up to independence, and for a period thereafter while local officers could be recruited and trained to take over and maintain as an efficient and effective level of government services as possible. On the other hand the government accepted that those expatriate officers whose careers were now being prejudiced should receive some compensation for loss of career, have their pension rights secured and, to the extent possible and for those wanting it, be found alternative employment. The more generous and available the compensation package the more likely expatriate officers would leave sooner rather than later, and before local staff were equipped to take over. Much of the problem lay not just in an accelerated 'wind of change' but rather in a sad neglect of local education.

In 1954 the government published its thoughts on the reorganisation of the Colonial Service, primarily to address these concerns in a Colonial Paper (306).[9] It asserted that upon self-government colonial officers were entitled to expect no less favourable terms of service than those on which they were already serving and, in the event of premature retirement resulting from constitutional change, they should receive compensation from the government of the territory concerned. The Colonial Paper made clear that the territory and the British government would enter into a formal agreement on these issues prior to self-government. Some felt that the 1954 Colonial Paper provided expatriate officers with more incentive to go rather than to remain in post as self-government was achieved and independence approached. Indeed, as expatriate officers took advantage of lump-sum compensation payments and left, many were being replaced with less experienced expatriate contract officers, including those financed by Britain under technical assistance arrangements.

In response to a situation where Nigeria would be independent by 1960, the territories of East and Central Africa were expected to move rapidly towards internal self-government and independence in the early 1960s, and a large number of pensionable overseas civil servants could be expected to leave, the government put forward proposals in a White Paper.[10] This was to offer to pay, under technical assistance, the cost of the inducement allowances required to encourage expatriate staff to remain in post or to be recruited on contract. The individual overseas governments would continue to pay the basic local salary and other costs. It would cover some 21,000 pensionable and contract staff already serving overseas in all territories still a colony as at 1 October 1960 (that is, including Nigeria) except for the Bahamas, Brunei, Bermuda and Hong Kong. The scheme was estimated to cost about £14 million a year. These proposals were enshrined in the Overseas Service Act, 1961. The scheme became known as the Overseas Service Aid Scheme and those employed under it became known as OSAS officers. The Act also extended the scheme to other people, as appropriate, working in such public sector bodies as universities and statutory corporations: this became known as the British Expatriate Service Scheme and those employed under it became BESS officers.

## An overview of Britain's colonial development assistance efforts

The Sinclair Report,[11] commissioned in 1958 to make recommendations on the future capital structure of CDC but largely rejected by the government, calculated that for the period 1946–55 total colonial investment was financed by CD&W funds (£155 million); CDC (£64 million); the London market (£190 million); and local revenues (£600 million). In addition, the author estimates that close to £100 million was provided by Britain as grants-in-aid. Finally, Morgan (see note 1) put a figure of £1100 million for private direct investment.

Thus, of an estimated public and private investment of some £2100 million, over this twelve-year period Britain provided official assistance of about £220 million (11 per cent); local net revenues provided £500 million (24 per cent); and private funding £1290 million (65 per cent). Of total public investment of some £1000 million, British official assistance accounted for about 18 per cent (including grants-in-aid).

As regards CD&W funds, most might start by providing an analysis of what they were spent on and what impact they had. Little if anything can be said about the latter drawing on public documents: formal ex-post evaluation of individual schemes or plans do not exist. The statistics available from the Department's 1970 publication[12] and other papers and Acts reveal the following picture.

Total CD&W expenditure (under Section 1 of the Acts) over the post-war years can be summarised as follows. Average annual expenditure was £12 million (1946/47–1955/56); £16 million (1956/57–1959/60);

£18 million (1959/60–1963/64); and £10 million (1964/65–1969/70). In the second half of the 1960s expenditure declined further as the Department took responsibility for development assistance to the remaining colonies under the aid programme more generally. Morgan (1980, Vol IV, pp. 8–11) estimated the proportion of the colonies' gross domestic product (GDP) which CD&W funds accounted for. In Africa it was seldom more than 1 per cent, except in Malawi, and was even more negligible in the case of Zambia. Only in the smaller territories of the West Indies (and Malta) was it more significant and therefore somewhat more important for their economic wellbeing.

In the period 1946–70 total expenditure amounted to £362 million, of which £21 million was in respect of research. Of the £341 million issued for all other purposes, £329 million was in the form of grants, and only £12 million as loans, mainly for industrial development. The main areas were physical infrastructure (£119 million), education (£73 million), renewable natural resources (£66 million), health (£30 million) and water and sanitation (£23 million). Under Section II of the 1959 Act (and subsequent amendments) Exchequer loans amounted to £90 million, of which £71 million went to Africa. Grants-in-aid for the weaker colonies, voted annually by Parliament, were a more important source of financial support than history has given them credit for.

All this may be very interesting but it is not the whole story. As donors are very conscious of today, what is relevant is the overall economic and social progress made by the colonies which, however, is beyond the scope of this book. As economists understand, aid is generally fungible without it being provided within an overall development framework. It is clear that, however well-directed and managed, CD&W funds were not sufficient in volume terms to make a material difference to the economic and social development of most of the colonies. Arguably, just as important a contribution to colonial development was the work of the Colonial Service on the ground and to a lesser extent the Colonial Office's influence on colonial development policies and plans, using the availability of CD&W funds to encourage development planning. The Colonial Office could not control events in the colonies, only influence them, even though the Colonial Secretary was responsible to Parliament for what actually happened.

# 3
# The Creation of the Department: From Colonial to Overseas Development

## The post-war policy transition

During the 1950s there were two related forces at work internationally which fundamentally changed Britain's thinking and policy towards poorer countries and territories beyond its shores. That part of the globe coloured red was declining rapidly and expected by the middle of the following decade to be very small indeed. At the same time there was growing international recognition that the poorer developing countries of the world needed the assistance of the richer industrial countries to achieve economic and social progress.

The Gladestonian principles of financial self-sufficiency had already been substantially modified, though the government had continued to hold the belief that by the time of political independence the colonies would also have achieved economic independence. But the tide of political change was outstripping economic progress. The expectation that on independence CD&W assistance would give way to accessing the London capital market on commercial terms was increasingly being found to be illusory. Thus some independence settlements included the provision of development assistance. However, this generally only meant continuing to provide after independence the unused amounts of already allocated CD&W funds (albeit under a different Vote) though, initially, with no commitment to doing more. Those colonies receiving grants-in-aid to cover recurrent budget deficits were expected as a matter of general government policy to be weaned off such assistance. But in many cases the pressures for better government services in advance of the economy's ability to resource them meant that such assistance grew rather than diminished, and some countries were in need of budgetary aid after independence (for example, Malawi).

The post-war era witnessed a growing consciousness of the economic and social deprivation of the mass of the people in developing countries. The motives for helping were essentially two-fold. The first was the moral imperative: many felt that those countries whose wealth enabled them to do so should provide resources to the poorer countries. Allied to this, some considered that Britain in particular should compensate its former colonies for earlier exploitation and neglect, though British governments have never accepted that view. The second was a complex set of issues around self-interests, some more enlightened than others. The large and possibly widening disparity between rich and poor could be a politically de-stabilising force in the world; in the Cold War context the West wished to have developing countries adopt a pro-Western, or at least a non-aligned, stance and not be seduced into the Soviet Union camp; economic progress in the poorer countries was mutually beneficial in economic and trade terms; and for some, development assistance was a means of promoting their own exports (*plus ça change*).

The problems facing developing countries were moving up the agenda of the United Nations. This was hardly surprising as the membership of the UN became augmented by a growing number of independent developing countries who wanted their concerns addressed. There were growing pressures for the industrialised countries to agree a target for the provision of resource flows to developing countries. Furthermore the US, which then provided some two-thirds of all resource flows to developing countries, was pressing for a more equal sharing of the burden. The Organisation for Economic Co-operation and Development (OECD) formed a Development Assistance Committee to co-ordinate and harmonise members' development assistance policies, initially established as the Development Assistance Group.

Meanwhile, in addition to bilateral assistance from donors, a multilateral aid system was being created. The IBRD (the original institution of the World Bank group) had been established in 1944. The UN established central technical assistance programmes, and created a number of Specialized Agencies such as the Food and Agriculture Organization (FAO), the UN Education, Scientific and Cultural Organization (UNESCO) and the World Health Organization (WHO). The International Labour Organization (ILO), established in 1919, also became part of the UN. The work of these bodies was financed by contributions from the member states of the UN on an assessed rather than a voluntary basis, and therefore mainly by the richer countries. The work of these Specialized Agencies was partly regulatory, world-wide, and partly consisted of promotion of economic and social development in developing countries.

Thus within two decades Britain faced a very different international situation. At the end of the 1930s it still had the largest empire the world had ever known, with the exception possibly of Persia, and accepted a special responsibility, however defined, for the people of its colonies spread around the globe. By the end of the 1950s it had lost most of its major colonies and expected to see most of the others, particularly in sub-Saharan Africa, become independent within a few years. It was becoming only one of several major rich industrial countries that were being looked to, internationally, to help sovereign developing countries achieve greater prosperity, through bilateral assistance programmes (country to country) and support for the growing multilateral aid system. The one almost constant theme was the mix of motives that prevailed: from moral duty and mutual interest, to enlightened and sometimes not so enlightened self-interest.

The Association for World Peace, a group of socialist British MPs with Harold Wilson as its Secretary, published a pamphlet in 1952.[13] It made the moral and enlightened self-interest case for reducing poverty in developing countries. An advocate of disarmament, it pointed out that fears about unemployment that this could give rise to should be allayed by re-allocating resources to promote overseas development. It disparaged the efforts of private enterprise and dismissed CD&W funds as geared to developing infrastructure for foreign private investors. It pointed to the Atlantic Charter in which President Roosevelt and Prime Minister Winston Churchill pledged freedom from hunger, and Article 55(a) of the UN Charter which declared that 'the UN shall promote . . . higher standards of living, full employment and conditions for economic and social progress and development'.

The pamphlet went on to support the findings and recommendations of a UN Experts Committee set up by a UN Resolution which had reported in 1951.[14] It estimated that to achieve a 2 per cent per capita growth rate developing countries (including the then remaining colonies) would need a total investment level of about $19 billion annually. Of this some $5 billion might come from domestic savings and about $12 billion would need to come from the industrialised countries. The then current flow of external resources to developing countries was thought to be $1–1.5 billion. Thus the industrialised countries needed to provide by way of private and official flows some 3 per cent of their GNP – for Britain the figure would be $350–400 million annually, or about 1 per cent of total public expenditure.

The UN report urged an increase in IBRD lending. But its main recommendation was the creation of a UN International Development

Authority to co-ordinate official flows and to provide substantial grant aid to developing countries which would be subscribed by the industrialised countries. These ideas were further developed in Harold Wilson's book,[15] published in August 1953, in which he argued for a World Assembly to which the international development authority would be responsible. However the UN report also emphasised the important role and policies of developing-country governments which would re-emerge as a recurring theme of development policies in later decades.

## Britain's response to a changing situation

The Commonwealth Relations Office (CRO) – prior to 1925 known as the Dominions Office – had responsibility for Britain's relations with the independent Commonwealth. This was clearly a growth industry ever since the independence of the Indian sub-continent, whereas the geographical ambit of the Colonial Office was in decline. In the context of both an increasing international debate about the problems of developing countries and the prospect of a rapidly growing independent membership of the Commonwealth among their ranks, the CRO produced a White Paper in 1957[16] about the newly independent Commonwealth and the way Britain could best help its development.

There were three main themes running through the White Paper. First, the ability of Britain 'to play an effective part in the provision of resources for development depended upon the maintenance of the strength of sterling and the successful development of the United Kingdom's own economy'.

A second key theme was the crucial role of the private sector, both local and foreign, in economic development. It argued that private capital from Britain was well adapted to direct investment in enterprises overseas and through subscribing to public loans on the London market. It went on to state: 'Foreign private investment forges the most permanent trading links and exchange of technical skills. Commonwealth countries need to adopt sound economic policies and practical measures that will attract it.'

The third important and related theme concerned the provision or otherwise of British public funds for Commonwealth development. The White Paper repeated Britain's special responsibility for the colonies, in recognition of which public funds were provided through such means as grants-in-aid, the CD&W Acts and the Colonial Development Corporation. However, this special responsibility 'ceases when they achieve independence'. Although Britain retains the 'closest interest in their well being and economic development it does not envisage government to government loans as a normal means of assisting such countries [. . .] Their interests can better be served if they build up their credit and thus make use of the facilities for raising money on the London market or elsewhere'.

The first of these three themes had the merit of being honest, and reflected the preoccupation with the balance of payments as well as the general resource costs of providing aid. The second flowed naturally from a Conservative government that was urging others to adopt the sorts of policies it was seeking to implement at home. The third, while to some extent a reflection of the other two, appears to have been a defence of the status quo rather than offering any new vision: arguably it was flying in the face of a rapidly changing political and economic reality. However, within a year (1958) the introduction of Commonwealth Assistance (CA) loans for independent Commonwealth developing countries, to be provided under Section 3 of the 1949 Export Credit and Guarantees Act, was announced. There had been no discussion of this in the White Paper or, indeed, of the increasing problems which many of the independent Commonwealth countries and the colonies were having in accessing the London market, which this measure sought to help address.

Even the rather more positive message in the White Paper concerning the provision of technical co-operation pointed out that the bulk of United Kingdom expertise was supplied through 'ordinary trading connections'. However, it cited the technical co-operation agreement with Ghana on its independence that year which provided for the training of public servants in Britain and the supply of experts to fill technical and scientific posts; it was prepared to enter into similar arrangements with other colonies as they became independent. It promised newly independent Commonwealth countries continued access to Britain's scientific bodies working on overseas issues. It also referred to the Colombo Plan, under which Britain had provided technical assistance to countries in the Colombo Plan area in Asia (Commonwealth and foreign) amounting to nearly £2 million over the five years since 1951, and its more recent pledge of £7 million over the next seven years. Perhaps as a reflection of the times, the White Paper devoted more than two pages to technical co-operation in the field of nuclear science – half the total space allocated to technical co-operation generally.

On independence the CRO took over responsibility for administering any development assistance settlement involved. By 1960 this usually included the uncommitted and unspent balances of the country's CD&W Section I allocation (such as in Nigeria in 1960) and in some cases Exchequer loans under Section II of the CD&W 1959 Act (such as in Jamaica in 1962). These were provided under a new CRO Commonwealth Grants and Loans Vote, which significantly had no statutory backing except for the annual Appropriations Act on the grounds that they did not represent a continuing new policy.

Commonwealth Assistance (CA) Loans, announced in 1958, were administered by the Export Credit & Guarantees Department though the CRO, which was, together with the Treasury, responsible for policy. The loans were provided on quasi-commercial terms only for the purchase of British goods and services, either for specific projects or general capital goods imports. Early beneficiaries of these loans included India and Pakistan which had previously not benefited from any development assistance from the British government either before or after independence. Britain pledged a total of £125 million of CA loans for India's Third Five-Year Plan (1961–65) for both projects and, exceptionally for India, general purpose imports from Britain. One of the projects Britain helped finance was the building and subsequent expansion of the Durgapur steel works, a plant which was to feature in aid discussions some thirty years later. Part of the loans for general purpose imports (£3.5 million) was earmarked for steel products for which there was surplus capacity in Britain. Pakistan received £35 million of CA loans in connection with its Second Five-Year Development Plan (1960–65). These were used for a variety of agreed projects and purposes including ships and buses, and also jute machinery under the 'surplus capacity' initiative (see below). Another major beneficiary was Nigeria, which received CA loans of £12 million on independence in 1960 to fund projects identified in its 1956–60 Development Plan.

In addition to rolling over CD&W Act funds at independence and providing CA loans, other forms of assistance were sometimes agreed as part of an independence settlement, as noted above in the case of Ghana. Examples also include Malaysia: a £2 million grant to help finance development in North Borneo and Sarawak; Tanzania: up to £4 million for its Development Plan, in addition to its unspent allocation of CD&W funds of over £5 million; and Nigeria: a grant of £5 million to build higher education institutions. These were provided from the CRO Commonwealth Grants and Loans Vote. This was separate from Britain agreeing to compensate expatriate members of Her Majesty's Overseas Civil Service for loss of career and taking over their pensions. Finally, it is worth noting that Britain provided a grant of up to £20.86 million towards the Indus Basin Development Scheme following the Indus Waters Treaty signed between India and Pakistan. The international Fund, created to finance major water and irrigation developments in Pakistan following the Treaty, and amounting to $457 million, was the first of its kind. It reflected the political and economic importance of co-operation between the two countries. Britain's contribution was authorised by Parliament under the Indus Basin Development Fund Act, 1960.

In this transition period towards overseas development and before the creation of the Department the Conservative government issued two further White Papers in 1960[17] and 1963.[18] They were the first comprehensive accounts of Britain's overseas aid policies, including assistance to non-Commonwealth developing countries and embracing both Britain's bilateral assistance and support for the multilateral aid system. The 1960 White Paper was short and largely factual; the 1963 White Paper rather longer and analytical. The essential message in these White Papers was more positive and forward-looking than that in the 1957 White Paper, though they cautioned against believing that aid would or should be the main force in raising living standards in developing countries rather than efforts of the governments and people of those countries; or that Britain could increase its aid effort without regard to the health of the British economy and other demands on public expenditure. That said, the 1963 White Paper recognised that 'over a large part of the world poverty and malnutrition still persisted; disease and illiteracy are still widespread; and the increase in population exerts a remorseless pressure on resources'. It also acknowledged that 'the difference between the standards of living in the industrialised and developing nations has not diminished – on the contrary it has increased'. It also, with much foresight, pointed out that 'although the era of aid, viewed in the perspective of history, may be a transitory one, it does not follow that it will be short, still less that its end is in sight'.

On foreign private investment the 1963 White Paper emphasised Britain's historic role in many regions of the world. It recognised, however, the tendency in recent years for the flow of capital to developing countries to level off or even decline. It supported OECD efforts to draw up a convention for the protection of foreign investors, which would help developing countries attract and retain private capital. It also supported the OECD's study of the feasibility and desirability of multilateral investment insurance – something which took more than a quarter of a century to materialise in the form of the World Bank's Multilateral Insurance and Guarantees Association (MIGA).

The 1963 White Paper provided a detailed account of Britain's aid to the colonial territories, the independent Commonwealth and to foreign (that is, non-Commonwealth) countries. As regards the last of these, it described how this began by providing aid to countries with which Britain had close historical links, such as Jordan, Libya (including budgetary aid), Nepal (both grants and loans), Sudan and Bolivia. Britain had also joined with other OECD countries to provide assistance to Turkey's Five-Year Development Plan and to provide consolidation credits (debt rescheduling) for Brazil and Argentina.

In 1962 the Chancellor of the Exchequer announced that Britain was ready to consider additional aid for the supply of British goods for which there was surplus productive capacity in Britain. Examples of this included, within the Commonwealth, India (steel products), Pakistan (jute machinery), Ghana (ships), the East Africa Common Services Organisation, which later became part of the East African Community (railway locomotives) and, outside the Commonwealth, loans to Afghanistan, Algeria, Cameroon, Senegal, South Korea, Syria and Vietnam.

Linked to this concern to promote exports of British goods, and a concern about the aid-tying practices of other donors, was the decision at about the same time to require the colonies and independent countries to buy British, to the extent that aid funds were used for imports, unless it could be shown that such goods could not be supplied on 'reasonably competitive terms'. There remained no formal restriction on the use of aid funds for local costs, apart from CA loans provided by ECGD and funds provided under the Chancellor's surplus capacity initiative. Britain's often stated formal position then and later was that it favoured an international decision to untie all aid, not least because it expected to be a net beneficiary of such a move.

Also discussed in the 1963 White Paper was the issue of terms of aid. It pointed out that more than half of Britain's aid in 1962/63 was on grant terms, which primarily meant grants-in-aid and the bulk of CD&W funds for the colonial territories, technical co-operation generally, and the funds channelled through the multilateral aid system. In 1954/55 the proportion of grants had been about 80 per cent: the decline was due not to a change in terms policy as such but because the proportion of total aid going as financial aid to the independent Commonwealth and other countries, which was generally on loan terms, had increased.

Conscious of the debt-servicing burden facing developing countries, the 1963 White Paper announced some easing of aid loan terms. Up to that point all loans (except CD&W Section 1 loans to the colonies) bore an interest rate equal to what the British government could borrow at, plus a small margin for administrative costs, and 80 per cent of loans had a maturity of between 20 and 25 years with a grace period of up to seven years before repayments of capital commenced. The concessions, subject to a 'strict assessment of need', were: i) a maturity of up to 30 years with up to a ten-year grace period on repayments of capital; and ii) a waiving of interest during the grace period. This second concession represented the first introduction of a grant element in Britain's aid loans in that it provided for an interest subsidy, though many might say that lending at a fraction over HMG's gilt rate to a developing country which carried a material risk was itself concessional.

Finally, one should record passages from two of the Queen's Speeches of that time. The 1959 speech included the passage: 'The improvement of conditions in the less developed countries of the world will remain an urgent concern of my Government. They will promote economic co-operation between nations and support plans for financial and technical assistance.' In 1963 the Queen's Speech went a step further and contained the following reference to aid policy: 'My Government will also be providing an *expanding* programme of financial and technical assistance' (author's italics). Meanwhile, in 1960 Britain had supported the UN General Assembly resolution that the industrialised countries should provide total net resource flows (official and private) to developing countries of at least 1 per cent of GNP.

## Aid volume

The 1963 White Paper contains several statistical appendices giving figures on the government's 'aid' to developing countries. Before summarising these, a health warning is relevant. The 'aid' provided is limited to official flows from the government but it is not based on today's definition of official development assistance (oda). It included all flows emanating from the government, regardless of the terms on which they were provided (that is, they included all flows from grants to loans on quasi-commercial terms). The way oda has been defined since the 1960s is explained in Chapter Ten. The following figures drawn from the White Paper exclude military assistance.

One can see from these statistics a significant growth in aid to the colonies in the five years to 1961/62 as many were moving towards independence. This included CD&W funds (both Section I and II), grants-in-aid, CDC loans and other exceptional assistance.

*Table 3.1* Total official gross financial grants and loans (£ million)

| Bilateral Aid | 1957/58 | 1958/59 | 1959/60 | 1960/61 | 1961/62 | 1962/63 (Est) |
|---|---|---|---|---|---|---|
| Sub-Saharan Africa | 20 | 17 | 24 | 51 | 81 | 61 |
| North Africa | 5 | 3 | 6 | 5 | 3 | 3 |
| West Indies | 6 | 7 | 8 | 8 | 9 | 8 |
| South America | 2 | 6 | 2 | 3 | 7 | 4 |
| Asia & Middle East | 16 | 34 | 50 | 45 | 40 | 43 |
| Other (inc Med/Europe) | 16 | 17 | 17 | 17 | 10 | 14 |
| **Sub-total** | 62 | 86 | 110 | 130 | 154 | 138 |
| Multilateral Aid | 19 | 24 | 20 | 21 | 6 | 10 |
| **Total Aid** | 81 | 110 | 130 | 151 | 160 | 148 |
| Bilateral aid comprised (£ millions) | | | | | | |
| Colonial Territories | 47 | 49 | 58 | 72 | 96 | 61 |
| Independent Commonwealth | 5 | 26 | 40 | 46 | 45 | 63 |
| Other (foreign) | 10 | 11 | 12 | 13 | 14 | 15 |

*Source:* 1963 White Paper: Aid to Developing Countries (Cmnd 2147).

Geographically the main beneficiaries were territories in Sub-Saharan Africa. This period also saw a substantial growth in assistance to the independent Commonwealth following the decision to provide CA loans under Section 3 of the ECGD Act, which focused heavily on the Indian sub-continent. In 1962/63 Sub-Saharan Africa and South Asia/ Middle East accounted for 75 per cent of all British bilateral aid and set a pattern which was to be continued by the Department after its creation in 1964. Assistance to non-Commonwealth countries remained relatively modest, and in 1962/63 the Commonwealth (including the colonies) accounted for 93 per cent of total bilateral assistance. As noted above, the terms of Britain's assistance overall hardened as the growth in CA loans plus Exchequer loans under Section II of CD&W Acts outstripped colonial grants.

## Machinery of government changes

By the close of the 1950s the situation that then prevailed made the existing machinery of government untenable in anything save the short term. There were three overseas departments which may have been appropriate before the Second World War but which afterwards seemed increasingly out of line with Britain's international relationships. The work of the Colonial Office would be further greatly diminished by 1965, leaving only Hong Kong, Gibraltar and the Falklands as major political concerns, but each increasingly having more to do with Britain's relations with three foreign countries than with the domestic affairs of the colonies themselves. The independent Commonwealth, the responsibility of the CRO, remained an important dimension of Britain's foreign policy but increasingly just that.

Furthermore, responsibility for Britain's overseas aid efforts was now spread between the three overseas departments and the Treasury itself, plus, in a very minor way, some home departments. Bilateral aid took the form of CD&W funds and grants-in-aid to the colonies (the Colonial Office); technical co-operation and CA loans to the independent Commonwealth (the CRO) and technical co-operation and financial grants and loans to foreign countries (the Foreign Office). Responsibility for Britain's policy towards the World Bank Group lay with the Treasury, which in financial terms meant its subscription to the capital of IBRD and the International Finance Corporation (IFC), its private sector affiliate. It also administered Britain's contribution to the International Development Association (IDA), the soft-lending window of the World Bank established in 1960. Finally, Britain's contribution to the technical co-operation activities of the UN was funded either by the Foreign Office or, in the case of the UN's Specialized Agencies, the relevant home department.

The first proposal for a change in the machinery of government came from the Select Committee on Estimates in 1960[19] following its enquiry into the Colonial Office and Colonial Service. Evidence was given to the Committee by the then Permanent Under Secretary of State for the Colonial Office, Sir Hilton Poynton, giving his personal view in favour of a merger of the CO and the CRO. Amongst other things this would also facilitate the continued access of newly independent countries to the advice of the extensive professional advisory network available to the CO. The Committee recommended such a merger on grounds of efficiency and effectiveness, with the added political advantage that the word 'Colonial', which irritated territories with self-government, would disappear if a new Commonwealth Office were created.

The government recognised the inevitability of such a merger of the two Departments but did not think that one Secretary of State could cope with the workload involved over the next few years. It did, however, recognise the need meanwhile to bring together the provision of technical co-operation activities under one roof, regardless of the status of the recipient, to be known as the Department for Technical Co-operation (DTC). It was concluded that financial aid, except to the colonies, was more a matter of policy than detailed administration as at that time most financial aid was for general economic support rather than for individual projects requiring close appraisal and monitoring, and should therefore remain with the relevant overseas department. More controversially, the new DTC would take over responsibility for administering Britain's financial support for officers serving in Her Majesty's Overseas Colonial Service (HMOCS), notably the cost of the Overseas Service Aid Scheme (OSAS) which would represent about half its total budget for 1961/62 of some £29 million. However, for political reasons all policy matters bearing on HMOCS would be determined by, and emanate from, the Colonial Office. Finally the DTC took over responsibility for the central UN technical co-operation schemes, but not the work of the UN Specialized Agencies which remained with the home departments because of their wider international regulatory role.

Thus the DTC came into being in July 1961, staffed largely by civil servants drawn from the CO. It was essentially to be a service department for the three overseas departments which would retain responsibility for broad policy issues. Its Minister, the Secretary for Technical Co-operation – the first of whom was the Rt Hon Dennis (later Lord) Vosper – would be a minister without Cabinet rank. The new Minister presented his first White Paper to Parliament in April 1962,[20] outlining the ten broad activities it took over from the three overseas departments, and how these might be developed.

Within a little more than two years of the setting up of the DTC the machinery of government as regards overseas aid was being looked at again. This was in the context of a wider discussion of the structure of the overseas departments (the CO and CRO had remained separate departments but since 1962 had the same Secretary of State), and an awareness that the Labour Party was proposing a Ministry of Overseas Development, although exactly what its responsibilities might be was, at that stage, unclear.

There were two basic issues to be considered: whether there should be a single department responsible for the management of all overseas economic aid and what policy responsibilities it should have, more or less independently of the other overseas departments. As regards the former, the then Director General of the DTC, in evidence to a Parliamentary Committee, favoured a single department, in particular to integrate and retain aid management skills and better to co-ordinate the provision of technical co-operation and financial aid. He also thought it more appropriate for a single minister to be answerable to Parliament and responsible for putting aid spending proposals to the Treasury.

Reactions to the Director General's ideas varied. The CO was, not surprisingly, hostile. It could not envisage giving up any policy responsibility for aid while its Secretary of State was answerable to Parliament for what happened within each colony. This was particularly true of budgetary aid for those in receipt of it, as it was regarded as crucial for the effective provision and administration of basic public services for a territory. The CRO were less hostile but expected to be in the policy driving seat, particularly when it came to financial aid because of the wider Whitehall interests that were thought to be involved. The Foreign Office were rather more relaxed, possibly because it had had only very limited experience of handling aid to non-Commonwealth countries. The Treasury, like the CO and the CRO, favoured the status quo, but for a rather different reason: if a single department for aid were to be created it should be strong enough to stand up to the overseas departments, which the Treasury thought unlikely.

At the Labour Party conference in October 1963, Harold Wilson promised a separate Overseas Development Minister, and in a subsequent newsaper article[21] wrote that 'we shall be engaged not in a tip-and-run raid on world poverty but an all out war'. Following a visit to Africa,

Barbara Castle told the House of Commons:[22] 'They [donors] are giving help for reasons of national prestige or for political motives . . . or for reasons of rivalry in the cold war . . . Because the motives are wrong the help bears no relationship to the results in terms of maximum economic development'. In early 1964 the Fabian Society started work on a blueprint for the new ministry, stressing a minister of cabinet rank and sufficient independence to resist pressures from other ministries to arrange its programme according to non-development criteria. The ministry should not be about aid but about development, independent of foreign policy, or trade or the economy. The recipients must believe that the Labour government is entering into a partnership and not dispensing charity.[23] These references have been taken from the authorised biography of Barbara Castle by Anne Perkins.[24]

Sir Robert Carr, then the Secretary for Technical Co-operation, prompted ministerial discussion, following Labour Party statements on the issue, by himself proposing a single Ministry of Overseas Development (ODM) but one which would manage all aid within detailed policies set down by the overseas departments. This school of thought envisaged that eventually there would be only one department for external affairs (that is, a Foreign and Commonwealth Office) and that such an ODM would then in effect become its executing agency.

However, the 1964 General Election intervened. The Labour Party manifesto, *The New Britain*, said that:

> poverty is an ever-present fear for more than half the world's population. It presents the western industrialised nations with a tremendous challenge which we ignore at our peril: for there is a growing danger that the increasing tensions caused by growing inequalities of circumstances between rich and poor nations will be sharply accentuated by differences of race and colour.

It went on to say that Labour would

> discuss with other countries proposals for expanding the trade of developing nations; and increase the share of our national income devoted to essential aid programmes not only by loans and grants but by mobilising unused industrial capacity to meet overseas needs.

It then promised that:

> To give a dynamic lead in this vital field, Labour will create a Ministry of Overseas Development to be responsible not only for our part in

Commonwealth development but also for our work in and through the specialist agencies of the United Nations. This new Ministry will help and encourage voluntary action through those organisations that have played such an inspired part in the Freedom from Hunger campaign. We must match their enterprise with Government action to give new hope in the current United Nations Development Decade.

The Conservative Party manifesto, *Prosperity with a Purpose*, made reference to using the growth in wealth 'to aid developing countries still battling against widespread poverty'. It took credit for its support internationally for proposals to expand developing-country trade; for having reached an aid level which was more than double that of six years earlier; and for having established the DTC. 'As the British economy expands so will the level of aid progressively rise'.

The Liberal Party manifesto, *Think for Yourself*, said a lot about international affairs and that 'a joint Western programme of aid and trade is essential to defeat world poverty' but said nothing further about the future role or size of the British aid effort.

Following the Labour victory in the 1964 election the new Prime Minister, the Rt Hon Harold (later Lord) Wilson MP, announced the setting up of a new Ministry of Overseas Development (ODM). This reflected the longstanding interest of Wilson in international development, and no doubt also the influence of Professor Thomas Balogh, his Economic Adviser both in opposition and after he became Prime Minister.[25] He appointed the Rt Hon Barbara (later Lady) Castle MP as its first minister with a seat in Cabinet, which also reflected her longstanding interest in colonial affairs and independence movements in Africa. The new minister proposed that the Department should be responsible for all policy aspects of overseas aid as well as its management: bilateral and multilateral aid, financial aid and technical co-operation. The Department would respect the policies of the other overseas departments, and that in the case of the colonies all aid should be provided in close consultation with the Colonial Office. The Department would take responsibility for 'development' aid and the Colonial Office would retain responsibility for budgetary aid.

The Colonial Office vigorously opposed the arrangement, wanting to retain responsibility for all aid to the colonies. However the new Secretary of State for the Colonies accepted the Prime Minister's conclusion that development should become the responsibility of the Department, provided he retained control of budgetary aid. Officials were left to agree a concordat by which the two departments would work together. After protracted negotiations a concordat between the Department and the Colonial Office was embodied in a 'Circular Despatch from the Colonial Secretary to Governors etc', dated 10 May 1965. It reflected the Prime Minister's conclusion regarding who should have lead responsibility for development assistance and budgetary aid. It drew a broad distinction between the CO's responsibility for the economic and financial policies of a colonial territory and therefore its development plans for which it would need to rely on the professional staff of the Department for advice, and the Department's responsibility for development assistance, while recognising the need for a close working relationship between the two departments on all aspects of a territory's economic and social affairs.

Finally, it was agreed between the Departments that 'the reasonable needs of the dependent territories had a first charge on the aid programme'. This phrase in one sense meant little because of the difficulty in defining what their reasonable needs were. On the other hand the Colonial Office and subsequently the unified Foreign and Commonwealth Office set considerable store by it for decades to come. They felt, correctly, that in some measure it set the dependencies apart from any rigorous application of some theoretical development model for the geographical distribution of aid, and that even if as a matter of policy the Department did not generally wish to finance certain types of activity this would not be binding on the dependent territories.

Thus was the Department conceived and its relationships with the other overseas departments established in outline. In telling the history of the Department over the following decades, just how that relationship evolved will be explored. For the moment it is sufficient to note that the setting up of the Department probably hastened the merger of the CO and CRO in 1966 as the Commonwealth Office. In 1968 the Foreign Office and the Commonwealth Office merged to form the Foreign and Commonwealth Office. This contained a Dependent Territories Division which became a joint FCO/ODM Division within the FCO.

Meanwhile Castle, as the new Minister for Overseas Development, and her new Permanent Secretary, Sir Andrew Cohen KCMG KCO OBE, together with the many other civil servants transferred from the DTC to the Department, set about making the new Department operational.

## Some policy reflections

Much had been learned from the institutional experience of providing assistance to the colonies. It required a substantial change over time in the structure and staffing of the Colonial Office and the colonial service. Both became more 'professional'. The former found itself responsible to Parliament for the welfare of the colonies but not in control of their administration. The influence of both was enhanced by the provision of aid and their insistence that such help should (after 1940) be in support of strategic development plans for the individual territories. The colonial service was increasingly staffed by professionals geared to designing and implementing such plans. It is a matter of debate as to whether they were there primarily to serve the Empire or to serve the territory and its people they were responsible for.

One of the major handicaps of the Colonial Office in its early years was the lack of communications with its territories. Following the problems in the West Indies in the late 1930s, a regional comptroller-general was appointed to oversee assistance to the Caribbean. There were discussions about the feasibility of establishing other regional offices, particularly in West Africa, but these were not progressed. Placing staff overseas in regional and country offices was to be a growing feature and strength of the Department in later years, particularly as information technology improved.

The concern with discharging trusteeship responsibilities gave way in the 1950s to a wider international concern with helping to reduce poverty in poor countries more generally. The rather narrow concept of economic development also gave way to a broader recognition of the importance of economic and social development and the linkages between issues such as education, public health and agricultural development. The Gladstonian principle of financial self-sufficiency was transformed into recognition of the need for longer-term support for development, as reflected in the 1963 White Paper, including for independent countries. Aid might be a passing phase in history but it would be with us for a very considerable period of time.

CD&W Section 1 funds were increasingly provided on grant terms though not yet entirely on the basis of the poverty of the country rather than the purpose for which the aid was provided. But even in 1940 there was already concern about the level of indebtedness of some of the colonies. Later, constitutional advance towards self-government, and then independence, undermined their perceived creditworthiness and further limited their access to commercial capital markets.

These concerns were to raise increasingly important policy issues later regarding the future terms of official aid and how to deal with growing indebtedness.

As regards independent countries, whether Commonwealth or foreign, Britain did not accept that it should provide official financial assistance until 1958. Even then government assistance was not on what today would be regarded as concessional terms, and it was fully tied to the purchase of British goods and services except for the provision of local costs.

The unique aspect of Britain's assistance to the colonies under successive CD&W Acts was that they provided for specific amounts of financial support over a large number of years (albeit with annual limits). The 1957 White Paper denied official financial assistance to independent countries, and successive White Papers (until 2006) discussed policy but without indicating future levels of aid. The latter was the preserve of the annual Public Expenditure Survey, which allowed government continually to re-assess its spending priorities.

# 4
# The Department's Mission: 1964–2013

The primary purpose of this chapter is to trace the stated mission of the Department from 1964 to the present (2013). For the most part it does not seek to assess the extent to which it adhered to its stated mission or to evaluate its effectiveness: that is for later. Nor does it seek to put the Department's stated mission in the context of contemporary development theories or thinking, for which the reader is referred in particular to Chapter Five.

## The work of the new ministry

The Department produced its first White Paper (that is, a statement of government-wide policy) in 1965, simply entitled 'The Work of the New Ministry'.[26] In explaining its motives and objectives, it stated: 'The objective of the British aid programme is to help developing countries in their efforts to raise living standards . . . and therefore promote economic and social development (para 1). It went on to

> recognise the advantages of providing aid through international organisations . . . [and] intend to give highest priority to technical assistance . . . [which] is often a prerequisite to make good use of financial aid . . .

> Countries which are members of the Commonwealth have a special claim on us . . . we have special obligations towards the territories still dependent on us [. . .] By the criteria we have discussed more foreign countries could make a claim on our aid . . . but [there are] obvious limits in our present economic circumstances to what we can do (para 5).

Aid will be most effective where it forms part of a coherent and co-operative effort to implement a well prepared development plan. Our contribution [is] best where it is big enough to play an effective part or where [there are] arrangements for the co-ordination of all donors' aid (para 6).

The provision of aid is to our long term advantage . . . but [this] must be secondary to the primary purpose of aid [. . .] A clear distinction must be kept between aid and commercial credits [. . .] To describe as aid transactions that do not entail a sacrifice would incur the risk of frustration and ill will (paras 7 and 8).

The solutions to the problems of developing countries are neither simple nor obvious. They will involve new experiments, new methods, new institutions, new relationships. There are many paths to development. Our aim is to help the developing countries to find and pursue them (para 9).

In policy terms it was not a major departure from the 1963 White Paper discussed in Chapter Three, though its reference to the special claims of the independent Commonwealth was new. However, the 1965 White Paper demonstrated more enthusiasm for the tasks ahead: this was not surprising given its new minister, Barbara Castle, and its substantial dedicated staff from both the DTC, administrative and professional, and subsequently from the Colonial Service itself. It also benefited from the creation of a substantial Economic Planning Staff (the EPS), which was part of the general exodus of academic economists from universities into Whitehall early in the Wilson Administration – later to be complemented by those having served time in developing countries. Castle took particular credit for creating a strong EPS and, on the advice of Professor Tommy Balogh, for appointing Dudley Seers as its first Director General.[27] She regarded this as essential to challenge the administrative Civil Service cadre and introduce new thinking. It included helping her challenge her own Permanent Secretary, the larger-than-life Sir Andrew Cohen, with whom she had a good relationship: they were known as 'the elephant and castle'. Unfortunately for the Department, Castle was 'promoted' to become Minister of Transport after only eighteen months. Some believe that this was in large part because the Prime Minister wanted to reach a compromise with Ian Smith following Southern Rhodesia's Unilateral Declaration of Independence, which he expected Barbara Castle strongly to oppose.[28]

The 1965 White Paper confirmed the responsibility of the Department for all bilateral aid (except for the Colonial Office's policy responsibilities for budgetary aid to the remaining colonies) and multilateral aid, including the UN Specialized Agencies with a significant development role, except WHO for which the Department of Health continued, as it still does, to have lead policy responsibility. There were two caveats. First, the White Paper acknowledged the Treasury's lead role in managing relations with the World Bank Group: it provided the Executive Director of the World Bank and IMF, who headed up the joint Washington office. That said, all the funds for the World Bank were on the Department's budget and it provided staff in the Washington office to help deal with World Bank business. The year 1965 marked the Department's long-standing, if sometimes rocky, love affair with IDA, the soft-lending arm of the World Bank (see Chapter Seven). The second caveat was to acknowledge (para 74) the need for joined-up government: 'our aid programme must be administered in harmony with the policies of all the departments concerned with our economic and overseas affairs.' We shall see later how this worked out.

Another emerging policy issue signalled in the White Paper was a stagnation in aid and rising indebtedness. Debt servicing as a percentage of exports for developing countries was on average about 15 per cent – a modest level by the standards of the 1980s and 1990s, but at the time seen as serious. But with the increased use of commercial credits, the relatively hard terms of much bilateral aid, and increasing multilateral aid loans a future problem could be foreseen, particularly if standards of economic management declined. As a response to this the Department decided to soften its own terms of aid. Concessional rates of interest on its long-term aid loans were reduced, including zero for the poorest countries.

The importance of the work of the CDC was acknowledged. In order to help the CDC provide more equity in agricultural enterprises and local development finance companies the Department persuaded the Treasury that new Exchequer Advances to the CDC for such purposes should be free of interest during the 'fructification' period. Previously, interest during this period was rolled up and added to CDC debt to government.

Finally, like earlier ones, the 1965 White Paper touched on the issue of the tying of aid to national procurement, and again said that it would like to see a collective untying of bilateral aid by all donors. Meanwhile, it stipulated that its bilateral aid to be used for imports by developing countries should be sourced from Britain.

In summary the White Paper represented a positive start for the new Department. It emphasised poor countries and the importance of the effective use of aid but deliberately avoided any prescriptive development policies. It recognised Britain's comparative advantage in providing technical assistance, particularly to poor Commonwealth countries through the provision of individuals with relevant skills and overseas experience, and the wealth of knowledge in its scientific institutions. It supported the multilateral aid system and the co-ordination of bilateral aid at the country level and through the Development Assistance Committee of the OECD. It provided a broad agenda for the next few years.

The White Paper was followed by the Overseas Aid Act 1966. Although it ran to seven pages for legal and technical reasons, it was only Section 1, paragraph 1 that really mattered in broad policy terms. This conferred on the Minister the power 'for the purpose of promoting the development of, or maintaining the economy of, a country or territory outside the United Kingdom or the welfare of its people, to furnish any person or body with assistance whether financial, technical or of any other nature'. This placed no restrictions on the Minister provided any assistance was for the purposes stated. This was later incorporated into the 1980 Overseas Development and Co-operation Act.

### India

Before moving on to the shift in policy set out in the next White Paper a decade later, it is worth reflecting on how the Department's mission changed in relation to India. Historically India had not benefited from any official flows from Britain when it was a colony because it had 'responsible government', and after independence in 1947 it was also denied any help. This changed in 1958 when relatively short-term loans on quasi-commercial terms and tied to British exports (Commonwealth Assistance Loans) became available under Section 3 of the ECGD Act (see Chapter Three). India became the largest recipient. The ECGD Act, Section 3, powers lapsed with the passing of the 1966 Overseas Aid Act, and these loans were followed with aid loans from the Department's budget and on increasingly concessional terms. In the case of India they did, however, remain wholly tied to British exports until the 1980s (see the section in Chapter Five on debt relief). In 1964/65 Britain's bilateral aid to India amounted to 27 per cent of total bilateral aid. In later years the EPS, using its theoretical model for aid distribution, argued for India to receive a much larger proportion of the Department's bilateral aid, but the FCO argued for a limit of no more than 30 per cent (which it peaked at in 1975).

In 1971 an internal policy guidance note (PGN 71 (3)) was produced under the influence of the EPS. Its basic message was that where a country had appropriate policies and allocated resources efficiently to promote development it should be eligible for commodity aid (that is, support for general capital and intermediate goods imports), later in the 1980s known as programme aid, and later once again budgetary aid (see Chapter Six) rather than more targeted project aid. At the time, India was judged to be the only country to qualify for this form of aid. This judgement was probably twenty years premature: it has only been since the 1990s that India has adopted policies (under the influence of Manmohan Singh, then its Finance Minister and subsequently Prime Minister) which have led to its remarkable record of economic growth, though there remains widespread poverty.

## More help to the poorest

The Conservative Party Manifesto of 1970, *A Better Tomorrow*, stated briefly: 'Britain must play a proper part in dealing with world poverty. We will ensure that Britain helps the developing countries by working for the expansion of international trade; by encouraging private investment overseas; and by providing capital aid and technical assistance to supplement their own efforts.' After the Conservative Party won the 1970 election there was no follow-up White Paper fleshing out what this would mean in practice.

In 1974 the Conservative Party manifesto, *Putting Britain First*, was silent on aid. However the Labour Party manifesto, *Britain Will Win with Labour*, stated: 'The Government has accepted the United Nations target of 0.7% of the Gross National Product for financial aid to developing countries in need throughout the world and will seek to move towards it as fast as possible. We shall direct our aid towards the poorest countries and to the poorest people and give emphasis to rural development.'

It should be noted that this manifesto commitment to reaching the UN aid target of 0.7 per cent of GNP (as soon as possible) is weaker than the 1970 manifesto commitment to reach it during the Second Development Decade (that is, at least by 1979). Furthermore, what matters is what the government says in a White Paper and the outcome of successive public expenditure surveys.

The Department's second White Paper was issued in October 1975.[29] It was prepared largely under the influence of the Rt Hon Judith Hart MP, who was to hold the post of Minister of Overseas Development on three separate occasions. She was Minister for eight months prior to the

1970 election and again between March 1974 and June 1975 whilst the White Paper was in draft: it was published later in 1975 after the Rt Hon Reginald Prentice MP had become Minister for the second time. Many of the policies in the White Paper were reflected in Hart's book, *Aid and Liberation*, which she wrote whilst in Opposition between her first and second terms in the Department.[30] In it she emphasised that growth was not enough for development, nor was it a criterion for allocating aid; improving rural living standards rather than increasing dualism should be a priority.

The context in which the White Paper was prepared had three dimensions. First, it was the experience of the last decade or so that while the middle-income developing countries had been growing on average at about 6 per cent per annum, though only some 3–4 per cent in terms of per capita income, the poorer countries were doing much less well. For countries with a per capita GNP of under $200 (1972) growth had been on average about 4 per cent and population growth had meant that per capita incomes had grown only marginally. Second, the world had just experienced the first oil price shock (1973) which impacted directly on oil-importing developing countries. It also caused a recession in the richer countries which reduced other commodity export prices.

Also in 1973, Robert McNamara, then President of the World Bank, made a powerful speech about the importance of rural development in the poorer countries if the living standards and quality of life of poor people were to be enhanced. He committed the World Bank to focus more of its resources on this challenge and what at the time became fashionably known as integrated rural development, that is, addressing not just livelihoods but also a range of other basic services, including education, health and economic infrastructure.

The essential message conveyed in the 1975 White Paper was that the Department would 'ensure that a higher proportion of British aid should directly benefit not only the poorest countries but the poorest people in those countries. As most of these people live in rural areas . . . our new aid strategy is to give a special emphasis to rural development' (Chapter 2, paragraph 21):

> The geographical distribution of bilateral aid would be a function of relative poverty; aid provided by others [a reference to francophone Africa, generously aided by France, on the one hand and paucity of aid to the Indian sub-continent per head of population on the other]; the absorptive capacity for aid by the country (to be enhanced by

technical co-operation); and performance criteria related to efforts made by countries themselves to reduce poverty. A balance of payments problem was not itself a reason for aid if it was brought about by poor economic management.

Britain's special responsibilities to its remaining Dependent Territories were also recognised; in 1974 these, despite their relative wealth and small populations, still accounted for 17 per cent of bilateral aid. It has to be said that, the Dependencies apart, it was a real challenge to increase the proportion of aid going to the poorest countries as so much of it, apart from the relatively small technical co-operation programmes to the middle-income countries mainly in South America, already did so. The 1975 White Paper made no commitments as to the future levels of aid or a timetable for achieving the UN aid target of 0.7 per cent of GNP.

The White Paper expressed strong support for the World Bank Group, particularly the International Development Association (IDA), and the UN and its Specialized Agencies. It also addressed in Chapter IX the new dimension of the European Economic Community (EEC), which Britain joined in October 1972. On aid it continued to urge the EEC to widen aid support for countries beyond the 46 African, Caribbean and Pacific (ACP) Associated States, in particular for the poorer countries of Asia. On trade, Britain argued for generous terms of access to the EEC market for both agricultural and industrial products for the Associated States, and improved trade arrangements for other developing countries.

Re-reading the full text of the White Paper nearly forty years on, one is nevertheless struck by some of the caveats and cautious wording. For example, Chapter III, paragraph 4, states:

it is sometimes argued that a direct method for trying to ensure that aid is used to benefit the poorest section of the community is for the donor to specify in advance the economic or social sectors . . . or particular beneficiary groups . . . to which it wishes to confine, or preclude the use of, its aid [. . .] we do not propose to follow this kind of approach.

In fact, following the White Paper the Department initially adopted a vigorous policy of concentrating on rural development, as did many other donors. Indeed some poor countries which were heavily dependent upon British aid, and which saw the Department as the 'donor of last resort' for a range of necessary capital expenditures, pleaded for it not to be so exclusive.

The White Paper was also surprisingly cautious in its statements on aid-tying and the provision of aid for local costs, particularly in the context of a rural development initiative. In Chapter III it acknowledged that such programmes involved a high proportion of local costs but in paragraph 9 was only able to say that the Department was 'ready to consider allowing in exceptional circumstances a limited part of our financial aid to meet local costs of individual projects'. In fact, outside India a substantial proportion of the Department's country aid programmes for the poorest countries was made available in the 1970s (and beyond) for financing local costs. Whereas the Department of Trade and Industry (DTI) had to be consulted when the Department wished to use aid to purchase goods in third countries, only the Treasury had to be consulted on local cost provision (see Chapter Nine). By the latter half of the 1970s, with sterling floated, the Treasury was more relaxed on the issue: it was commonplace for the poorer countries in Africa, as well as, for example, Bangladesh and Nepal, to be allowed to spend 40–50 per cent of their aid allocations on local costs.

The underlying principles of the 1975 White Paper – focusing aid on the poorest countries and helping the poorest people in those countries – continued for a long time, including during the Conservative Administration 1979–97; indeed up until the next White Paper in 1997 after another Labour administration came into office. But there were undoubtedly significant waiverings and diversions during this long period which will be explored later. However, it was the Labour government, in 1977, that first introduced the Aid and Trade Scheme (see Chapter Nine).

## Aid cuts and the 1981 Aid Review

Potentially more important for the Department than the introduction of ATP was the advent of the Thatcher government of 1979 whose General Election Manifesto gave no space to overseas aid.

To fully understand the impact of the aid cuts which were imposed by the new Thatcher government one must appreciate that in the last years of the Labour administration the Department secured a 6 per cent real terms per annum growth in its aid budget and Labour's final three-year Public Expenditure Survey provided for similar growth in aid into the early 1980s. As a result the Department had embarked upon a major increase in its commitments, both in terms of its bilateral aid activities and multilaterally, in particular to IDA. As it turned out the new Thatcher government made significant public expenditure reductions which it believed were made necessary by the economic circumstances of the time. For the Department this involved a 6 per cent cut in-year for 1979/80, followed by a 14 per cent real terms cut for the Public Expenditure Survey period 1980/81–1982/83.

The cuts had a profound impact on the work of the Department. The increased commitments to IDA and the projected increases in Britain's contribution to the EC budget for aid, which were inescapable, put a tight squeeze on the bilateral aid programmes. The Department met all its contractual commitments, but it had to give up many near-commitments and future plans.

Although later in the 1980s the Foreign Secretary Sir Geoffrey (now Lord) Howe argued for some increases in aid, in a recent interview with the author he said he made no apologies as Chancellor for reducing overall public spending, including in aid, when the Conservatives took power in 1979.

In addition to the overall public expenditure constraints, Mrs (later Baroness) Thatcher's view of aid, which she famously once referred to as 'hand-outs', was generally negative. She was supported in this by Sir Keith Joseph, a senior Cabinet Minister, the writings of Lord Bauer, and later Sir Alan Walters, one of her senior policy advisers. An official inter-department Aid Policy Review was conducted. By 1979 the Department had few friends in Whitehall: the FCO felt the Department had effectively sought to run its own foreign policy and ignored the political relevance of aid to the influential middle-income developing countries; and the Department of Trade and Industry was anxious to secure what it saw as the potential commercial benefits of aid, particularly through an expansion and more aggressive use of the Aid and Trade Provision (ATP) scheme.

The review of aid policy was conducted within Whitehall and never published. Instead, on 20 February 1981 Sir Neil Martin, Thatcher's first Minister for Overseas Development, made a statement to Parliament following the completion of the review. It included the following passages:

> Our ability to support development overseas is dependent on the state of our economy and the need to strengthen it. Nevertheless, the Government will continue to provide aid to the developing countries on a substantial scale. Official aid continues to be an essential element in development, especially for the poorest countries . . .

> We believe that it is right at the present time to give greater weight in the allocation of our aid to political, industrial and commercial considerations alongside our basic developmental objectives

We need to maintain the strength of our ties with the Commonwealth, to which the greater part of our bilateral aid now goes, and to fulfil our obligations to our remaining dependencies. We must also be able, when necessary, to offer help and encouragement to other friendly countries

Since 1978 about 5 per cent of the bilateral aid programme has been made available for the aid-trade provision for sound developmental projects – which are also of commercial and industrial importance for British firms – in developing countries to which we do not normally provide aid, or where the planned allocation is already committed. In order to maintain the value of this provision in real terms, its share of the bilateral aid programme will now be increased

Our commitments to international agencies and bodies will absorb a larger proportion of the aid programme over the next few years. As we need more room for manoeuvre in bilateral aid, we shall need to look critically at our expenditure on multilateral aid programmes

Much can be done with our aid programme, which is to the mutual advantage of the developing countries and ourselves, and we shall therefore concentrate on using it in that way.

The essential message was that greater weight would be given to political, industrial and commercial concerns alongside the basic developmental objectives of the aid programme, which according to the text was to relieve poverty, especially in the poorest countries. Giving greater weight to political and commercial considerations meant continuing to focus on the Commonwealth; reducing the potential impact on bilateral aid of a cut in the overall aid budget by looking critically at new multilateral aid commitments; and maintaining the real value of the ATP so, as a consequence, it was accepted that its share of total bilateral aid would increase. The statement promised to maintain a substantial aid programme, despite the plans to reduce it. The reaction in Parliament to the statement was expectedly mixed, but Dame Judith Hart suggested that it 'basically endorses the aid strategy of the Labour Government' and congratulated the Foreign Secretary and others for 'their powers of persuasion and influence on their free market, monetarist and anti-aid colleagues at a crucial point'. Hansard (col 466) does not record whether or not her tongue was in her cheek at the time.

This was undoubtedly an important political statement though its significance was over-rated. Political and commercial considerations had always been important – most aid went to the Commonwealth and others with whom we had historical links; bilateral aid was tied to British goods and services (except for local costs) and Britain was a staunch supporter of the multilateral aid system which was also key to its position internationally. But within the development community, including, it has to be said, the staff of the Department itself, it was feared to be a fundamental change of policy. It was seen as a major shift from a long-term view of Britain's interest in a more prosperous world to a focus on more short-term political and commercial gains. Some felt that the positive references to helping poor countries and the poorest people were no more than necessary platitudes to avoid creating undue hostility in Parliament. It nevertheless provoked, among other things, the Real Aid Campaign by academics and NGOs which interpreted virtually everything the Department did subsequently as driven by political and commercial considerations.

The mission of the Department was stalled mainly by the lack of funds with which to do anything new. The Treasury was unsympathetic to an expansion of the ATP (for which see Chapter Nine), and the FCO's geographical ambitions were for a relatively modest increase in technical co-operation for some middle-income countries in South America and South East Asia, though they also, like the DTI, for political reasons generally favoured bilateral aid rather than aid to the multilateral aid system.

The events of 1984 were to prove an important inflexion point in allowing the Department to maintain its basic mission. If the Treasury had any one prejudice it was in respect of the FCO, which it regarded as being over-indulged overseas and weak on financial management at home. In the public expenditure climate of the early 1980s it sought to reduce the FCO Diplomatic Wing's budget. The response of the Planning Staff in the FCO at that time was to seek to negotiate future public expenditure settlements with the Treasury on the basis of a combined FCO (Diplomatic Wing and Aid Wing) figure, allowing the Foreign Secretary, advised by Diplomatic Wing officials, to decide the division of funds. This was politically seen off by the all-day Overseas Aid debate in the House of Commons on 22 November 1984 in Opposition time.

The debate was prompted by serious famine in the Horn of Africa, with terrible scenes of human suffering seen on British television screens. This was just at a time when the government's new public expenditure plans had been published covering the year 1985/86. By this time the aid budget had been planned to be stabilised in real terms except, however, for a technicality. In order to provide help for the Falklands following the war and for the upgrading of the Gibraltar dockyard, the Department had been given additional funding which was now coming to an end. As a result the published figures for total aid showed a further real terms cut of 2 per cent for the next financial year (1985/86) based on the government's own inflation forecast of 5 per cent. The debate was an extraordinary event: the government whips could find none of their usually reliable right-wing backbenchers to speak against aid and more than 40 Conservative backbenchers abstained on the 10 o'clock division by sitting in their seats – no doubt encouraged by Bowen Wells, a respected Conservative member of the Foreign Affairs Sub Committee on Overseas Aid and supporter of the aid programme.

This single event had important consequences. The absolute size of the aid budget was not again put under serious threat, even though successive Conservative Foreign Secretaries were unable to achieve any significant increases in the aid budget. FCO planners (and ministers) dropped any ideas about a combined FCO Public Expenditure Settlement. The NGOs intensified their campaign against the government's aid policies and the unfortunate Rt Hon Timothy Raison MP, then Minister for Overseas Development, who struggled valiantly that evening, was later eventually replaced in September 1986 by the Rt Hon (now Lord) Chris Patten.

The Prime Minister put Patten into the Department, as he once said, in order to take the 'sting out of the aid debate' (which she had created) and which he did with considerable success. In his first public speech he noted that the media had said he had been sent to the 'salt mines' but that he did not see it like that. He wooed the NGOs – admittedly partly by exponentially increasing the Department's funding for their work overseas but, importantly, by convincing them that not everything the Department did was driven by short-term political and commercial expediency.

He was succeeded three years later by the Rt Hon Lynda Chalker MP, who was both the FCO Minister for Africa and the Minister of Overseas Development. She held those posts for more than a decade and in 1992, on losing her Wallasey constituency, became Baroness Chalker, with additional responsibilities in the House of Lords until 1997. Like Patten, Chalker defended the Department's basic mission and earned world-wide respect for her concern for development, particularly in Africa, defending human rights, urging better governance, and responding to humanitarian crises.

## The fall of the Berlin Wall

With the collapse of the Berlin Wall and the Soviet Union, the Department had an important strategic decision to make. Despite its basic mission of helping to reduce poverty in the poorest countries, should it become marginalised in Whitehall or offer to use its expertise in this new area and help the countries of the ex-Soviet Union and Eastern and Central Europe, which were to be called Countries in Transition, to convert a market economy? The FCO had been given £50m to help Poland but without any capacity to spend it effectively.

The Department decided to offer to help, though the FCO (Diplomatic Wing) was reluctant to give up control. However a compromise was eventually reached involving dual control. A joint FCO/ODA Division was created, initially with dual reporting lines, and jointly staffed by the Department and the Diplomatic Wing. This resulted in the Department taking over effective control of assistance to all the transition countries because of its aid management expertise. It also led the Department into large humanitarian aid operations, including some in close liaison with the military (notably in Bosnia and Kosovo). Some might say it was a diversion from the Department's basic mission but there was considerable poverty in many of these countries of Central and Eastern Europe and an urgent need to help transform their economies to reduce poverty and to set them on the path to join the European Union. The level of aid to the transition countries reduced as many joined the European Union and benefited from its internal budgetary mechanisms.

## The Fundamental Expenditure Review 1995

The Conservative administrations between 1979 and 1997 did not produce a new White Paper on Aid. However, during 1995 the Department was required, like all government departments, to undertake a Fundamental Expenditure Review (FER) which was intended to provide a more robust framework within which to conduct annual public expenditure surveys. The FER Report was made publicly available and its conclusions as agreed by ministers were set out in the 1996 Departmental Report. As in all FERs, the Department was required first to ask whether its expenditure programme was justified and should continue. The answer to this first question was yes: 'There is a strong moral case for using part of the nation's wealth to improve the quality of life and reduce poverty and suffering in poorer countries and the provision of aid is in the UK's interest too in that it helps create a more prosperous and stable world.'

The FER also re-affirmed the advantage seen in having all aspects of overseas aid managed 'through a single administrative unit'. It went on to consider the aid programme's basic goal and purpose and recommended a new Mission Statement which read as follows: 'ODA's purpose is to improve the quality of life of people in poorer countries by contributing to sustainable development and reducing poverty and suffering.'

Finally, the FER tackled the age-old issue of the geographical spread of Britain's bilateral country aid programmes. It noted:

> compared with a few years ago, ODA is working in more countries and undertaking more complex activities, while the resources available for bilateral programmes have been shrinking and are expected to continue to decline [. . .] it would be difficult to sustain ODA as an effective player in so many countries in terms of achieving developmental impact and enhancing UK influence [and] that key decision criteria for determining further concentration should be the relative need for aid, ODA's effectiveness (sufficient UK capacity to deliver development impact and influence others in the development community), and British national interest.

Had the FER stopped there some might think that the decision criteria were sufficiently wide so as to make further concentration of the Department's bilateral programmes difficult to achieve. However, ministers agreed that for many countries, particularly middle-income ones, the Department should run down its own-administered programmes and leave the Diplomatic Mission to run modest delegated British Partnership Schemes (previously known as the Heads of Mission Small Projects Scheme and Small Gifts Scheme). This was achieved at the relatively modest price of a somewhat more generous allocation of aid for these purposes.

## Eliminating world poverty

In its General Election Manifesto of 1997, *New Labour Because Britain Deserves Better*, the Labour Party stated the following:

> Labour will also attach much higher priority to combating global poverty and under-development. According to the World Bank, there

are 1.3 billion people in the world who live in absolute poverty, sub-
sisting on less than US$1 a day, while 35,000 children die each day
from readily preventable diseases.

Labour believes that we have a clear moral responsibility to help com-
bat global poverty. In government we will strengthen and restructure
the British aid programme and bring development issues back into
the mainstream of government decision-making. A Cabinet minister
will lead a new department of international development.

We will shift aid resources towards programmes that help the poorest
people in the poorest countries. We reaffirm the UK's commitment to
the 0.7 per cent UN aid target and in government Labour will start to
reverse the decline in UK aid spending.

We will support further measures to reduce the debt burden borne by
the world's poorest countries and to ensure that developing countries
are given a fair deal in international trade. It is our aim to rejoin
UNESCO.

The Labour Party manifesto also pledged to set out a timetable for
'sustained progress towards the UN aid target within the next ten years',
targeting bilateral aid where it was most needed, and ending the tying
of aid.

When the Labour administration was elected in May 1997, the Rt
Hon Clare Short MP was made Secretary of State for International
Development. The new Secretary of State was determined that its role
should be clearly seen as concerned with international affairs affecting
developing countries in which it was a partner with others in Whitehall,
rather than a Department concerned only with the provision of aid.

Short already had a reputation for plain speaking and she quickly
established within the Department clarity of purpose. She established
that the sole purpose of the Department was to eliminate or at least
reduce poverty in the poorest countries of the world, and that expenditure within her responsibility should not have a dual purpose. Thus
she fought for and achieved the abolition of the ATP scheme (of which
more in Chapter Nine). This was initially opposed by the DTI and its
new Secretary of State. On leaving an appearance before the House of
Commons Select Committee on International Development to go to a
meeting with the new DTI Secretary of State about the future of ATP,
she was given a copy of a letter to the Prime Minister by the Secretary

of State for Trade and Industry arguing for a retention of the ATP scheme. She cancelled the meeting, went back to the Department and wrote to the Prime Minister in uncompromising terms. The scheme was abolished.

Similarly, she considered that while the work of the British Council was to be valued she saw no reason why the Department should provide it with part of its grant-in-aid. She surrendered some £30 million to the FCO so that it should be its sole sponsoring department on the condition that at least that amount should continue to be used for development purposes. And in that vein she reviewed all the Department's programmes.

The 1997 White Paper[31] put a new stamp on the Department. Following an intensive review of all its policies, the White Paper did two things. First, it made clear that the Department's sole objective was to reduce world poverty through sustainable development. Second, it effectively mobilised all relevant Whitehall departments to the same end, be it in relation to debt, conflict resolution, liberalisation of international trade and protecting the environment. For Short's views on the 1997 White Paper and later development issues, including her relationship with the Prime Minister, Tony Blair, and the then Chancellor, Gordon Brown, see also her book, *An Honourable Deception?*, written shortly after her resignation in 2003.[32]

Most importantly the White Paper endorsed the International Development Targets (IDTs) which had been agreed in the DAC in 1996[33] and which Britain had been instrumental in establishing. These were:

1. a reduction by one-half in the proportion of people living in extreme poverty by 2015 (popularly defined as living on less than $1 per day);
2. universal primary education in all countries by 2015;
3. eliminating gender disparity in primary and secondary education by 2005;
4. a reduction by two-thirds in mortality rates in infants and children under age 5 and a reduction by three-fourths in maternal mortality by 2015;
5. access through primary health care systems to reproductive health services for all individuals of appropriate ages as soon as possible and no later than 2015;
6. implementation of national strategies for sustainable development in all countries by 2005 to ensure that current trends in the loss of

environmental resources are effectively reversed at both global and national levels by 2015.

Despite a new firmness of purpose, the White Paper contained considerable continuity of policy. It re-asserted the importance of sound economic policies at a macro-economic level – responsible monetary policy and public finances to contain inflation and to allow the private sector to flourish, including a continuation of privatisation measures. In this the new Secretary of State led the policy rather than simply follow the Treasury. Her concern was that within the need for fiscal responsibility governments should focus more of their resources to directly reduce poverty, improve basic services and meet the IDTs.

The IDTs had emerged from various UN Summits over nearly a decade and were given added importance when in 1996 the OECD donors collectively committed themselves to a partnership with developing countries and countries in transition, the success of which would be measured against these key targets. The Department set itself the objective of ensuring that the IDTs would be kept at the forefront of the development agenda and pursued with vigour. In addition to the original IDTs the WHO agreed two further targets for improvement in people's health – in relation to HIV infection rates and reductions in TB and malaria mortality. Furthermore the second World Water Summit, in The Hague in September 2000, recognised the disappointing progress made over the previous twenty years in the areas of safe drinking water and sanitation. It agreed a new target for access to safe water and improved water resource management, though it was surprisingly silent on sanitation.

## 'Making Globalisation Work for the Poor'

In 2000 a further White Paper, 'Eliminating World Poverty, Making Globalisation Work for the Poor', was issued which focused on the challenges of globalisation.[34] It was intended to supplement, not replace, the 1997 White Paper. It committed the government as a whole to a set of policies to help ensure that the trend towards globalisation would benefit poor countries and, within them, poor people.

The White Paper took for granted that globalisation was an inevitable process, and defined it as:

the growing inter-dependence and inter-connectedness of the modern world. The process is driven by technological advance and reductions in the costs of international transactions, which spread technology and ideas, raise the share of trade in world production, and increase the mobility of capital. It is also reflected in the diffusion of global norms and values, the spread of democracy and the proliferation of global agreements and treaties, including international environmental and human rights agreements.

It went on to state:

managed wisely, the new wealth being created by globalisation creates the opportunity to lift millions of the world's poorest people out of their poverty. Managed badly and it could lead to their further marginalisation and impoverishment. Neither outcome is predetermined; it depends on the policy choices adopted by governments, international institutions, the private sector and civil society . . .

The White Paper set out the government's commitment to work with others to manage globalisation so that poverty would be systematically reduced and the Millennium Development Goals (MDGs) achieved, as well as to promote economic growth that is equitable and environmentally sustainable. The MDGs emerged from the IDTs and were endorsed at the 2000 UN Millennium Development Summit.

## The International Development Act 2002

Following the 1997 and 2000 White Papers, Parliament passed the 2002 International Development Act. This was intended to further focus the aid programme on reducing poverty. Although the Act is drafted in fairly general terms it did for the first time include the requirement (Part 1, Section 1 (i)) that the Secretary of State 'may provide any person or body with development assistance if he is satisfied that the provision of the assistance *is likely to contribute to a reduction in poverty*' (author's italics).

The Act also went on to refer to sustainable development. Part 1, paragraphs 2 and 3 state:

2. In this Act development assistance means assistance provided for the purpose of
   a. furthering sustainable development in one or more countries outside the United Kingdom, or
   b. improving the welfare of the population of one or more such countries.

3. For the purposes of sub-section 2(a) 'sustainable development' includes any development that is in the opinion of the Secretary of State prudent having regard to the likelihood of it generating lasting benefits for the population of a country or countries in relation to which it is provided.

It is also relevant to note that British overseas territories continued to receive a special mention in Part 1, paragraph 2 of the Act:

The Secretary of State may also provide any person or body with development assistance in a case where the requirement of Section I (i) is not met if assistance is provided in relation to one or more of the territories for the time being mentioned in Section 6 of the British Nationality Act of 1981 (British Overseas Territories).

## 'Making Governance Work for the Poor'

For the 2005 General Election each of the three main parties produced a manifesto committing to the achievement of the UN aid target within a clear time-frame (2013).

The new Labour government issued a further White Paper in 2006[35] whilst the Rt Hon Hilary Benn MP was Secretary of State for International Development. It built upon the previous White Papers and focused on promoting both national and international good governance. It was the first White Paper to confirm a target date for Britain meeting the UN target for oda of 0.7 per cent of Gross National Income by 2013. It reinforced Britain's commitments made at the 2005 G8 Summit, in particular to Africa, in the context of concentrating development assistance on countries with the largest numbers of poor people, particularly in sub-Saharan Africa and South Asia; and on fragile states, especially those vulnerable to conflict.

## 'Building our Common Future'

The Department produced a further White Paper in July 2009.[36] It emphasised both continuity of its mission and the need for change to respond to the global economic crisis, which it recognised could reverse progress towards the MDGs. There was to be a particular focus on addressing the causes of low growth, climate change, and conflict and fragility in many of the poorest countries. It committed the Department to allocating at least half of new bilateral aid to conflict-affected and fragile states.

## Public Service Agreements

With the introduction of the two-yearly Comprehensive Spending Reviews under the 1997 Labour government also came Public Service Agreements (PSAs). These are designed to translate broad policy statements into more specific, time-bound objectives and targets for the coming three years. Each department in Whitehall negotiated its PSA with the Treasury, but they were in effect a contract with Parliament intended to better hold departments to account for the monies voted to them by Parliament and hence by the taxpayer. During the period of the Labour government (1997–2010) the Department had five successive PSAs. The format and focus of these has evolved over the years but they each embraced the MDGs, increasingly reflected joint targets with other parts of Whitehall, and asserted the importance of strengthening the international aid system.

The PSA published in October 2007 covered the period 2008–11.[37] It was more narrative in style than previous PSAs, without numbered objectives, and is more akin to a mini-White Paper setting out actions for the coming three years. It re-affirms the centrality of the MDGs and the fact that 'in this global environment, international co-operation is also needed on issues that go beyond the delivery of traditional aid programmes: issues such as trade, the environment and climate change, and conflict and security'. As before, it focused on working through the bilateral development programmes, working with the multilateral development institutions, and influencing the international system. In terms of the Department's bilateral programmes, for the first time it emphasised the importance of focusing on countries with the largest number of poor people (that is, South Asia as well as Africa) and on working with fragile states, which it defines as governments unable or unwilling to deliver core functions to the majority of its people, and which it lists as Afghanistan, Cambodia, Democratic Republic of Congo (DRC), Ethiopia, Kenya, Nepal, Nigeria, Sierra Leone, Sudan, Yemen and Zimbabwe.

This PSA explicitly recognised the problem of attributing the Department's own efforts to results in partner countries, and while measuring progress globally 'will focus on measuring progress [against the MDGs] in the 22 countries where the Department can make an impact . . . [t]his choice of countries is based on the numbers of poor people; the size of the UK bilateral programme; the impact of a wider set of multilateral and bilateral programmes and policies; and the overall influence of the UK on policy development'. They were, in Africa: DRC,

Ethiopia, Ghana, Kenya, Malawi, Mozambique, Sierra Leone, Rwanda, Sudan, Tanzania, Uganda, Zambia and Zimbabwe; in Asia: Afghanistan, Bangladesh, Cambodia, India, Nepal, Pakistan and Vietnam; and Yemen in the Middle East. It retained the target of allocating 90 per cent of its bilateral aid programme to low-income countries but dropped the reference in earlier PSAs to improving the performance of its project portfolio. In terms of delivery, the PSA cites the role of a number of other government departments (FCO, HM Treasury, Department for Environment, Food and Rural Affairs, Department for Business, Enterprise and Regulatory Reform, Ministry of Defence, Department of Health), giving even greater emphasis to joined-up government than before.

Some of the changes in the five successive PSAs have more to do with improving presentation than strengthening their substance. However, there have been important changes of emphasis. First, later PSAs highlight the importance of mobilising and making more effective the international aid system. The last two PSAs both recognise the work the Department was doing to elaborate new development policies that will strengthen efforts of the international community and developing countries to reduce poverty. But most significant of all, there was the emphasis on joined-up government, with many targets being shared with a range of other government departments.

The manifestos for the three main parties for the May 2010 General Election each re-affirmed a commitment to the UN 0.7 per cent aid target by 2013 despite the difficult fiscal position.

The 2010 Coalition government initially produced three important documents. The first was the Coalition Agreement[38] itself which committed the new government 'to honouring Britain's aid commitments to allocate 0.7% of GNI to overseas aid from 2013', while at the same time ensuring 'greater transparency and scrutiny of aid spending to deliver value for money for British taxpayers and to maximise the impact of our aid budget'. The former reflected both Conservative and Liberal Democrat party manifestos and the latter the need to reassure the electorate at a time of severe cuts in public spending generally. Its specific commitments to help achieve the MDGs, including through stronger political and economic governance, debt forgiveness for the poorest countries, an increasingly joined-up government approach to conflict resolution and reconstruction, and a strengthening of the international aid system, reflected a continuation of the previous government's policies. Importantly, the Coalition Agreement pledged that it 'will keep aid untied from commercial interests and will maintain

DFID [the Department for International Development] as an independent Department focused on poverty reduction'. It is notable that for the first time a British Prime Minister, David Cameron MP, made a commitment to a time-bound achievement of the 0.7 per cent UN aid target at the September 2012 UN General Assembly.

The second paper[39] set out the reviews it intended to undertake to achieve these objectives, emphasising 'direct action to deliver the MDGs, wealth creation, governance and security, climate change and global partnerships'. The initial results of these reviews were contained in its further publication[40] in March 2011. This specified the number of people that would benefit from British aid in terms of the MDGs, including in terms of education and health improvements, particularly for girls and women, and of helping people work their way out of poverty. It promised greater results and impact, and to be more transparent and accountable, by establishing a new Independent Commission for Aid Impact, reporting directly to Parliament.

The reviews of bilateral aid programmes resulted in a decision to end bilateral aid to 17 countries either because they no longer needed aid (China and Russia), or could be better helped by others. This leaves 27 countries on which the Department will focus its efforts, plus three aid-dependent Overseas Territories: St Helena, Pitcairn and Montserrat. The reviews of multilateral aid programmes concluded that Britain should cease core support for four agencies which they believed provided poor value for money: the ILO, the UN International Strategy for Disaster Reduction, UN-Habitat and UNIDO. In addition, other organisations were judged to have serious weaknesses and would be placed on 'special measures'; these included the International Organisation for Migration, FAO, the development programmes of the Commonwealth Secretariat and UNESCO – for which core funding would cease after two years unless progress were made in their performance.

## Inter-departmental consultation

Government policies as reflected in White Papers are agreed by either the full Cabinet, a Cabinet Sub Committee, or a less formal ad hoc group of interested ministers, sometimes by correspondence. The Prime Minister will have endorsed the policy, and the doctrine of collective responsibility requires all ministers to accept and, as necessary, support it. Therefore, what is not said is as significant as what is. For example, the lack of a timetable for meeting the UN aid target in the first four White Papers was significant in that it reflected a lack of collective government commitment to a policy that would have breached the strongly held position of the Treasury that public expenditure priorities should be determined in the round over a specific time period, having regard to the economic circumstances then prevailing.

The absence of a new White Paper on overseas development during the Conservative governments of 1979–97 can best be explained by the fact that no Minister of State for the Department during that period was confident that collective agreement by those ministers concerned, including the Prime Minister, was possible on a text that would have been acceptable to themselves. The outcome of the 1980 Aid Policy Review as put to Parliament was a poor substitute for a White Paper and exposed the underlying tension between continuing to pursue the basic mission of the Department, which had a wide measure of support, and wishing to give greater weight to short-term political and commercial considerations. Better, therefore, to live with the ambiguity than expose the tensions further by seeking to elaborate an aid policy in a White Paper.

With or without an extant White Paper the official Joint Aid Policy Committee (JAPC) provided the forum for seeking to agree broad policy issues relating to aid which might bear on the interests of other departments. It was chaired by the Department's Permanent Secretary and comprised officials from the FCO, DTI and HM Treasury. Its main function was to seek agreement on the allocation of the agreed aid budget over the coming three or so years between individual aid programmes. In general the JAPC sought only minor changes to the Department's proposals, though it might be argued that during the period 1979–97 the Department was more likely to feel the need to take account of the views of other Whitehall departments at working level before formal proposals were put to the JAPC. For the twenty years 1977–97, there was a JAPC Sub Committee on Aid and Trade (SCAT) that sought (some may say fought) to reach agreement on the management of the ATP (see Chapter Nine).

## Seeking resources

First, however, the Department had to secure its funding in what used to be called the annual Public Expenditure Survey, and after 1997 was known as the Comprehensive Spending Review (CSR), conducted biennially. This was a matter primarily for the Department and the Treasury to thrash out. It was a time of the year when each Whitehall department needed to look after its own interests, so one could not expect any help from another quarter, and the JAPC played no role. The PES/CSR process is the nearest thing the government has for deciding rationally on the allocation of total public resources deemed available for spending by the Treasury, having regard to macro-economic considerations. The process is essentially a political one, and is driven largely by the party electoral manifesto, subsequent events and the ministerial personalities involved.

In formulating a bid for additional aid resources successive ministers for the Department might reasonably argue in support of their party's commitment to the UN aid target of 0.7 per cent of GNI, even though until recently no party had set a timetable for achieving it. Depending upon the political and economic climate, the Department's bid might be couched either in terms of making progress towards the UN target (usually rather modestly) or at least not falling further behind it. The former argument appears to have had little success in the second half of the 1960s or in the mid-1970s, and the latter argument carried little weight in the 1980s and early 1990s. An additional and sometimes more cogent argument was how Britain's performance compared with that of other G7 and EU donor countries, particularly in later years. The fact that Britain was lagging behind other major international players, and by implication therefore might carry less influence, was an argument that appealed to successive Foreign Secretaries during the Conservative administrations of 1979–97. The main problem for the Department in this argument was the USA: it did not accept the UN aid target in principle and performed very poorly against it in practice, and its superpower status depended on large defence expenditure. A further perceived logical flaw in the argument was the UK government's strongly held belief that it 'punched above its weight', a phrase associated particularly with Sir Douglas (now Lord) Hurd, when he was Foreign Secretary.

There were at various times more immediate arguments for additional resources, though given the nature and composition of the aid budget they were seldom compelling, except possibly in political terms. One such argument was the ever-increasing aid demands of the EU, which were politically difficult to resist and which therefore would continue to encroach on Britain's bilateral aid programmes unless the total aid budget was increased. Another was the international response in helping 'countries in transition', following the collapse of the Soviet Union. A third arose from the prolonged crises (such as Kosovo and Afghanistan) which not only made medium-term demands on the aid budget but which could have been regarded as inappropriate were they to be met by reductions in aid elsewhere.

It was sometimes noted that the aid budget accounted for less than 1 per cent of total public expenditure and that even a substantial increase in aid would not materially impact on the Treasury's total public expenditure arithmetic. Unfortunately this carried little or no weight with the Treasury, which fought each expenditure round on the basis of trade-offs at the margin. Allied to this sort of thinking was the judgement as to whether it was better to settle with the Treasury early (while it still had 'uncommitted' funds to negotiate with) or to hold out until towards the end in the hope of getting more but with the risk of the Treasury having conceded to others what little it had left. The former might mean having to settle for less than one might otherwise get; the latter might mean coming to the attention of the Prime Minister and being subject to the Star Chamber, a small sub-committee of Cabinet ministers, chaired by a senior minister whose Department's budget was no longer in contention, to arbitrate on outstanding expenditure settlements. For most of the Department's history the latter course of action was considered either high-risk and to be avoided or, in recent years, unnecessary. When the Department was under the Foreign Secretary, he might consider taking his Diplomatic Wing bid to the Star Chamber, in which case he would have wanted to have settled the aid bid, as indeed would the Department to avoid the Foreign Secretary being offered a trade-off between the two bids. The outcome of these bids is best seen by examining the actual change in the size of the aid budget over time (in nominal and real terms), which is shown in Chapter Ten.

## The changing status of the Department

As outlined in Chapter Three, the Department was established in 1964 as a separate Ministry of Overseas Development (ODM) with a Secretary of State in the Cabinet, a step driven partly by politics and partly by the need to change the machinery of government in response to a changing world. When the Conservative Party, under the Rt Hon Edward Heath MP, was returned to government in 1970 the Department became the responsibility of the Foreign Secretary and was renamed the Overseas Development Administration. It had its own Minister of State and remained a separate department with its own Permanent Secretary and staff. It reflected a view that aid was one tool of foreign policy and should ultimately be the responsibility of the Foreign Secretary. Many feared, however, that this was a return to the Conservative ideas of the early 1960s whereby a separate Department would be an executive institution implementing FCO policies (see Chapter Three). Although the morale of staff in the Department plummeted, these fears proved largely unfounded. Certain important issues were referred to the Foreign Secretary, but for the most part aid decisions were made by the aid minister.

In 1974, the next Labour government, with the Rt Hon Harold Wilson MP again its Prime Minister for the first two years, re-established the Department as a separate Ministry of Overseas Development. The jointly staffed Dependent Territories Division of the FCO continued in existence, as did the official inter-departmental machinery for discussing aid policies. Again, in 1979 with the return of a Conservative government, ODM became ODA, responsible to the Foreign Secretary. But, as in 1970, the Department had its own Minister of State and separate administration headed by a Permanent Secretary. There was again an expectation by many that the new ODA would be more subservient to the demands of the FCO Diplomatic Wing and the Department of Trade and Industry (DTI). Fortunately for the Department, the Treasury was generally opposed to using scarce aid resources in the richer developing countries or more generally for short-term political purposes, and even more antipathetic to the DTI's interventionist policies of promoting sometimes uncompetitive exports using aid funds.

So what has been the significance and impact of the variations in the status of the Department? The Foreign Secretary of the day is one of the three most senior ministers in government after the Prime Minister and therefore can be expected to wield considerable influence. To what extent, and in what direction, that influence is exercised when he is responsible for the Department depended upon his own political philosophy, and the confidence he had in his Minister of State and senior officials. He would of course receive advice from his own Private Office, no doubt influenced on occasions by other Diplomatic Wing officials. Throughout much of the Thatcher government and beyond it became standard practice for a member of the Department to be part of the Foreign Secretary's Private Office.

There were particular occasions when the Foreign Secretary needed to be consulted; otherwise other considerable demands on his time meant that he was bound to leave the day-to-day running of the Department in terms of its aid policies and management to his Minister of State. By definition there were occasions on which the Foreign Secretary could affect the level of resources available to the Department and shape the policy according to which those resources would be deployed. The key event that the Foreign Secretary needed to lead on was the annual Public Expenditure Survey (PES) exercise which would largely determine the level of resources the Department would have over the coming three years. The PES bid for aid would be submitted to the Treasury by the Foreign Secretary based upon a submission put forward by his Minister of State drafted by and discussed with the Department's senior officials. It usually resulted in meetings between the Foreign Secretary and the Minister of State and his/her senior officials. Diplomatic Wing officials, apart from his Private Secretary, were not involved in such meetings. In general, successive Foreign Secretaries during the Conservative administrations (1979–97) increasingly recognised the importance of aid as part of Britain's role internationally, and the importance of sustaining a substantial bilateral aid programme in the face of increasing multilateral aid obligations, particularly the growing aid demands of the European Commission.

PES negotiations were generally conducted between the Foreign Secretary and the Chief Secretary to the Treasury. Discussions were attended by the relevant senior officials from the Treasury and the Department. The Aid and Diplomatic Wing bids were normally discussed separately, something the Treasury, as well as the Department, preferred. However, in his own mind the Foreign Secretary was able to give different weight to his Aid and Diplomatic Wing bids in reaching agreement with Treasury ministers.

Following a PES agreement the Department would undertake an internal exercise to allocate the total agreed aid budget for the next three years among its various programmes. While the Department was the ODA under the Foreign Secretary, each country aid programme bid was required to be discussed, but not necessarily agreed, with the FCO Diplomatic Wing. Once the expenditure allocations were agreed internally at working level they were discussed and agreed with the relevant senior Diplomatic Wing officials at a meeting chaired by the Department's Permanent Secretary. They were then discussed inter-departmentally in the official Joint Aid Policy Committee.

Outsiders might expect these consultations to have been fairly 'bloody' affairs, particularly if the Department's officials were intent on pursuing its basic mission. But in the author's experience this was not so. Because multilateral commitments generally are spent over a long period, most of the policy issues in deciding the expenditure allocations for the coming three years related to the distribution of resources within the bilateral aid programmes. As regards country aid programmes, there would be two kinds of policy issue. The first was the extent to which bilateral aid to a particular country should be affected by its government's economic policies and political behaviour. This could give rise in the early 1980s to some serious disagreements between the FCO (Diplomatic Wing) and the Department, but this became rare by 1990 with the ending of the Cold War. The second was the extent to which Britain should retain modest programmes of technical co-operation with middle-income countries in South America and South East Asia. Here, Diplomatic Wing ambitions were indeed modest: at most the argument would be about an additional allocation of £10–15 million annually, and it was usually conducted in a quiet and resigned manner. The DTI's prime concern was the size of the ATP allocation. The Treasury had two roles: one was to test whether expenditure allocations reflected agreed policy objectives and represented value for money; the other was to ensure that there were sufficient funds set aside in an unallocated reserve to meet unanticipated demands rather than having to call on the Treasury's Central Reserve. The former usually meant supporting the Department, and the second required the Treasury to say that whatever the proposed size of the Unallocated Reserve it was not enough.

At each stage in the process the Department'sminister would be consulted, from setting out a broad strategy to setting detailed expenditure allocations. It was then submitted to the Foreign Secretary, who at this stage was unlikely to ask for changes. He then sent the proposals, with a covering letter, to the Prime Minister, copied to relevant colleagues: he did not invite his colleagues to approve it – instead he noted what he had decided and invited any comments. The Chief Secretary would routinely say that he wished the Unallocated Reserve were larger but he was content provided the Foreign Secretary was confident he could manage unanticipated demands on the aid budget without seeking recourse to the Central Reserve. The Secretary of State for Trade and Industry might make some reference to the need for flexible and speedy management of ATP and bemoan the increasing share of the aid programme that was being devoted to multilateral aid.

Was any of this very different when the Department was a separate ministry? The answer depends very much on the strength and inclination of the minister of the day. In the periods 1964–70 and 1974–79 the process of inter-departmental consultation was similar to that described above, except the FCO did not have an inside track. After 1997, initially under Clare Short, the Department had a more robust approach to inter-departmental consultation. She did not like official advice from the Department to have been diluted by any negotiations within Whitehall: the objective of the aid programme was unambiguous – poverty reduction – and how the aid budget should best be used to achieve it was a matter for the Department. That said, when it came to formulating and implementing international development policies, she wished the whole of Whitehall to be mobilised behind achieving them. In the current Conservative-led Coalition government the Department has retained its status as a separate Department for International Development.

When the Department was part of the FCO, the Foreign Secretary was also consulted on major multilateral aid negotiations because of their impact on future aid budgets. These would include the Department's position in the three-yearly IDA negotiations, its negotiating position within the EU on the five-yearly negotiations for the European Development Fund (EDF), and the annual EC budget discussions essentially negotiated in Brussels by the Treasury. In general Foreign Secretaries valued bilateral aid and would prefer to take a tough position on these multilateral negotiations while recognising the political realities and, in the case of the EC budget, potential trade-offs between aid and other issues.

The Foreign Secretary might also be consulted on issues likely to become controversial in Whitehall, often concerning proposals by the DTI for the use of the ATP, which the Department, supported by the Treasury, was opposed to, though which the Diplomatic Wing tended to be sympathetic towards.

## Comment

Would the Department have been better able to pursue its mission, and secure more resources for its work, had it remained a separate ministry under a Conservative government? That would have depended largely on the seniority of the minister and the influence that he or she could yield. Arguably Prime Minister Thatcher would not have appointed a minister for the Department as a separate ministry that could have begun to match that of the Foreign Secretary in terms of influence if he wished to exercise it. Most Foreign Secretaries under Thatcher increasingly appreciated the role of aid as part of Britain's international position and were sceptical of the DTI's ambitions regarding the ATP. This does not appear to have been so as regards Thatcher herself, which suggests that as a separate ministry the Department may have had an even more difficult time. It is true that while the Treasury in its international, financial and economic role was generally supportive of, and supported by, the Department, there was one important time in the year when they were bound to be adversaries (that is, during the PES negotiations over the size of the aid budget).

As a separate ministry, the Department's minister has been influential partly because Labour governments have been more sympathetic to international development concerns and partly because at times it has had senior and robust ministers, mainly women such as Barbara Castle, Judith Hart and Clare Short.

Despite some political twists and turns the basic mission of the Department has remained remarkably constant, namely to reduce poverty in the poorest countries. This is reflected in its successive White Papers, though each had its own emphasis. The 1965 White Paper was expressed in fairly general terms; the 1975 White Paper emphasised the importance of rural development. Even the 1981 Aid Review asserted that the basic purpose of the aid programme was the reduction of poverty, while concluding that greater weight should be given to political and commercial considerations. It only partially deflected the Department from its basic mission despite the aspirations of the FCO and the DTI. However, at that time it had substantially reduced resources with which to pursue its mission.

The biggest threat to the Department's mission became the ATP. As suggested earlier, when it was set up it was seen as a small price to pay to allow the Department to get on with its basic mission. But the DTI had increasingly threatening ambitions. The author shared a public platform with a senior DTI official in the mid-1980s to address business figures. The DTI official likened ATP to the Isle of Wight, saying that the the Department still controlled the mainland, which business needed to capture. As we will see in Chapter Nine, by the early 1990s the ATP was absorbing about 10 per cent of the Department's bilateral aid budget.

The second most important shift in policy in the early 1990s was for the Department to become involved in the transition countries of the former Soviet Union and East and Central Europe and also take financial responsibility for the European Bank for Reconstruction and Development (EBRD), though the Chancellor was its Governor. The Department secured some additional resources for this (see Chapter Ten).

The 1997 White Paper was more forthright than its predecessors and intensified the Department's focus on its basic mission: for the first time it explicitly made poverty reduction the sole purpose of the aid programme; it formally extended the remit of the Department beyond aid; and explicitly endorsed the IDTs (later to become, with some adjustments, the MDGs). The same was true of the 2000 White Paper which focused on globalisation, the 2006 White Paper which focused on governance for the poor and for the first time reflected

Britain's commitment to a timetable for achieving the UN 0.7 per cent aid target by 2013, and the 2009 White Paper which sought to respond to the changed global economic situation. This commitment has been endorsed by the current Coalition government.

This relative continuity has much to do with the dedication and leadership of the Department's succession of ministers, a generally bi-partisan approach in Parliament, particularly in the Foreign Affairs/ International Development Select Committees, at least with regard to the focus of the aid programme if not always its size, and the skills and commitment of the Department's staff. The ATP (see Chapter Nine) was initially a relatively small part of the aid budget, but having become a greater threat later was abolished in 1997. Aid to Britain's overseas territories also remained modest, though they have continued to be seen as having a special charge on the aid programme. The amount of funds going to middle-income countries, mainly in Latin America at the behest of the FCO, also remained modest. Britain continued its commitment to the multilateral aid system, in particular to those parts of it that the Department believed were effective. In all this, history played an important part given Britain's historic link with the Commonwealth, most of whose members were poor.

Whether the Department was independent or not arguably mattered less than most outsiders have believed. Rather it depended crucially on whether or not the government as a whole was committed to international development, and on the role of aid and other international policies in reducing poverty. It is the commitment of the government as a whole to reducing poverty overseas and the increasingly joined-up approach in Whitehall that made the difference after 1997.

# 5
# Development Policies

## Introduction

This chapter traces changes in development and aid policies over the life of the Department as it sought to pursue its mission. It reflects upon international development thinking and work of academia, and the extent to which the Department was influenced by, and influenced, such thinking.

## The historical context

When the Department was established in 1964 most developing countries with which it had a significant aid relationship had become independent in the previous twenty years or were about to become so. Political independence was seen as a first step towards national independence which for most countries meant state control of their economies and an ability to shape their own future development. This was true of most of sub-Saharan Africa, the Indian sub-continent and South East Asia. A number of developing-country political leaders and senior officials were trained in the Soviet Union and Eastern Europe and were influenced by their prevailing ideologies of socialism and state intervention. Many more political leaders and senior officials were trained in and had strong connections with the West, including, in particular, Britain. They were exposed to the thinking of Western governments which in varying degrees accepted the need for substantial state intervention. The 'socialist' parties in those countries, and the academic community, which with a few exceptions also emphasised the leading role of the state in order to achieve economic and social development, were important influences.

Against this background, and reinforced by nationalist sentiments, most developing countries following independence enhanced considerably the role of the state, and at a time when their technical competency for doing so was limited. Central banks replaced Currency Boards, with power to 'print money'. There was an inadequate recognition of the relationship between inflation and balance of payments disequilibria on the one hand, and fiscal and monetary policies on the other. There was considerable political concern that many of the largest private enterprises were in foreign ownership: economic independence required that many, and in some cases all, foreign enterprises of any size should be brought into state ownership. A major problem, particularly in Africa, was the lack of an indigenous entrepreneurial class in many countries except, of course, in the small-scale business sector and a large part of rural economies.

The political processes at that time can be divided generally between those newly independent countries that established early democratic structures such as India, Sri Lanka and a few in Africa (such as Botswana) and others which became dictatorships either periodically, such as Pakistan, or more or less permanently, such as Myanmar (Burma) and other countries in South America. Many countries in Africa became one-party states in the name of African socialism, notably Tanzania (under Nyerere), Zambia (under Kaunda), Ghana (under Nkrumah), and Guinea (under Sékou Touré). While for the most part rejecting 'scientific socialism' it advocated a major interventionist role for the state to achieve economic and social progress.

A preoccupation with industrialisation, and the concern to placate the more vocal urban populations, often led governments to adopt policies that discriminated against peasant agriculture to keep food prices for the urban dwellers artificially low. They were able to do this using their monopoly buying power to hold down prices to farmers for staple foods such as maize and rice through state-owned Marketing Boards which their previous colonial masters, particularly in Africa, had bequeathed them. In too many cases small farmers were not recognised as entrepreneurs who needed incentives if they were to adopt new farming methods and produce the surpluses required. Subsidies for foodstuffs were also made available either directly or through allowing Marketing Boards and state-owned food processing plants to be run at a loss, something that became more difficult to sustain as governments' overall fiscal positions became more precarious. Furthermore, the monopoly power of governments over export crops, which were originally designed to cushion price fluctuations, became a convenient source of taxation (most notably in the case of cocoa in Ghana). While development analysts have long been concerned about the nutritional consequences of export crops being given precedence over food crops, the early problem was the discrimination against agriculture generally. This was despite putting public funds into largely ineffective agricultural extension services. For a brief but insightful account of early policy obstacles to development see Harry Johnson's book on *Economic Policies Towards Less Developed Countries*[41] and *Markets and States in Tropical Africa* by Robert Bates.[42]

## Some early development thinking

The first White Paper (1965) was a statement of aid policy and explicitly said that developing countries needed to find their own path to development. That said, the Department, in particular the EPS, were influenced in their work by some early academic thinking, mainly that concerned with capital accumulation. First, there was the readibly understandable Harrod-Domar model of economic growth.[43] In a closed economy, economic growth was a function of domestic savings available for investment and the incremental capital-output ratio. In an open economy, domestic savings could be augmented by foreign private capital and foreign aid, though there was of course, as appreciated later, also the risk of capital flight. It was largely on this type of analysis that the UN and others argued that 1 per cent of developed countries' GDP should be transferred to the poorer countries (see Chapter Ten).

However, the Harrod-Domar model was a simple mathematical equation and offered little by way of an explanation of how its two elements might be determined. This was left to other development economists. One of these was W. W. Rostow[44] with his three stages of development. The first comprised a traditional society both in terms of social structures and, for the most part, static production functions to which modern science and technology was either not available or not widely applied. Thus there was a limit to output per head despite annual fluctuations due, for example, to weather or civil conflict. Rostow's second stage was the process of transition, when the pre-conditions for take-off were developed. For take-off (that is, sustained economic growth) to occur, Rostow set three related conditions: a rise in rate of productive investment to over 10 per cent of GNP; the development of one or more industrial sectors; and the emergence of a conducive political, social and institutional framework. This heroic attempt to provide a general theory of economic history offered some important insights into the challenges facing the Department, though the last condition was often given insufficient attention.

Not unrelated to Rostow's work was the considerable literature on economic and social dualism and disguised unemployment, a good example of which was the work of Professor W. A. Lewis.[45] Lewis argued that, particularly in densely populated regions, the marginal productivity of labour in peasant agriculture was zero, and therefore labour could be attracted to a growing modern sector without a reduction in agricultural output. Although intellectually attractive, Lewis's argument did not address the key issue of raising agricultural productivity and output in the context of rapid population growth. Furthermore, with its colonial heritage and experience in agricultural development the Department, at least implicitly, was drawn more towards the balanced-growth approach associated with Paul Rosenstein-Rodan.[46] Thus, in its first decade, depending on the circumstances and policies of the country concerned, bilateral aid focused on three broad areas: physical infrastructure, agricultural research and extension, and sustaining and improving public sector institutions, particularly in the ex-colonies.

However, perhaps the most influential piece of work which provided the intellectual basis for the 1975 White Paper, and much development thinking since then, was *Redistribution with Growth* by Hollis Chenery et al.[47] It was the product of a study by the World Bank and the Institute of Development Studies (University of Sussex). The two conferences held in 1973 were attended by Professor Dudley Seers (the first head of the EPS) and other senior economists from the Department. It noted that while average aggregate growth over the preceding decade had been better than expected the benefits of growth for the poorer groups had been variable. It identified the bulk of the poor as 'self-employed small farmers, rural artisans, and members of the rapidly growing urban informal sector'. For these, 'income growth is limited by lack of access to land, capital, and other public facilities, often by outright discrimination'. The authors proposed that country-specific national programmes should be developed to overcome these obstacles to the participation of poorer groups in economic development. They argued that this was not just a welfare issue but an important element in achieving economic development. The book was the basis for the basic-needs approach to development which dominated the Department's and other donors' thinking for some time to come.

The book also argued that aggregate growth in GDP was 'not designed as a measure of social welfare . . . [it] is a special case in which weights are proportional to the groups' existing share of national product'. It proposed the adoption of different weights, the most politically neutral being to give equal weights to the same proportional increase in income of each group. This led on to the attempted use of income weights in cost benefit analysis for individual projects, though the subjective nature of this approach and lack of engagement by most developing-country governments meant this proved of limited practical value.

As Frances Stewart wrote,[48]

Basic Needs always include the fulfilment of certain nutritional standards (food and water) and the universal provision of health and educational services. They sometimes also cover other material needs such as shelter and clothing, and non-material needs such as employment, participation and political liberty. Basic Needs is an approach to development not a strategy in the sense that it consists of giving priority to a certain type of objective of development but does not dictate the means by which the objective is achieved.

Subsequent and related influences on the Department's thinking were the writings of A. K. Sen,[49] which defined development as an expansion of human capabilities and the freedom of individuals to a life that they valued. This required anti-discrimination and redistributive policies. In a paper[50] presented to the IAB conference in 1999 Sen wrote:

It is not a switch (as often portrayed) from a state dependent view of development to a market reliant view. Rather, it involves rejecting a 'blood, sweat and tears' view of development in favour of celebrating people's agency and co-operation and the expansion of human freedom and capabilities.

In parallel with this was the work of Robert Chambers[51] which emphasised the importance of consulting the poor about what being poor meant and what their priorities were for improving their lives. This and related work had a considerable influence on the later work of the Department. For a succinct account of developing thinking in relation to poverty over the years see *Defining Poverty in the Developing World*, edited by Frances Stewart et al. and published in 2007.[52]

The Department was also strongly influenced by the 1987 report of the World Commission on Environment and Development, *Our Common Future* (commonly referred to as the Brundtland Report).[53] The Commission was established by the UN General Assembly in 1983 and was chaired by Gro Brundtland, former Prime Minister of Norway. It identified sustainable development as that which 'meets the needs of the present without compromising the ability of future generations to meet their own needs'. It concluded that this required, among other things,

> a political system that ensures effective citizen participation in decision making, an economic system that is able to generate surplus and technical knowledge ... a social system that provides for solutions for the tensions arising from disharmonious development, a production system that respects the obligation to preserve the ecological base for development, [and] a technological system that can search continuously for new solutions.

As such it offered a far-reaching vision of development and poverty reduction rather than just some technical fixes to safeguard the physical environment.

Another important piece of work which took forward the thinking of Chenery et al., and that of the Bruntland Commission was an Institute of Development Studies paper[54] produced by Robert Chambers and Gordon Conway; the latter, having started his career as an agriculturalist in the Colonial Service, and later, after working in India, having a distinguished academic career at Imperial College, London, became the Department's first Chief Scientific Adviser. The paper developed the concept of sustainable rural livelihoods, though it was equally applicable to the urban informal sector. It built on the works of A. K. Sen[55] related to entitlements and capabilities. As stated in its summary:

> A livelihood comprises people, their capabilities and their means of living, including food, income and assets. A livelihood is environmentally sustainable when it maintains or enhances the local and global assets on which livelihoods depend, and has net beneficial effects on other livelihoods. A livelihood is socially sustainable, which can cope with and recover from stress and shocks, and provide for future generations.

It has informed the work of the Department ever since, even though much of the aid it provided did not in later years address these issues directly.

## The Washington Consensus

During the 1950s and 1960s there had existed a substantial divide between the structuralist school of thinking in Latin America, led by eminent development economists such as Professor Raúl Prebish and Professor Dudley Seers, first Director General of the EPS, and what might for shorthand purposes be called the demand-management school. The structuralists believed that the root cause of fiscal deficits and inflation was the structure of developing countries' economies, particularly in Latin America – concentration of land ownership in the economic and political elite, a reliance on one or two primary commodity exports and limited domestic financial markets – combined with governments' aspirations for development involving substantial public sector recurrent and capital expenditure. Governments had a limited tax base and ability to increase revenue which led them into fiscal deficits and the printing of money, leading to high inflation. Thus, tackling fiscal deficits and inflation involved a restructuring of economies over time rather than short-term fiscal and monetary policies to reduce the inflation which would impede growth and poverty reduction.

The demand-management school emphasised the negative impact of fiscal deficits and high inflation on growth through the crowding out of private sector investment and the creation of uncertainty. They believed that more realistic (and market-determined) exchange rates would promote exports, including non-traditional exports. They also increasingly pointed out that the distortion of domestic prices accompanied by subsidies and rationing, leading to black market situations, resulted in the poor suffering most. The Department's focus on micro-economic issues and project assistance meant that it did not seriously address these issues until the late 1970s.

By the early 1980s there was a growing recognition within the international community, led by the Washington institutions, of the importance of developing countries adopting more appropriate monetary and fiscal policies that would restore economic stability and promote growth. There was also an increasing view that prices should be determined by the marketplace (including the price of foreign exchange) and that private enterprise, including foreign direct investment, should be encouraged rather than discouraged. The nationalisations of the earlier years should give way to privatisations. Developing countries were encouraged to adopt more outward-looking policies and embrace trade liberalisation. The following decade or so was certainly a controversial period in the development debate. Many developing countries and the international NGO community saw this so-called 'Washington Consensus' as being concerned only with monetary and fiscal rectitude and the positive role of the market, with its assumption that the poor would benefit from overall economic growth, known as the 'trickle down effect'. They, generally supported by the UNCTAD Secretariat, advocated slower adjustment programmes, more interventionist policies to help the poor even if that meant more lax monetary and fiscal policies, and criticised particularly the IMF for not sharing their view on public expenditure priorities when cuts were a condition of assistance.

However, perhaps the most balanced summary of the Washington Consensus was given in ten points by John Williamson (Chief Economist at the IMF) in 1990 and reflected in his 1994 book[56] and which the Department adhered to:

1. **Fiscal Discipline:** budget deficits, properly measured to include those of provincial governments, state enterprises, and the central bank, should be small enough to be financed without recourse to the inflation tax.
2. **Public Expenditure Priorities:** redirecting expenditure from politically sensitive areas, which typically receive more resources than their economic return can justify, such as administration, defence, indiscriminate subsidies, and white elephants, toward neglected fields with high economic returns and the potential to improve income distribution, such as primary health and education, and infrastructure.
3. **Tax Reform:** to broaden the tax base and cut marginal tax rates.
4. **Financial Liberalisation:** the ultimate objective of which is market-determined interest rates.
5. **Exchange Rates:** a unified rate set at a level sufficiently competitive to induce a rapid growth in non-traditional exports.
6. **Trade Liberalisation:** quantitative trade restrictions should be rapidly replaced by tariffs, which should be progressively reduced.
7. **Foreign Direct Investment:** barriers impeding the entry of foreign firms should be abolished; foreign and domestic firms should be allowed to compete on equal terms.
8. **Privatisation:** state enterprises should be privatised.
9. **Deregulation:** governments should abolish regulations that impede the entry of new firms or restrict competition.
10. **Property Rights:** the legal system should provide secure property rights without excessive costs, and make these available to the informal sector.

Since 1979 the Thatcher government had been pursuing its own structural adjustment programme of tighter fiscal and monetary policies within the UK to reduce inflation and to promote growth through the crowding in of the private sector and privatisation programmes which it expected to help reduce the public sector deficit and increase efficiency in the use of resources. It is not surprising therefore that the British government, including the Department, supported the Washington Consensus view of what developing countries needed to do to restore economic stability, promote growth and help reduce poverty. The Department supported the policies of the Washington institutions and increasingly supported World Bank-led structural adjustment lending through the parallel provision of non-project bilateral aid to poor countries ready to commit themselves to such programmes. The debate turned to whether such policies in developing countries were a sufficient condition or just a necessary condition to achieve the desired objectives of growth and poverty reduction. The Department never subscribed to the former view, and continued to believe that in addition to sound macro-economic policies, positive measures, including the reallocation of public expenditure resources and better governance, were necessary to achieve both growth and poverty reduction.[57]

The current global financial crisis has highlighted a number of changes that have taken place in recent years in the balance of economic power in the world. It never was the case that all developing countries were poor aid recipients dependent upon official capital flows from the rich OECD countries. But in recent years the increasing economic power of many upper-middle countries, and in particular BRIC countries (Brazil, Russia, India and China), has made them important suppliers of capital to OECD countries and new donors to the poorer developing countries. This in turn has drawn attention to the limited voting rights of these countries in the international financial institutions, a situation which many OECD countries, including Britain, accept needs to be changed. The financial crisis has also demonstrated that it is not only developing countries that have mismanaged their economies. While this may change the politics of aid conditionality, the fact that some of the peripheral euro-zone countries have had to accept painful restructuring of public finances in return for external assistance is likely to reinforce the view that such restructuring is a necessary complement to effective aid delivery. Perhaps the phrase 'we are all in it together' will have greater resonance internationally in future. Or, as Robert Zeollick put it on his departure as President of the World Bank in mid-2012, in respect of many of the stronger performing developing countries, 'there are things that the US and Europe should spend some time learning instead of teaching'.

## Good governance

The Department's ideas and policies on governance were set out most recently and comprehensively in its 2006 White Paper, though they featured strongly in the 1997 and 2000 White Papers under Clare Short and during the previous period under Lynda Chalker. As the DAC Peer Review of the UK (1997)[58] noted, 'in the late 1980s the United Kingdom was one of the first donors to speak out about good governance and to incorporate this idea into its aid programmes'. Concerns with governance beyond economic management rose up the international agenda increasingly during the 1990s. Initially, some regarded governance as less of a development issue and more an attempt by the West to impose its own political values on developing countries following the end of the Cold War. The issue was not just about whether governments allowed periodic elections which were (reasonably) 'free and fair', but also about whether they respected human rights and the rule of law. There was also a growing concern about transparency and accountability in the use of resources, and giving civil society a voice both at a national and community level. The issue of corruption from the top down became a major discussion point between the international community and developing countries. This reflected two related issues: first, the renewed concern with poverty reduction and the importance of how the use of local resources as well as aid contributed towards it; and second, the importance of maintaining public support for donor aid programmes. It was no longer sufficient for donors, including the Department, to be able to show that their own aid funds were properly used and accounted for, particularly with the increased provision of programme/budgetary support.

The ending of the Cold War by 1990 had made Western donors far more willing and able to address these issues rather than turn a blind eye. Jim Wolfensohn as President of the World Bank, once said that when he started the job the 'c-word' (corruption) was not in the Bank's public dictionary. By the time he left it was a major issue in the dialogue with developing countries. Likewise, if British High Commissioners had been instructed in the early 1980s to talk to their Presidents about governance issues (either economic or political) they would have been aghast. By the 1990s it was difficult to hold them back, including in public speeches (for example, in Kenya and Zambia).

In Africa, governance issues, including corruption, have been a major part of the aid dialogue in a number of countries at various times in recent years, notably Ethiopia, Kenya, Nigeria, Sudan, Uganda and Zambia, in addition to failing or failed states such as the Democratic

Republic of the Congo, Liberia, Sierra Leone, Somalia and Zimbabwe. The Department, together with the World Bank, the US and many European donors, has played an important role in seeking change for the better. There is no doubt that, over the past two decades, poor governance has significantly affected both the levels of aid which donors, and notably the Department, have been prepared to provide to particular countries, and the way in which it has been delivered.

The introduction of governance issues in the aid dialogue initially complicated the aid decision-making process, particularly with regard to programme/budgetary aid provided to countries adhering to an IMF/World Bank economic reform programme. If adherence to the economic reform programme coincided with at least moderately good political governance there was no dilemma for the Department, and equally in the reverse case. The dilemma arose when a country followed a reasonable economic reform programme but was found wanting on political governance. Initially greater weight was given to macro-economic performance but over time the emphasis shifted to political governance, including corruption and the diversion of local resources that it involved. With the increased focus on poverty reduction over the past decade or so, the Department, with others, has found it increasingly difficult to separate out these two issues. As Kofi Annan, then UN Secretary General, said in 1998, 'Good governance is perhaps the single most important factor in eradicating poverty and promoting development'.

One of the criticisms of the early dialogue on governance was that donors sought to impose conditionality using the standards by which they themselves believed they were governed. In some areas donors were more willing to accept that progress would only be achieved over time, in others they demanded more instant change such as the holding of 'free and fair' elections and stamping out high-level corruption. Since then researchers have contributed to a better analytical framework for understanding governance issues and have provided a set of principles that go beyond a Western model of liberal democracy. Hyden et al.'s *Making Sense of Governance*[59] identified six core principles that became widely accepted, including by the Department, and provided the basis for a more objective comparative assessment between countries:

- Participation: the degree of involvement by affected stakeholders.
- Fairness: the degree to which rules apply equally to everyone in society.
- Decency: the degree to which the formation and stewardship of the rules is undertaken without humiliating or harming people.

- Accountability: the extent to which political actors are responsible to society for what they say and do.
- Transparency: the degree of clarity and openness with which decisions are made.
- Efficiency: the extent to which limited human and financial resources are applied without unnecessary waste, delay or corruption.

The Department itself recognised that in engaging in the governance dialogue it initially had little capacity for political analysis. The Foreign Office regarded this as their territory, though the Department tended to the view that the Foreign Office were better at understanding short-term political events, and the personalities involved, than analysing the forces that would contribute towards, or resist, long-term political change. The Department joined with the Overseas Development Institute to develop a methodology for understanding the 'drivers for change'.[60] Such a framework facilitated a more systematic analysis of how political processes influence economic and social policies, both positively and negatively. It was intended as a tool to enable development practitioners to understand how formal and informal political actors and interests interact through institutional arrangements to influence decisions about how resources are used and hence how developmental outcomes are shaped. It provides a basis for helping create the conditions that will provide greater space within which the drivers of positive change can operate and to provide them with support. The Department now has a substantial cadre of governance professionals and a stronger capacity for political analysis.

## Poverty reduction strategies

Chapter Four outlined the greater focus of the international community on poverty reduction that was reflected in the adoption in 1996 by the DAC of the International Development Targets (IDTs) and which were enshrined, in a modified form, as the Millennium Development Goals (MDGs) in the 2000 Millennium Summit. Individual countries were urged to formulate Poverty Reduction Strategies setting out their own plans and priorities for meeting the MDGs and reducing poverty generally, based on strong government ownership and involvement of civil society, in return for more predictable international development assistance. Thus, relatively short-term structural adjustment programmes gave way to longer-term poverty reduction strategies.

However, criticism of early Poverty Reduction Strategy Papers (PRSPs) was that they were driven largely by the Washington institutions in a hurry to establish policy frameworks and plans for which they could provide support and which would qualify countries for debt relief under the Heavily Indebted Poor Country (HIPC) Initiative. Too little attention was given initially to the crucial importance of ownership by the country concerned and the need for proper consultation with civil society to ensure that the poor were given a voice in setting priorities. This has gradually been corrected in recent years, with pressure from the countries themselves and the bilateral donor community, including the Department. The adoption of well articulated PRSPs, with the involvement of civil society and greater ownership by countries, has been an important step forward in seeking to articulate more effective policies intended to help achieve the MDGs and reduce poverty more generally.

It was in the context of the development of PRSPs that Tony Blair, then Prime Minister, decided that he wanted to take an initiative on Africa in late 2000. Initially the Department urged No. 10 to wait and respond to Africa's own initiative which was then in train; a number of African countries were articulating a New Economic Programme for African Development (NEPAD). In the event, the upcoming 2002 General Election distracted No. 10's attention from Africa. The NEPAD programme was endorsed by the Assembly of African Heads of State and Governments in July 2001, focusing on peace and security, economic and political governance, and regional integration. It established an African Peer Review Mechanism, by which countries could examine the progress they were making and agree an agenda for the future. Subsequent to the 2002 General Election, Tony Blair revived his initiative and set up a Commission for Africa comprising a number of international and African leaders, and including Gordon Brown (then Chancellor) and Hilary Benn (then Secretary of State for International Development), which broadly endorsed the NEPAD agenda.[61]

The Department has always believed that economic growth is a pre-condition for meaningful poverty reduction. The issue has been what actions the Department should itself take to help bring it about, and in ways that would lead to more rather than less reduction in poverty. The early growth models emphasised capital accumulation and implicitly assumed that the technical progress necessary to raise productivity would in some sense look after itself, though self-evidently not in the smallholder agricultural sector. Thus, in the early years the Department focused on investing in physical infrastructure and agricultural research and extension as well as technical assistance, including training, to improve the effectiveness of the public sector. As referred to earlier,

*Redistribution with Growth* (1974), which called for an increase in the physical and human productive assets of the poor to achieve a more even pattern of growth, has been the basis of much of the Department's thinking over the following decades.

The emphasis since the 1980s on sound macro-economic policies, and providing a more attractive environment for private sector investment, including in the agricultural sector, was primarily about restoring economic growth. The error, now being corrected, was to believe that governments could largely leave the private sector to drive up productivity in agriculture. It is also the case that the more recent Poverty Reduction Strategies were as much about growth as achieving the specific MDGs which had increasingly been seen as an end in themselves. The Africa Commission Report (2005), initiated by the then Prime Minister, Tony Blair, in putting forward a 'coherent package for Africa' stated that 'recent years have seen improvements in economic growth and in governance. But Africa needs more of both if it is to make serious inroads into poverty'. Growth was given added emphasis by the World Bank in its 2008 World Development Report, *Agriculture for Development*, and in a speech by the Rt Hon Douglas Alexander MP, as Secretary of State for International Development.[62] The Coalition government has made wealth creation one of its six Departmental priorities.

## Forms of aid

It will be recalled that the 1965 White Paper accepted that there were several roads to development which developing countries needed to explore for themselves. The diversity of economic policies and political systems led the Department to focus its financial aid, for the most part, on specific project interventions while being relatively tolerant of the overall economic and political context in which it was operating. Aid for the most part was, and still is, a transaction between governments. It therefore focused on the role developing-country governments could play in promoting development, and project aid interventions have been guided by the development thinking of the day. This project-led approach was reflected in the Department's early attitude towards budgetary aid for newly independent Commonwealth countries from which it wished to extract itself as quickly as possible.

A similar approach was taken, over time, to manpower assistance. The general manpower support to governments under the OSAS and BESO schemes (see Chapter Two) was gradually run down and increasingly projectised. There were both demand and supply aspects to this.

Developing countries were themselves anxious to have their own nationals fill public service cadre posts as trained people became available, albeit usually with much less experience than their expatriate counterparts. The Department was content to see such generalised manpower support diminish and be replaced with Technical Co-operation Officers employed directly by the Department on time-bound contracts related to specific projects and institution-building activities.

This project approach led the Department, with its influential EPS, to focus on, and help develop, the concept of social cost benefit analysis by which to appraise individual investment projects. This was designed to identify investments which were economically viable after abstracting from the price distortions within the economy created by government intervention, in particular in foreign exchange and labour markets, and allowing for those other costs and benefits which could not be captured by a purely financial analysis, so-called externalities (such as the cost savings in time and vehicle maintenance achieved by investing in road improvements). In the context of rural development it encouraged detailed socio-economic surveys of rural communities, often focused on labour-supply constraints to adopting new farming methods and to increasing food and cash crop production, though with too little attention being given to the financial incentives for doing so. Although much early economic thinking favoured a measure of protection, cost benefit analysis was based on international prices and assumed, at least implicitly, that an open trading economy was beneficial.

The Department's shift in the 1970s towards integrated rural development and other programmes to help the informal sector meant that the emphasis on economic appraisal, together with narrow technical issues, gave way to closer attention to other concerns such as social and environmental issues. This was reflected in the changing balance of professionals' expertise within the Department during the 1980s (apologies to the administrative cadre that increasingly regarded themselves as development professionals). For example, in 1979 there was only one social development adviser; by the early 1990s there were nearly 50 such advisers, though in the early days they focused more on being internal advocates for a greater focus on poverty reduction than on objective social analysis. They subsequently made an important contribution to the understanding by the Department and others of the causes of poverty and how its aid interventions could more effectively help reduce poverty and address gender issues.[63] The 1997 DAC Peer Review of UK Aid recognised these efforts as 'a major contribution to this field'. They also made a significant contribution to international discussions on poverty and gender issues, including at the Beijing Summit on Women in the year 2000. Likewise, the few staff dealing with renewable natural resources increased to encompass environmental specialists, as did the numbers of engineering staff to deal with 'brown environmental issues'. Both contributed significantly to the Department's bilateral aid work and to the evolution of international policies at the local and global levels.

The problem with this emphasis on projects and the use of cost benefit analysis was that they did not take account of the broader macro-economic and political realities within which they were pursued. Many projects which were theoretically viable could not be sustained either financially or managerially. However, for projects in the infrastructure sectors which should be financially viable, the Department did seek to encourage more realistic pricing policies through policy dialogue and by insisting that highly concessional aid funds provided directly to governments to finance them should be on-lent to the parastatals responsible for implementing investment projects on 'commercial' terms, though this by itself was not able to overcome the distortions in the economy that increasingly prevailed. It also sought to strengthen management through the provision of technical assistance.

Much later, in the 1990s, the Department was seeking to appoint a new Chief Economist. One candidate (Alan Coverdale) who did eventually become Chief Economist, but sadly died shortly afterwards, was asked what he thought was the future of cost benefit analysis. He replied with singular insight: cost benefit analysis was about trying to identify the perfect project in a very imperfect world. Now the Department had a more ambitious project, to improve the world.

As noted in Chapter Four, the 1975 White Paper recognised the particular difficulties of the poorer oil-importing countries following the 1973 oil price hike. It supported the new IMF facilities including providing aid to soften IMF interest rates. It also supported the World Bank's introduction of non-project assistance under its Structural Adjustment Programmes beginning in the late 1970s, and agreed to provide non-project-related bilateral aid to some of these countries, mainly in Africa, which were known as the Most Seriously Affected countries, in support of IMF and World Bank assistance.

Equally, it is true to say that while the dominant period of project aid was in the first twenty years, as a form of aid it has remained important, the more so today in the context of public expenditure cuts being made while protecting the growth in the aid budget. In the past twenty years, and increasingly over the past decade, it has sought to be more transformational in its ambitions for project aid rather than just transactional.

The Department supported the Washington Consensus and what developed beyond it by providing 'programme aid' in conjunction with agreed IMF/World Bank economic reform programmes in the poorer countries. Initially it was seen as a short-term, if necessary, expediency. Within its limited budget prior to 1997 it meant the Department cutting back on investment projects, something the developing countries themselves were also having to do. The Department's short-term approach to programme aid was reflected in the fact that initially it was drawn in-year from its own unallocated reserve and made available only on an annual basis, provided that the developing country remained on track with the IMF/World Bank. This short-term, all-or-nothing approach made planning by developing countries extremely difficult. Only in the late 1990s did the Department begin to build programme aid into its three-year forward planning exercise and offer developing countries an indication of programme aid levels over the next three years provided they continued to adhere to agreed economic reform programmes.

For some time the Washington institutions, particularly the IMF, failed to appreciate the link between this form of assistance and the aid recipient government's budget. Calculations of need to support an adjustment programme were based on the projected balance of payments requirements of the country, and in the case of the IMF it was seen as a monetary transaction between itself and the country's central bank. Likewise, the Department initially focused on providing foreign exchange to finance imports without much regard to the content and structure of the recipient government's budget. It was the Department, however, in the 1990s that pointed out to the Washington institutions and other donors that funds provided to the central bank were largely passed on to governments to help finance their budgets. This was important in two respects. First, estimates of balance of payments requirements were somewhat elastic and uncertain. More importantly, linking programme aid to imports did not encourage medium-term budgetary planning by the countries concerned; nor did it give legitimacy to donors wanting to establish a dialogue on overall budget priorities and on improvements in financial management and accountability, both for its own sake and in order better to account for the aid being provided.

This led eventually to two important changes in the provision of more flexible and predictable development assistance. The first was the development of Sector Wide Assistance Programmes (SWAPs), which had two important advantages. First, it tended to avoid the 'all-or-nothing' approach to giving programme aid: except in an extreme situation, aid to a particular sector would not be terminated if the country went off-track with its overall economic reform programme. Second, they allowed the donor community collectively and the recipient government to establish a dialogue on policies and programmes for the sector as a whole within a medium-term perspective while avoiding a reversion to old-fashioned project aid. SWAPs provided a vehicle for improved donor co-ordination and gave the government greater confidence about the continuity of aid, though the approach could be time-consuming for all parties in establishing an agreed sector-wide development programme. They also enabled donors to help developing-country governments strengthen financial management in the sector concerned, for example in the education sector by tackling the problem of ghost teachers staying on the payroll. Education and health were seen as the most obvious candidates for a sector-wide approach, mainly in the low-income countries of Africa (such as Malawi, Zambia and Ghana). The Department took a leading role internationally in promoting this approach.

The adoption of the MDGs and poverty reduction strategies led to a more ambitious and comprehensive approach towards the dialogue between the international community and the poorest countries. In return for comprehensive and meaningful poverty reduction strategies, covering both macro-economic policies that would promote growth and pro-poor budgetary priorities and programmes relating to particular sectors that provided an overall medium-term framework for development assistance and debt relief under the Heavily Indebted Poor Countries (HIPC) initiative (see below), the international community agreed to provide aid increasingly in the form of general support for the government's budget, on the basis that governments were prepared to be helped to improve financial management and accountability.

Again the Department led the way internationally in promoting this approach, though even it had vigorous internal discussions. Some, particularly economists, argued for wholesale conversion to general budgetary support. Many of the other technical staff felt threatened and were concerned that their influence at the sector level would be diminished, and favoured the continuation of SWAPs. There was a genuine concern that most of the poorer countries still needed expatriate technical assistance to help design, implement and manage programmes effectively, which governments might not appreciate and therefore not seek. The transfer and diffusion of new technologies in both the public and private sector, in the latter case through direct foreign investment, has for some time been recognised as an important part of modern growth theory, but seen as often difficult to achieve. Many other donors have been more reluctant to adopt the budgetary aid approach, and the Department itself has continued to recognise the crucial importance of assisting with institutional capacity-building.

The initial high level of non-project financial aid (nearly two-thirds) was an inheritance by the Department of the government's policy in the early 1960s of providing substantial loans to the independent Commonwealth (particularly India and Pakistan) for agreed imports, and the remnants of budgetary aid to the colonies and newly independent countries. As the Department developed its own project aid activities, this proportion fell to just over a quarter and was until the early 1980s largely accounted for by programme assistance to India. It has increased steadily since, first with the provision of short-term programme aid for countries in crisis (mainly in Africa) and then with the provision of general budgetary support to help finance poverty reduction strategies where the fiduciary risk has justified it. More recently the Coalition government has emphasised more specific results in terms of reducing maternal mortality and more children (particularly girls) in schools as a result of British bilateral aid, though this is not reflected in a substantial change in the form in which financial aid is being delivered.

Changes in development aid policy and practices have put an increasing premium on co-ordination between donors and with their partners. However, aid co-ordination has long been a feature of the aid scene. Annual aid consortia meetings, usually chaired by the World Bank, or

*Table 5.1*  Bilateral financial aid[a] 1965–2010/11

| Percentage provided as Programme Aid/Budgetary Support[b] | | | |
|---|---|---|---|
| 1965 | 64 | 1990/1 | 37 |
| 1970 | 53 | 1995/6 | 32 |
| 1975 | 42 | 2000/1 | 56 |
| 1980 | 36 | 2005/6 | 59 |
| 1985 | 27 | 2010/11 | 53 |

[a] Excluding humanitarian assistance, advances to CDC and debt relief.
[b] Excludes sector-wide assistance programmes, not classified as poverty reduction budget support.
*Source*: Departmental statistics.

round-table meetings for the least developed countries, usually chaired by UNDP, have been common since the 1970s. The early focus was on the development plans put forward by developing countries and the level and nature of commitments which donors were prepared to make. Economic reform programmes agreed between the IMF/World Bank and developing countries provided a more specific context after the 1980s in which donors committed both project and non-project (programme) aid. Later, SWAPs facilitated better donor co-ordination and more coherent policies and programmes being agreed with developing countries at the sector level, and PRSPs provided a more comprehensive framework at the country level for donor co-ordination, particularly with the emphasis on general budgetary support. This paved the way for more wide-ranging discussions in the Development Assistance Committee (DAC) of the OECD, together with developing countries, with a view to achieving greater harmonisation of donor aid practices and procedures in support of developing countries' poverty reduction strategies.

Before ending this section some indication of the range of bilateral project aid expenditure is in order. Table 5.2 provides a partial analysis of the sectors/purposes to which it has been allocated. However, in the first twenty years or so technical assistance was not allocated by sector for statistical purposes. In the past decade or more spending departments have been allowed to allocate expenditure on projects for up to six, and more recently eight, purposes. Table 5.2 is therefore an imperfect attempt to indicate the spread of activities to which project aid has been applied since 1987/88. It shows a relative increase in the social sectors, with the use of SWAPs for education and health, and for governance activities, and a relative decline in physical infrastructure and livelihoods. Readers may be surprised at the relatively small proportion of expenditure attributed to the environment directly, but this reflects the fact that most effort has been in policy dialogue and project appraisal.

Whilst it is left to the last chapter to offer some thoughts on the development impact of the Department, some comment is relevant here. To some extent it mattered less on what the Department used its aid for than the policies that it encouraged. If it used its funds to encourage transformational change in the ways recipient governments behaved, that would be clearly beneficial. That might be at a project level through mutual learning that would be replicated or it might be at a macro-economic level, changing the ways governments managed their economies.

*Table 5.2*   Project aid by sector/purpose

|  | 1987/88 | 1990/91 | 1995/96 | 2000/01 | 2005/06 |
|---|---|---|---|---|---|
| Education | 81 (20%) | 116 (20%) | 111 (16%) | 110 (14%) | 225 (14%) |
| Health | 19 (5%) | 40 (7%) | 88 (13%) | 184 (23%) | 390 (24%) |
| Social | 2 (−) | 3 (−) | 7 (1%) | 21 (3%) | 280 (17%) |
| Economic | 182 (45%) | 269 (46%) | 237 (34%) | 166 (21%) | 316 (19%) |
| Livelihoods | 74 (18%) | 89 (15%) | 122 (17%) | 127 (16%) | 103 (6%) |
| Governance | 21 (5%) | 39 (7%) | 87 (12%) | 150 (19%) | 295 (18%) |
| Environment | 24 (6%) | 19 (3%) | 44 (6%) | 34 (4%) | 40 (2%) |
| **Total** | **406** | **581** | **696** | **793** | **1649** |

*Source*: Departmental statistics.

## Environmental issues

The Department has been strongly involved in environment issues at both country and international levels over a long period of time. Its early work in addressing rural development and increasing agricultural productivity in the context of rapid population growth led to an appreciation of the problems of declining soil fertility, particularly in marginal areas. Large-scale deforestation has threatened the livelihoods of forest dwellers and led to soil degradation. Intensive large-scale irrigation schemes have given rise to increasing salinity levels in countries such as Pakistan, where the Department was involved in costly remedial measures together with the World Bank by the late 1970s. Large-scale dams for hydro-electric and irrigation purposes have often been associated with erosion of slopes and siltation of the lakes created, which needed preventative and remedial attention. Rapid urbanisation and the growth of slum areas have threatened the health of poor people, particularly with the pollution of water supplies and lack of sanitation. All these and other local and global environmental issues associated with development made the Department aware of the importance of sustainable development if poverty was to be reduced and the environment safeguarded for future generations. Appraisal of environmental factors for projects became standard practice, with a full environmental impact assessment being required for large projects thought likely to pose significant environment issues.

As global environmental issues such as biodiversity, climate change and depletion of the ozone layer went up the international agenda in the 1980s, the Department for the Environment (DOE, later DEFRA) was able to look to the Department for a source of advice and expertise on how to engage with developing countries. Well before 1997 and the emphasis on joined-up government, the Department had established both a strong central policy department and a strong regional and country-level network of professional advisers who were regarded as important members of their multi-disciplinary teams.

In the 1990s a number of international agreements on specific environmental issues were negotiated and agreed, all of which required some measure of donor assistance to developing countries, including:

1. The UN 1992 Convention on Climate Change agreed at the Rio Earth Summit and the 1997 Kyoto Protocol, with the objective of stabilising greenhouse gas concentrations in the atmosphere at acceptable levels (a follow up to Kyoto is still, in 2012, the subject of intense international debate);
2. The Convention on Biological Diversity which came into force in 1994 with the objective of conserving biological diversity and the equitable sharing of the use of genetic resources;
3. The Montreal Protocol signed in 1997 by which nearly all countries agreed to eliminate or reduce the use of chemicals which damage the ozone layer. Developing countries were given a longer timeframe to implement control measures and a multilateral fund was established to help them meet the incremental costs of them phasing out ozone-depleting substances, to which the Department was a significant contributor.

The Department was fully engaged with DOE/DEFRA in negotiating these agreements. These specific international environmental issues necessarily had to be seen in the broader context of sustainable development and seeking to involve in varying degrees the entire international community. The major international conferences, such as the Rio Earth Summit in 1992, the Rio+10 Summit held in South Africa in 2002, and the Rio+20 Summit in 2012 all addressed a broad sustainable development agenda which required developed and developing countries to agree on a wide range of issues requiring mutual co-operation. Sustainable development requires a better management of both local and global environmental resources. The Department therefore had and will continue to have an important role to play, and not just because the volume and nature of future development assistance was and remains a key issue in engaging developing countries.

In 2005 the Poverty Environment Partnership – a network of 30 international development and environment agencies including NGOs and of which the Department was a member – launched the Environment for the MDGs initiative 'to galvanize support for the significant scaling up of worldwide investment in environmental management to help win the fight against poverty to achieve the MDGs'. A synthesis paper was produced for the 2005 World Summit[64] in which the key message was: 'greatly expanded public and private investment in the productivity of environmental assets can generate strong returns to poverty reduction'. It emphasised the high returns available to investing in environmental assets that would benefit the poor, and challenged the so-called Environmental Kuznets Curve hypothesis that environmental assets will be degraded in the early stages of economic development, only to improve after some income threshold has been passed.

In 2006 the Department produced a publication[65] which summarised its view of the roots of the problem of continued environmental degradation as: unsustainable consumption patterns of the non-poor, and lack of access to land resources and secure income by the poor, which forces them to prioritise short-term needs over long-term environmental sustainability; inadequate understanding of the causes and impacts of environmental degradation; vested interests and corruption; lack of transparent, responsive and accountable government; failure to recognise the value of environmental goods and services which leads to inappropriate policies and perverse economic incentives; and population increase which leads to increasing pressure on limited resources.

Meanwhile, climate change had become a central development issue. As Hilary Benn said in an introduction to a publication by the Department,[66] 'Climate change will put international action to eradicate poverty and achieve the MDGs at risk. Responding to this risk is an opportunity to move away from the science and towards action to reduce poor peoples' vulnerability to the climate'. As the Stern Review[67] recognised, poor countries and within them poor people are most vulnerable to climate change, which impacts particularly on agriculture, health and water supplies.

Douglas Alexander, then Secretary of State for International Development, in his speech in New York (April 2008), set out five 'development tests' against which to judge the effectiveness of the international response on climate change: a credible, fair and ambitious global deal; helping countries grow in a low carbon way; a reformed carbon market; building climate-resilient economies and societies (that is, through adaptation); and reforming the international system. In its 2007 Budget the government announced an Environmental Transformation Fund with an international window of £800 million, to be operational from April 2008 and jointly managed by the Department and DEFRA.

It was envisaged that this should form part of an international fund, co-ordinated by the World Bank, which would finance programmes focused on poverty reduction and environmental protection and help developing countries to tackle climate change. The current Coalition government has included climate change as one of its six Departmental objectives.

When the Global Environment Fund was established in 1991 it was limited to financing the incremental cost to developing countries of reducing greenhouse gas emissions, and initially at least donor contributions did not count towards the UN aid target in order to get developing countries on board. Some will continue to argue that help with adaptation to climate change caused largely by the rich countries should be additional to oda, but provided the increasing aid commitment of many donor countries is honoured, and the fact that climate change and development are inextricably linked, this arguably now seems less relevant.

## Debt

The story of debt relief began, and in recent years again became associated with, aid. The Department has been closely associated with debt issues throughout the entire period since 1978.

The first international debt relief initiative was agreed at an UNCTAD conference in 1978 in relation to past aid debts. It was agreed that for the UN category of Least Developed Countries (LDCs) past aid loans should be converted to grants: what was known as Retrospective Terms Adjustment (RTA). Donors implemented this in different ways. Britain signed bilateral agreements forgiving past aid debt and reported internationally to the DAC annually the amounts of principal and interest payments forgone. It affected gross aid flows but not net official development assistance (oda), except in one very minor respect. Principal repayments of aid loans were added to the aid budget and recycled, thus net oda remained the same. However, interest payments on aid loans went to the Treasury. In the case of RTA, the Treasury required compensation from the aid budget for interest receipts forgone, which reduced the amount of net oda the Department had available in-year. The initial amount was only some £2.5 million annually, and declined over time. Whether or not the recipient country benefited in future years from the RTA initiative depended on how the Department decided to allocate its future aid budgets. The only condition Britain set for providing RTA was that the country should respect basic human rights, which at the time excluded Myanmar (Burma) and Zambia.

Partly because the Department had little regard for the concept of Least Developed Countries (LDCs) as defined by the UN, it persuaded the Treasury that for Britain the initiative should include all the poorest countries, including those such as India, Pakistan, Kenya and Ghana. However, the vast bulk of aid debt was owed by India (some £900 million out of a total of £1.2 billion) and both the FCO and DTI opposed the writing-off of such a large sum. Agreement was eventually reached within Whitehall that RTA could apply to India provided that at least one-third annually of the aid debt forgiven was used for projects tied to British exports and that another third would be used to finance the local costs of projects in India. Thus the main benefit to India and the Department was that the quality of the British aid programme was enhanced. Until then all British aid had been tied but in future it enabled the Department to work with Indian institutions to develop innovative projects in areas of rural development in which it could make a difference.

By the early 1980s, and following the second oil price increase, the seriousness of the problem of indebtedness of developing countries was increasingly recognised. Nearly all the oil-importing countries were heavily indebted, the commercial banks were no longer ready to increase their exposure, and export credit agencies were increasingly reluctant to maintain insurance cover except in a few, mainly middle-income, countries. It was evident that many developing countries were no longer just having a liquidity crisis but would never be able to repay their debts in full. The finance ministries of the OECD countries feared a systemic failure of the international banking system in the event of large-scale defaults, particularly by the large middle-income countries. In the late 19th and early 20th centuries developing countries had financed their infrastructure development largely by accessing the international bond markets financed by a large number of institutions and individuals: the risk of failure of individual ventures was spread amongst a wide number of players. But since the 1950s most external commercial lending had been concentrated in the hands of a fewer number of large banking institutions (which were 'too big to fail' in modern parlance).

Hence, in the case of Latin America, 'Brady Bonds' were introduced by which the banks agreed to reschedule debt at a discount, guaranteed by the US Treasury. The poorest countries, particularly in Africa, were in an even more difficult situation and many were already defaulting on their debt repayments both in respect of export credits and of uninsured commercial loans. In Britain successive Chancellors at the Treasury recognised that many of these heavily indebted poor countries would never be able to repay these debts in full and that there was much political credit to be gained by recognising this and taking initiatives which were in effect cost-free.

The Treasury leads on debt issues within Whitehall, though in the 1980s it had limited technical capacity. The Department, together with the Bank of England and the Export Credits Guarantee Department (ECGD), formed a small group with the Treasury to begin to work out what level of debt forgiveness on export credits might be sufficient to achieve debt sustainability for a limited group of the poorest, heavily indebted, countries, mainly in Africa but excluding Nigeria, a major oil exporter, which was by far the largest debtor of all in absolute terms. Given all the uncertainties about future economic variables and performance this was a highly speculative exercise. However, the initial tentative conclusion was that 33 per cent debt forgiveness for export credits, accompanied by parallel action by the commercial banks in respect of uninsured lending, would be necessary. This was the basis of the initiative put forward by the then Chancellor at the 1988 G7 Summit in Toronto and which became known as the Toronto terms. It was subsequently agreed by the Paris Club, which is the informal group of OECD creditors which decides on the terms of bilateral export credit debt relief for countries following internationally agreed economic reform programmes. In 1990 the Paris Club agreed up to 50 per cent debt relief for these countries following the 1990 G7 Summit in Trinidad. In 1994 the Paris Club creditors agreed the 'Naples Terms', which provided up to 67 per cent debt relief.

These successive initiatives reflected a growing recognition of the seriousness of the debt problem of these countries and their inability ever to repay the bulk of their debt. Pressure was put on the commercial banks to provide similar debt relief on their uninsured lending, which many did. In some cases (such as Mozambique, Sierra Leone and Guyana) deals were struck by which the commercial banks accepted buying back their debt at up to a 90 per cent discount, with donors, including the World Bank and Britain, financing the remaining 10 per cent or so required to be paid by the debtor country. These initiatives also reflected the strong international NGO pressure on the rich countries to provide debt forgiveness. The Jubilee Campaign in the UK ('Drop the Debt') was particularly vocal and influential as more recently has been the campaign to Make Poverty History in the context of the

2005 G8 Summit, held in Gleneagles in Scotland. These groups pressed for both 100 per cent bilateral debt relief and debt forgiveness by the multilateral institutions such as the IMF, World Bank and the regional development banks for the poorest, most heavily indebted countries.

The international financial institutions were initially reluctant to concede debt relief on the grounds that they were banking institutions and to provide debt relief from their own resources would undermine their ability to continue to recycle funds for future lending. This was particularly true of the IMF; the World Bank did make a profit from its IBRD hard window operations to the middle-income countries, part of which could be used for debt relief for the poorer countries.

In 1996 the Heavily Indebted Poor Country (HIPC) initiative was launched by the World Bank and IMF, which recognised the need for multilateral as well as bilateral debt relief on an exceptional basis for some of the poorest countries, and the Enhanced Naples/Cologne terms of 1995 subsequently provided for bilateral debt relief of up to 80 per cent.

The HIPC initiative required a Trust Fund to be established by which bilateral donors would provide funds particularly for the IMF and the African Development Bank to receive assistance to help finance such debt relief, with the Department being a major contributor. Ideas such as IMF sales of gold to finance its HIPC debt relief did not attract sufficient support amongst its members.

At the 1999 G8 Cologne Summit a substantially enhanced HIPC initiative was agreed and endorsed by the international community in September 1999. This provided for bilateral debt forgiveness of 90 per cent and possibly more (up to 100 per cent where this was thought to be necessary). In fact, Britain provided 100 per cent on all its official bilateral debt. This further initiative focused upon poverty reduction and the need for countries to establish and implement Poverty Reduction Strategies.

More flexibility was introduced as regards the need for a three-year track record of agreed economic reform. Temporary debt relief from annual debt servicing due was made available at what is called the Decision Point by which time a country had to have achieved a track record in economic reform, with irrevocable forgiveness of the stock of debt at Completion Point three years later, provided the country was still following an agreed economic reform programme.

In 1997 Britain announced a separate Commonwealth Debt Initiative for lower-middle-income Commonwealth countries following sound economic policies and good governance which relieved their remaining aid debt to Britain. Debts to CDC (formerly the Commonwealth Development Corporation) have also been forgiven for HIPC countries as these count as official debt.

In 2005 Britain held the Presidency of the G8 and the Edinburgh Summit agreed that some HIPC countries were still encountering an unsustainable debt burden in respect of the multilateral finance institutions. A Multilateral Debt Relief Initiative (MDRI) was agreed by which 100 per cent of the remaining debt of HIPC countries to the soft-lending arms of the World Bank (IDA), the African Regional Development Bank (AfDB) and to the IMF should also be forgiven. This was subsequently agreed by the Boards of the three bodies. Finally, Britain announced its own Multilateral Debt Relief Initiative by which it agreed to meet 10 per cent of qualifying non-HIPC countries' debt service payments to IDA and AfDB until 2015, and similar assistance to 17 HIPC countries in 2005/6, until the MDRI was fully implemented.

For some countries that had defaulted almost entirely on their export credit and uninsured commercial debts, regularising their position with export credit agencies and commercial banks could mean agreeing future debt-servicing levels that were higher than actual payments in the recent past. Likewise, where a country had defaulted on its IMF debt and no further IMF lending was permissible, ways had to be found to enable the Fund to become engaged again. This involved a Rights Accumulation Programme, usually over a three-year economic reform programme, by which the country earned the 'right' to refinance its arrears with longer-term concessional funding under the Enhanced Structural Adjustment Fund (ESAF). Again, until HIPC and the 2005 MDRI initiative, this meant that a developing country's actual debt service payments would be increased. Thus, many early announcements by HIPC countries that they would devote their debt relief to poverty reduction programmes, while politically attractive and well-meant, were sometimes less than they appeared, at least at first.

The Department remained engaged within Whitehall and internationally on all the above initiatives. The aid programme directly met the cost of RTA, the CDI initiative, Britain's contribution to the HIPC Trust Fund and the UK MDRI initiative. It has not directly met the cost of ECGD's export credit debt relief except for the amount above the 90 per cent agreed at Cologne. It meets amounts above 90 per cent because ECGD's Accounting Officer had to be satisfied that any debt forgiveness is justified in terms of it being uncollectible or not worth the administrative costs of seeking to do so. The Accounting Officer and the Treasury agreed that on this basis it would be difficult for ECGD itself to provide debt relief beyond 90 per cent.

Export credit debt forgiveness initially did not count as oda, and when it did in the few years prior to 1997 the Department did not negotiate its annual PES settlement in terms of the level of Britain's net oda against the UN aid target. It was thus largely a free good both to the Chancellor (being uncollectible) and to the Department (since it did not impact on the size of its future aid budget). Ironically after 1997 it stopped being a free good to the Department since making progress towards the 0.7 per cent UN aid target was a key factor in determining the CSR outcome. After 1997 the Treasury estimated the likely oda contribution of the export credit debt relief and used this as a factor in negotiating the Department's aid budget for the coming three years. In addition to sweeping debt relief for the HIPC-eligible countries, exceptional debt relief has been provided to non-HIPC countries such as Nigeria and Iraq.

Successive debt relief initiatives have in theory benefited HIPC countries and others by many billions of dollars. In its peak year to date, 2006/07, it cost Britain some £2013 million, of which £147 million was met by the Department's aid budget, £90 million by CDC, and £1,776 million by ECGD. For more details, readers are referred to the latest edition of the Department's Statistics on International Development (www.gov.uk/government/organisations/department-for-international-development/ about/statistics).

In addition to debt relief itself the Department has been engaged with other donors to fund programmes of technical advice and assistance to HIPC and other countries (such as Nigeria) to strengthen their debt management capacity and help them to develop a strategy to plan and manage any future borrowings, to avoid getting into an unsustainable debt situation again, often using the Crown Agents' expertise in this area. Too often governments had had little idea what their debt liabilities were.

## International trade

From its inception the Department always had an interest in international trade issues. The original structure of the EPS included an International Division which in part was concerned with trade issues, though primarily it dealt with commodities and international price stabilisation schemes (such as for tin and coffee) that existed in those days and which the

Department was generally supportive of. The rationalisation of the EPS in the early 1980s led to the abolition of this Division, and with it most of the Department's capacity for dealing with international trade issues. In any event it had no formal locus within Whitehall for participating in wider international trade issues, for which the DTI took the lead. However, the Department at a macro-economic level supported the Washington Consensus view that greater trade liberalisation and more outward-looking policies by developing countries would promote growth and development, which in turn also required developed countries to reduce their tariff and non-tariff barriers.

Only in 1995 did the Department's Fundamental Expenditure Review (FER), accepted by ministers, recommend that other government departments should make more use of the Department's knowledge and experience of development issues in formulating Britain's international policies. Based on the FER conclusions the Department adopted a specific 'aim' in 1996 'to promote international policies for sustainable development and improve the effectiveness of multilateral development institutions'. This included issues beyond aid, including trade, investment, food security, migration and debt. As David Pedley pointed out in his 2002 Evaluation,[68] the FER gave the Department a seat at the official Whitehall Trade Policy Group, but with limited influence. Between 1995 and 1997 the lack of influence, in David Pedley's view, stemmed from a lack of resource input, and therefore a knowledge and understanding of trade issues, within the Department. The Department's contributions to international trade issues were seen as fairly predictable: arguing for better developing-country access to the markets of the richer industrialised countries, particularly for agriculture and other non-traditional export sectors, without addressing the issue of reciprocity. Within Whitehall these attitudes were seen as predictable positions based more on instinct and special pleading than evidence-based policymaking and an understanding of wider trade issues and the positions of those the Department sought to influence.

With the formation of the Labour government in 1997 and the change in the status and role of the Department, together with the new government's determination to have a more joined-up approach to international policy issues, and a new Secretary of State equally determined to have the Department fully engaged, the position and influence of the Department in trade policy issues changed materially. More strongly resourced central departments were established.

In 1998 the International Economics Policy Department (IEPD) set itself the following objectives for the coming three years: to ensure that

the government's international policies on trade, agriculture and investment take account of its development objectives; to help promote these
objectives both within the EU and multilateral fora; and to promote the
development of trade capacity in developing countries (which included
promoting the capacity of developing countries to participate in a rules-
based multilateral trade system). By 2000 its objective was expressed
in a single sentence: 'to promote greater participation in international
trade by poor people and countries and to increase the benefits and
minimise the costs of international trade to the poor.' This was reflected
in specific objectives to build capacity in developing countries to pursue pro-poor trade reforms, and to better articulate trade issues in their
Poverty Reduction Strategy Papers.

The Everything but Arms initiative (EBA) announced by the EC in
September 2000, which proposed that all Least Developed Countries'
products be allowed duty-free access to EU markets for everything
but arms was controversial within Whitehall. DEFRA were concerned
with the impact on Britain's sugar beet industry, while the FCO were
concerned about the reaction of Caribbean countries to possible loss
of preferential markets, particularly with respect to sugar cane, rice and
bananas. The Department was influential in Britain adopting a positive
position on EBA and securing a phase-in of these tropical products over
a five-year period in the final agreement. EBA was agreed to by the EU
in February 2001 and provided duty- and quota-free access for all Least
Developed Countries, though the rules-of-origin regime imposed limita-
tions on the extent to which countries are able to benefit.

In 2005 the Department produced its 'Trade Matters' publication.[69] It
provided a number of examples where improved opportunities to export
had benefited relatively poor people in developing countries. It emphasised the need for practices by the richer countries that distort global
trade to be dealt with so that trade could play 'its vital role in creating
economic growth and jobs needed to help fight poverty. The benefits
of trade eclipse both aid and debt relief because they offer people the
chance to earn their way out of poverty and promise a time when poor
countries will no longer be dependent on aid'. It also pointed to the
potential benefits of developing countries importing goods at cheaper
prices than they could be produced locally. It went on to say that 'the
lesson of history is that the alternative to open markets – protecting
your own goods by hand outs and taxes against competition – doesn't
work in the long run'. It added that 'for all the shortcomings the WTO
calls for it to be scrapped are misplaced . . . it is an institution vital to
the prospects of the poorest countries in turning trade into a way out

of poverty'. This reflects both the policies set out in the 2000 White Paper on Globalisation and the Department's approach to the Doha Development Round.

## The Doha Development Round

The WTO Ministerial meeting in Doha reached a measure of agreement on the basis for the new trade negotiations. Clare Short was the only development minister to attend and spoke forcibly and knowledgeably about a new round, which she called the Doha Development Round. She set out an ambitious development agenda and endorsed the World Bank's view that the continued opening of markets to trade could lift an additional 300 million people out of poverty – helping to make the Millennium Development Goals on poverty reduction a reality. In 2005 the Hong Kong Ministerial Summit agreed to abolish all export subsidies by 2013 and to give 100 per cent duty- and quota-free market access to all Least Developed Countries. However the Doha talks were suspended in July 2006 by the WTO Director General because of a persistent impasse between countries. They were resumed in January 2007, but the G4 (the US, EU, India and Brazil) failed to reach agreement on a trade deal in June 2007 that could be put to the WTO as a whole, with Brazil and India being reluctant to agree concessions, which under the Most Favoured Nation clause would have to be accorded to other countries such as China. Despite further attempts to revive the talks, the WTO Director General, Pascal Lamy, acknowledged in a speech to the Brookings Institution in October 2012 that a comprehensive agreement in the Doha Round 'is out of reach in the short term'.

The Rt Hon Gordon Brown MP became Prime Minister in June 2007, and made several ministerial changes in forming his Cabinet, including changes to ministerial portfolios. The Rt Hon Douglas Alexander MP was made Secretary of State for International Development and also assumed responsibility for trade policy. A joint Trade Policy Unit was created between the Department and the new Department for Business Enterprise and Regulatory Reform (DBERR) to advise ministers on international trade policy issues.

# 6
# Natural and Manmade Disasters: The Department's Response

## Introduction

The Department has responded to the acute needs of people in poorer countries arising from natural and manmade disasters since its inception in 1964. This moral and political obligation was inherited from an earlier period. The Colonial Office provided exceptional assistance to British colonies at times of natural disasters arising from drought, floods, earthquakes and hurricanes, in Africa, Asia and the Caribbean, when colonial administrations were judged unable to cope with their consequences, both in terms of humanitarian suffering and the need for reconstruction. The Commonwealth Relations Office provided similar, if limited, assistance to the independent Commonwealth, notably to the Indian Sub-continent, and the Foreign Office did likewise in independent non-Commonwealth countries, notably in South America. The first recorded provision of disaster relief provided by Britain was in 1755 when Parliament voted £100,000 to help Portugal to deal with the Lisbon earthquake.[70] However, outside the developing world natural disasters have largely been dealt with by national (and local) governments which generally have had the resources to cope. Exceptionally, developed countries have been offered and accepted outside assistance, particularly of a specialist nature. In 1982 the Foreign Office made a transfer of £250,000 to the Department's expenditure baseline on the understanding that it would respond exceptionally to natural disasters other than in developing countries.

Humanitarian assistance generally involves the provision of material aid (including food, shelter and medical care), personnel and advice in order to save lives, alleviate suffering and maintain human dignity during and in the aftermath of manmade crises and natural disasters; reduce the incidence of refugees and internally displaced; hasten recovery and protect and rebuild livelihoods and communities; reduce risks and vulnerability to future crises, including strengthening preparedness measures. For these purposes the Department provides funding to a number of international agencies (the Red Cross/Red Crescent Movement [ICRC and IFRC], WFP, UNICEF, OCHA, UNHCR and WHO) and to British NGOs for their humanitarian assistance programmes in individual countries. As a percentage of the Department's total aid programme, humanitarian assistance was generally 1–3 per cent in the period 1965–1989/90, since when it has generally been between 5–10 per cent (see Table 6.1).

*Table 6.1*   Total British humanitarian assistance[a]

| | Total (£m) | % of total bilateral aid[2] | | Total (£m) | % of total bilteral aid[b] |
|---|---|---|---|---|---|
| 1965 | – | – | 1990/91 | 38 | 2 |
| 1966 | 1 | 1 | 1991/92 | 71 | 4 |
| 1967 | 1 | 1 | 1992/93 | 143 | 7 |
| 1968 | 2 | 1 | 1993/94 | 180 | 9 |
| 1969 | 4 | 2 | 1994/95 | 201 | 9 |
| 1970 | 5 | 2 | 1995/96 | 142 | 6 |
| 1971 | 9 | 3 | 1996/97 | 122 | 6 |
| 1972 | 17 | 6 | 1997/98 | 95 | 5 |
| 1973 | 19 | 7 | 1998/99 | 126 | 5 |
| 1974 | 5 | 1 | 1999/2000 | 226 | 9 |
| 1975 | 8 | 2 | 2000/01 | 180 | 6 |
| 1976 | 10 | 2 | 2001/02 | 193 | 7 |
| 1977 | 9 | 2 | 2002/03 | 295 | 9 |
| 1978 | 22 | 3 | 2003/04 | 311 | 8 |
| 1979 | 10 | 1 | 2004/05 | 333 | 10 |
| 1980 | 19 | 2 | 2005/06 | 448 | 10 |
| 1981 | 21 | 2 | 2006/07 | 383 | 7 |
| 1982 | 16 | 2 | 2007/08 | 431 | 12 |
| 1983 | 20 | 2 | 2008/09 | 449 | 10 |
| 1984 | 29 | 2 | 2009/10 | 435 | 11 |
| 1985 | 61 | 5 | 2010/11 | 361 | 8 |
| 1986 | 26 | 2 | | | |
| 1987/88 | 35 | 3 | | | |
| 1988/89 | 38 | 3 | | | |
| 1989/90 | 37 | 2 | | | |

[a] Excludes bilateral food aid for the period 1965–79, data for which are not available, and regular core contributions to the multilateral agencies including UNRWA and UNHCR.
[b] Total bilateral gross public expenditure, excluding advances to CDC.
*Source*: Departmental statistics.

In 1974 the Department centralised the management of bilateral humanitarian assistance, after a long period when it had been left largely to the geographical departments concerned. In the 1990s in the poorer countries where the Department had long-term development country programmes, there was some tension between the humanitarian assistance department, however styled, and the geographical departments, particularly in the case of long-running humanitarian crises. This reflected the gradual erosion of the dichotomy between humanitarian crises on the one hand, and development on the other. In recent years the Department has increasingly integrated conflict and the occurrence of natural disasters with its longer-term development policies and programmes, and again passed responsibility for both back to the geographical department. At the same time it has strengthened its central policy and co-ordinating capacity.

These changes are reflected in funding mechanisms. In the 1970s and 1980s, except for a small humanitarian aid allocation, responses to natural disasters were financed from the Department's own in-year contingency reserve. However, when a major humanitarian crisis emerged the Department would seek additional funding from the Treasury. The latter frequently responded sympathetically, though first they required the Department to identify any unplanned savings that could be expected to arise in its other programmes during the year. There has always been close interest in Parliament about how humanitarian crises are funded. The Select Committee in the House of Commons has often examined the Department on this and has tended to be critical of the government whenever it suspected that other planned development programmes had been cut back and that the Treasury had not been sufficiently forthcoming with additional funding. In recent years each geographical division has been expected to hold its own contingency reserve for any unanticipated aid requirements and only come to the centre, and possibly the Treasury, for help when this had been exhausted. Given the long-running nature of many crises in recent years it has also been possible to programme funding for them in future years as part of the Department's overall forward aid planning process.

## Background

Natural disasters have occurred as long as recorded history, and before. Climate change appears to be giving rise to more frequent and severe natural disasters and humanitarian crises around the world, particularly in Africa and South Asia in the recent past, and probably making them less predictable in future. In recent decades, however, early warning systems have been put in place that enable countries such as Bangladesh and those in the Caribbean to be prepared better, and local systems have been put in place better to deal with their consequences. Unfortunately less investment had been made in early warning systems in the Pacific that might have reduced the enormous loss of life and human suffering caused by the tsunami disaster at the end of 2004. That said, the last major tsunami was in 1883, caused by a volcanic eruption on the uninhabited island of Krakatau in Indonesia. It caused a seismic sea wave over 30 metres high, which swept over parts of Java and Sumatra killing an estimated 36,000 people and affecting many more.

Since the second half of the 20th century most conflicts have taken place within state borders with the notable exceptions of the Vietnam war, the Middle East wars of 1948 and 1967, the Suez Conflict of 1956, and the periodic fighting between India and Pakistan over Kashmir. Intra-state wars have included wars of independence from colonial rule (regarded by some as inter-state wars); the prolonged civil wars in Angola, Mozambique, Somalia, Sri Lanka, Sudan and Zaire (now the Democratic Republic of the Congo – DRC); the series of conflicts leading to the break-up of the former Yugoslavia; and other civil wars that have erupted in Africa (such as in Ethiopia, Liberia, Nigeria, Rwanda, and Sierra Leone), in Asia (Cambodia, Indonesia and Sri Lanka) and in South America (Colombia and Peru). This list of recent conflicts does not exhaust the causes of acute humanitarian suffering resulting in large-scale movements of population within and across borders, known respectively as internally displaced persons and refugees. The suppression of democracy and human rights in countries such as Myanmar (still Burma to many), North Korea and Zimbabwe has only added to the list of human suffering both within their borders and beyond.

Much prolonged conflict was sustained by outside support during the Cold War period and the proliferation of small arms subsequently. Violent conflict peaked in Africa in the early 1990s when half of sub-Saharan African countries suffered from civil unrest. This was also a time when more cross-border conflict took place, notably with a number of countries intervening inside DRC either to deal with their own internal conflicts or for material gain. The number of countries in Africa experiencing open conflict has declined steadily since then to nine by 2005 (Burundi, DRC, Guinea-Bissau, Ivory Coast, Kenya, Nigeria, Somalia, Sudan and Uganda). This has been brought about by the more active involvement of the African Union and regional organisations such as the Economic Organisation of West African States (ECOWAS), and the international community following the end of the Cold War.

It is estimated that the forcibly displaced populations in Africa reached a peak of about 23 million in the early 1990s, of which nearly six million were refugees from their own countries and some 17 million were internally displaced. By 2005 these numbers were estimated to have fallen to 15 million, three million and 12 million respectively.[71] These figures were drawn from a number of sources and are not directly comparable with UNHCR's own figures (see below for its global estimates).

## International humanitarian assistance architecture

The Red Cross and Red Crescent Movement comprises the ICRC (International Committee of the Red Cross), national societies and the IFRC (the International Federation of Red Cross and Red Crescent Societies); they were founded in 1919 to facilitate and promote the work of national societies, and in particular to co-ordinate international assistance to victims of natural and technological disasters, and in health emergencies. The Movement officially proclaimed seven Fundamental Principles at its international conference in Vietnam in 1965: humanity, impartiality, neutrality, independence, voluntary service, unity and universality.

With the establishment of the United Nations in 1945, and the Universal Declaration of Human Rights of 1948, the UN Relief and Works Agency (UNRWA) was established following the Middle East War of 1948 to help Arab refugees in Palestine (which it has continued to do ever since). UNRWA is funded by voluntary contributions from donors. The Department has provided annual contributions to the Agency since its inception, which since the year 2000 has averaged about £20 million per annum. It has also provided help for Palestinian refugees in Jordan and the Lebanon.

In 1950 the UN General Assembly established the Office of the UN High Commissioner for Refugees (UNHCR). Its mandate was renewed every five years until 2003 when the General Assembly agreed it should continue to exist 'until the refugee problem is solved'. The mandate of the General Assembly empowers UNHCR to provide international protection and humanitarian assistance to refugees and 'other persons of concern while finding durable solutions to their situation'. As of the beginning of 2006, UNHCR estimated that the population of concern was 21 million, including 8.6 million refugees and 6.6 million internally displaced persons. In accordance with one of the principles of the UN that it will not interfere with the actions of a member state within its borders which do not affect other nations, UNHCR can only provide assistance to internally displaced persons with the agreement of the government of the country concerned. The work of UNHCR is funded by voluntary contributions from the international community, including the Department.

The World Food Programme (WFP) was established in 1963 as the food aid arm of the UN system and has its headquarters in Rome. It was created to make food surpluses available to food-deficit countries, to provide emergency food relief, and to support longer-term rehabilitation, reconstruction and development through the provision of food aid. Its (first) 1994 Mission Statement, influenced by the Department, states that 'the central objective of food aid should be the elimination of the need for food aid'. It included the following core policies and strategies for the provision of food aid: to save lives in refugee and other emergency situations; to improve the nutrition and quality of life of the most vulnerable people at critical times in their lives; and to help build assets and promote self-reliance of poor people and communities, particularly through labour-intensive works programmes.

The Food Aid Convention was originally signed by contributory states in 1968. Under the Convention the EU has a minimum obligation to provide 1,670,000 tons of cereals each year. Of this, 927,700 tons are provided by the European Commission's food aid programme funded by the EC budget and with the costs attributed to member states. The balance is provided bilaterally by the member states; Britain's minimum obligation has been 110,700 tons annually. This is allocated bilaterally, on a country basis, and multilaterally through the WFP.

The Department has long taken the view that food aid should be provided mainly in support of humanitarian assistance operations. Influenced greatly by the works of the late Professor Hans Singer of the Institute of Development Studies, the Department has argued that the provision of long-term food aid to a country can distort agricultural markets and be a disincentive to poor farmers to produce food locally. It has sought to provide only the minimum food aid under the Food Aid Convention obligation and to the extent possible only for humanitarian assistance purposes. It has urged others to do likewise, and for the WFP to focus its efforts primarily on humanitarian crisis situations, something which it has done increasingly since the mid-1990s.

The Office of the Co-ordination for Humanitarian Affairs (OCHA) is the over-arching co-ordinating body within the UN, reporting to the Secretary-General. It also chairs the Inter-Agency Standing Committee which comprises the UN humanitarian agencies, the Red Cross/Red Crescent Movement and non-governmental organisations. In recent years its role has been strengthened to help the UN and the wider international community better to respond to the growing complexity of humanitarian crises brought about by conflict (see the section below on the international policy response, p. 111).

The Office of the High Commissioner for Human Rights (OHCHR) was created in its present form in 1997 and the High Commissioner reports to the UN Secretary-General. Its mission is to protect and promote all civil, cultural, economic, political and social human rights for all and to prevent the occurrence or continuation of human rights abuses throughout the world, in accordance with the UN Charter and international human rights law. OHCHR plays a critical role in monitoring and reporting on human rights violations in conflict-affected countries.

The European Commission Humanitarian Organisation (ECHO) is the humanitarian assistance arm of the European Commission's external assistance programme. It is funded from the EC budget, financed by member states, to which Britain has contributed about 20 per cent. It administers the EU's 'multilateral' food aid obligation under the Food Aid Convention, as distinct from that provided bilaterally by individual member states. Over the years, and consistent with its own policy on food aid, the Department has argued for ECHO to provide food aid only for humanitarian purposes, though with limited success. In 1984 the EU agreed that developing countries could request that food aid could be provided in the form of financial assistance instead. ECHO is the second largest provider of humanitarian assistance and the Department co-ordinates closely with ECHO, together with other international agencies, in responding to humanitarian crises. In 2005/6 ECHO provided some £340 million of humanitarian assistance, of which £65 million represented Britain's contribution via the EC budget. However, ECHO has continued to provide food aid in non-emergency situations which, in 2005/6, also amounted to about £340 million.

## The period 1965–89

In terms of the Department's humanitarian assistance, this period was characterised mainly, though not exclusively, by responses to natural disasters. The prolonged civil wars in Africa led directly to humanitarian suffering and made people more susceptible to drought and floods which their governments were poorly placed to respond to. The Disaster Unit created in 1974 was established with a small administrative staff and which called upon the aid budget's in-year contingency reserve, retained to meet unanticipated aid requirements. The Unit provided a central means for assessing need: it liaised with international bodies and British NGOs to which it provided funding to enable them to respond to humanitarian crises.

Between 1965 and 1989/90, total humanitarian assistance amounted to £424 million (see Table 6.1). Unfortunately information by country is not available for the 15 years prior to 1980. During the period 1980 to 1989/90 (see Table 6.2) the Department provided a total of £302 million in humanitarian assistance, the bulk of which (£248 million – 82 per cent) was to Africa, almost exclusively to sub-Saharan Africa. During this decade there were four main and continuing recipients of humanitarian assistance: Ethiopia, Mozambique and Sudan in Africa, and Bangladesh in Asia. Between them they accounted for 62 per cent of all humanitarian assistance provided worldwide during that period. Assistance to Bangladesh was to help cope with periodic monsoon floods, and to Ethiopia mainly to help alleviate suffering caused by persistent droughts, particularly the serious drought of 1984–85 when the Department paid for some 2,000 missions flown by RAF Hercules aircraft to deliver food and shelter in the 14 months to December 1985. The remainder was provided to countries such as India and Kenya to help them deal with the consequences of floods and droughts, and to other countries to help cope with the aftermath of earthquakes (Pakistan, Mexico and Turkey) and volcanic eruptions (Colombia).

In the case of Mexico, the Royal Engineers and the Fire Service Inspectorate provided on-the-ground assistance, and in the case of Colombia the RAF Hercules delivered urgently needed supplies. These early interventions by the Ministry of Defence raised the issue of how much the Department should pay for these services. While the MOD was required by the Treasury to charge full costs, the Department argued that it should only meet the incremental costs to MOD of such operations. A charge based on the latter was eventually agreed for the above and subsequent operations.

## The period since 1990/91

This period saw many humanitarian crises as a result of natural disasters to which the Department continued to respond. But it was also a period of major conflict around the world even though the number of violent conflicts in Africa declined substantially from its peak in the early 1990s. Since 1990, there have been several major conflicts, other than in Africa, where Britain has had major and immediate political and security interests – Bosnia and Kosovo in Europe, and Afghanistan and

*Table 6.2* Main and recurring recipients of humanitarian assistance: 1980–2010/11 (£m)

| | Angola | DRC | Ethiopia | Malawi | Mozambique | Somalia | Sudan | Zimbabwe | Total Africa | Iraq | Afghanistan | Bangladesh | Total Asia/ Mid East | Former Yugo- slavia | Total Europe |
|---|---|---|---|---|---|---|---|---|---|---|---|---|---|---|---|
| 1980 | - | - | 1 | - | - | 1 | - | - | 9 | - | - | - | 4 | - | - |
| 1981 | - | - | - | - | - | 1 | - | - | 15 | - | - | 3 | 6 | - | - |
| 1982 | - | - | 5 | - | - | 1 | - | - | 13 | - | - | - | 3 | - | - |
| 1983 | - | - | 3 | - | - | - | 3 | - | 15 | - | - | 1 | 5 | - | - |
| 1984 | - | - | 2 | - | 1 | - | 4 | - | 23 | - | - | 4 | 6 | - | - |
| 1985 | - | - | 27 | - | 4 | - | 8 | 1 | 55 | - | - | - | 3 | - | - |
| 1986 | - | - | 8 | - | 2 | - | 7 | - | 24 | - | - | - | 1 | - | - |
| 1987/88 | - | - | 13 | - | 6 | - | 2 | - | 24 | - | - | 8 | 9 | - | - |
| 1888/89 | - | - | 12 | - | 7 | - | 8 | - | 36 | - | - | - | 1 | - | - |
| 1989/90 | - | - | 10 | - | 6 | - | 8 | - | 34 | - | - | 2 | 2 | - | - |
| Total (£m) | - | - | 80 | - | 26 | 3 | 40 | 1 | 248 | - | - | 18 | 40 | - | - |
| % world-wide | - | - | 26% | - | 9% | 1% | 13% | - | 82% | - | - | 6% | 13% | - | - |
| 1990/91 | 1 | - | 20 | - | 5 | - | 8 | - | 44 | 3 | - | - | 5 | - | - |
| 1991/92 | 1 | - | 18 | - | 6 | 3 | 19 | - | 58 | 34 | - | 4 | 51 | - | - |
| 1992/93 | - | - | 13 | 6 | 10 | 16 | 9 | 2 | 83 | 4 | 1 | - | 14 | 39 | 39 |
| 1993/94 | 13 | - | 10 | 2 | 10 | 5 | 15 | - | 86 | 9 | 1 | 2 | 25 | 52 | 58 |
| 1994/95 | 8 | - | 13 | 12 | 10 | 1 | 12 | 1 | 108 | 7 | 1 | 1 | 31 | 46 | 53 |
| 1995/96 | 11 | - | 5 | 6 | 10 | - | 4 | 2 | 57 | 7 | - | 2 | 22 | 38 | 41 |
| 1996/97 | - | - | - | 1 | - | 1 | 3 | 5 | 31 | 6 | 9 | - | 27 | 43 | 46 |
| 1997/98 | - | 6 | 3 | 2 | - | - | 4 | 6 | 24 | 3 | 7 | - | 14 | 20 | 22 |
| 1998/99 | - | - | 4 | 3 | - | - | 24 | 6 | 47 | 6 | 3 | 16 | 29 | 4 | 7 |
| 1999/2000 | - | - | 3 | - | 12 | - | 3 | 6 | 32 | 7 | 5 | - | 31 | 107 | 121 |

*(continued)*

Table 6.2  Continued

| | Angola | DRC | Ethiopia | Malawi | Mozambique | Somalia | Sudan | Zimbabwe | Total Africa | Iraq | Afghanistan | Bangladesh | Total Asia/ Mid East | Former Yugo-slavia | Total Europe |
|---|---|---|---|---|---|---|---|---|---|---|---|---|---|---|---|
| 2000/01 | - | - | 13 | - | 9 | - | 5 | 7 | 50 | 10 | 6 | 3 | 47 | 34 | 41 |
| 2001/02 | 2 | 8 | 8 | - | - | 2 | 6 | 7 | 44 | 8 | 50 | 2 | 84 | 5 | 11 |
| 2002/03 | 7 | 12 | 27 | 7 | 1 | 3 | 16 | 23 | 153 | 19 | 44 | - | 83 | - | 4 |
| 2003/04 | 4 | 15 | 19 | 1 | - | 3 | 22 | 25 | 126 | 110 | 11 | - | 129 | - | 4 |
| 2004/05 | 2 | 16 | 7 | 5 | - | 4 | 78 | 14 | 166 | 21 | 7 | 25 | 113 | - | 3 |
| 2005/06 | 4 | 44 | 9 | 2 | - | 16 | 98 | 26 | 264 | 5 | 3 | - | 88 | - | 2 |
| 2006/07 | 1 | 52 | 2 | 3 | 1 | 8 | 83 | 16 | 226 | 10 | 2 | - | 64 | - | 3 |
| 2007/08 | 1 | 46 | 5 | 2 | - | 14 | 91 | 18 | 221 | 20 | 8 | 13 | 100 | - | 1 |
| 2008/09 | 1 | 33 | 34 | - | 2 | 18 | 53 | 21 | 241 | 16 | 20 | 7 | 174 | - | 3 |
| 2009/10 | - | 40 | 63 | 1 | - | 32 | 59 | 19 | 294 | 8 | 7 | 1 | 103 | - | 1 |
| 2010/11 | - | 47 | 6 | 1 | 1 | 30 | 84 | 2 | 212 | 3 | 1 | 3 | 109 | - | - |
| Total(£m) | 56 | 319 | 282 | 54 | 77 | 159 | 763 | 207 | 2567 | 316 | 186 | 79 | 1343 | 388 | 460 |
| %worldwide | 1% | 6% | 5% | 1% | 3% | 3% | 14% | 4% | 51% | 6% | 4% | 2% | 26% | 8% | 9% |

*Source:* Departmental statistics.

Iraq in Asia and the Middle East. In each case British forces have been heavily involved, and humanitarian assistance by the Department has played an important role, albeit dwarfed by the military costs. As the figures in Table 6.2 show, whereas in the 1980s more than 80 per cent of all humanitarian assistance went to Africa, in the period that followed (to 2010/11), over 30 per cent went to Asia, the Middle East and Europe, and some 60 per cent to Africa. In absolute terms, in the 1980s £248 million was provided to Africa and £40 million to Asia and the Middle East. In the subsequent period to 2010/11, £2.6 billion went to Africa, over £1.3 billion to Asia and the Middle East, and £460 million went to Europe. Thus, humanitarian aid to other parts of the world was not directly at the expense of Africa; rather, there was a very large increase in humanitarian assistance globally.

With the increasing scale and complexity of humanitarian operations which the Department found itself responding to, the Emergency Aid Department (EMAD) was established in the early 1990s, headed by a senior civil servant and provided with enhanced manpower resources. The ability to assess and to respond to need was enhanced by the Emergency Logistics Team contracted from the Crown Agents, subsequently renamed the Emergency Relief Team (ERT). This provided the Department with the capacity for sending short-term missions better to assess needs on the ground and to provide a better understanding of how the Department could help and which agencies were best placed to implement humanitarian operations. It also enabled the Department to deliver humanitarian assistance directly in difficult circumstances on certain occasions. The Conflict and Humanitarian Aid Department (CHAD) was created in 1997 with a wider mandate to develop policies aimed at conflict prevention and resolution. This has progressively involved greater co-operation with the FCO and the MOD, and dialogue with the international community. In recent years CHAD has been renamed the Conflict, Humanitarian and Security Affairs department (CHASE), and the ERT has become known as the Operations Team, still provided under contract from the Crown Agents. CHASE has become more of a policy and service department for others in the Department, reflecting the increasing integration of conflict and natural disasters into development policy, and the importance of focusing on the international system. Since 1997 the Department has entered into partnership agreements with a number of UN and other international agencies to assist them strengthen their own capacity to deliver their mission. These partnerships are set out in International Strategy Papers drawn up jointly by the Department and the agencies concerned (including OCHA, OHCHR, UNHCR, WFP and ICRC).

The 2006 White Paper 'Making Governance Work for the Poor' addressed these issues at some length, as an integral part of achieving the Millennium Development Goals. It promised to 'concentrate more development assistance . . . on fragile states, especially those vulnerable to conflict [. . .] work to help states promote peace and security' and 'where states are unable to protect their citizens . . . work with our international partners to prevent, manage, and respond to, conflict' and work with others for 'a more effective UN system to deal with humanitarian crises'. This reflected the fact that in 2005 of the 34 countries furthest from meeting the MDGs 22 countries were either still in the midst of violent conflict or were just emerging from it.

Relations with the rest of Whitehall in relation to conflict prevention and peace-building were formalised in 2001 with the creation of two Conflict Prevention Pools, one for Africa (the ACPP) and another for the rest of the world (the GCPP). The objective of each Pool was to improve the governments' contribution to conflict prevention and peace-building by joining up British expertise across the three Whitehall Departments in development, diplomacy and defence (the Department, the FCO and the MOD). The model for this was Britain's help for Sierra Leone. At ministerial level, inter-departmental Committees provided policy oversight – for the ACPP, chaired by the Secretary of State for International Development, and for the GCPP, chaired by the Foreign Secretary. As part of the 2007 CSR the two conflict pools were merged, with DFID taking the lead within Whitehall.

The three Departments have worked jointly to support the activities of the African Union (AU), sub-regional organisations and individual countries. The main activities have been in relation to security sector reform; disarmament, demobilisation and re-integration; enhancing African peace support operations capacity; political dialogue and peace processes; NGO/civil society grassroots peace-building programmes; support to the African peace and security architecture; media projects in conflict-affected areas; and research and conflict analysis. A Performance Report for the period 2001–05 was produced which set out the work of the ACPP and reviewed progress.[72]

## Montserrat

This chapter would not be complete without a special mention of the natural disaster which befell the Overseas Territory of Montserrat, a small island in the Caribbean. It is unique in that the volcanic eruption which began in 1995 affected the lives of all its 11,000 inhabitants and wiped out the capital, Plymouth, virtually all its infrastructure, including the airport, and means of livelihood. The only links with the outside world were now a small ferry and a helicopter hired by the Department, while aid funds were also being used to build a small jetty in the north. Apart from limited domestic revenues the island was dependent largely on British development assistance. Eventually a new airport was built in the north to restore regional fixed-wing air links.

As the volcanic eruptions got worse during 1996 and 1997, many people left the island, originally mainly for neighbouring Antigua, and then for Britain. In 1997 the government announced a scheme for assisted relocation outside the island both regionally and to Britain, which in the latter case included permission to remain and work, and receive social security benefits. It was estimated that some 3,000 people went to Antigua, another 1,000 to other Caribbean islands, and some 3,000 came to Britain. In the case of Antigua, special assistance was provided to the government and NGOs to provide housing and new means of livelihood.

In mid-1997 the Chief Minister resigned and David Brandt, a vocal critic of London, was elected in his place. The new Chief Minister made several visits to London to demand faster and larger assistance to the island, and was quite intransigent in his demands despite all the efforts being made. This prompted Clare Short, during a local constituency newspaper interview, to quip that the Chief Minister would next be asking for 'golden elephants', intended to be a criticism of Brandt's attitude. Unfortunately, it was highlighted by the national media, taken badly by the islanders (to whom she apologised) and by Foreign Office ministers (to whom she did not). Sadly the islanders who remained or later returned have been unable to return to their previous life, and many remain in Britain and elsewhere.[73]

## The international policy response

The experience of the last 20 years has led to important developments in both the international community's and the Department's approach to humanitarian crises. It has led to a more co-ordinated, international, response to crises and to a more integrated and holistic approach to conflict situations. The Department has increasingly focused its efforts on encouraging the international community to respond collectively to crises and seeking to prevent them.

In 1999 Tony Blair, then Britain's Prime Minister, made a wide-ranging speech to the Chicago Economic Club. He covered a number of economic, political, security and environmental issues and began by justifying the NATO military action in Kosovo, describing it as a just war to stop ethnic cleansing and worse. He went on to describe what he believed to be the emergence of a new doctrine of international community in a globalising world (later described as 'the Blair Doctrine'). He sought to qualify the principle of non-interference in the internal affairs of sovereign nations:

> Acts of genocide can never be a purely internal matter. When oppression produces massive flows of refugees which unsettle neighbouring countries then they can properly be described as threats to international peace and security. [. . .] When we decide when and whether to intervene . . . we need to bear in mind five major considerations: are we sure of our case; have we exhausted all diplomatic options; are there military actions we can sensibly and prudently take; are we prepared for the long term; do we have national interests involved?

He went on to argue for reform of international institutions and for support for the UN as the central pillar for a world ruled by law and international co-operation, with a Security Council that works.

In the same year, the UN Secretary-General, Kofi Annan, posed the following question: 'if humanitarian intervention is, indeed, an unacceptable assault on sovereignty, how should we respond to a Rwanda, to a Srebrenica – to gross and systematic violations of human rights that affect every precept of our common humanity?' At the UN Millennium Review Summit in 2005, the international community gave its answer; 191 world leaders agreed that the primary responsibility for the protection of vulnerable populations lies with their respective governments. They agreed also that the international community has a duty to support national governments to protect their civilians. The agreement went on to say that

> in exceptional circumstances, and when all other options had been tried, the international community, through the UN, would be prepared to take collective action, in a timely and decisive manner . . . should peaceful means be inadequate and national authorities are manifestly failing to protect their populations from genocide, war crimes, ethnic cleansing and crimes against humanity.

Neither Tony Blair's speech, nor the 2005 UN World Summit endorsed by the UN General Assembly, sanctioned international military action without the authority of the UN Security Council. Chapter Seven of the

UN Charter already provided for international action when the events in one country adversely impacts on regional and global security. But the debate moved on about when and whether such military action would be justified. For some, interventions were justified in Bosnia, Kosovo, Afghanistan and Iraq, even in the absence of a full mandate by the UN Security Council. However, the inability of the UN Security Council to agree any international response to the situation in Syria demonstrates the limits of this approach.

In 2003, 17 donors, including the Department, agreed the Principles of Good Humanitarian Donorship, subsequently endorsed by the DAC. According to the Principles, humanitarian action should be guided by humanity (saving lives and alleviating suffering wherever it is found), impartiality (without discrimination between or within affected populations), neutrality (not favouring any side in armed conflict) and independence (autonomy from the political, economic, military and other objectives that any actor may hold). It goes on to set out: i) further general principles of good donorship, including respect for international law and human rights, flexible and timely funding, involvement of beneficiaries, strengthening the capacity of affected countries and local communities, assisting in ways supportive of recovery and long-term development, and support for the central and unique role of the UN, the special role of the ICRC, and non-governmental organisations; and ii) good practice in donor financing, management and accountability.

Managing humanitarian operations where outside military forces are involved has raised important policy issues and concerns. Both the international agencies and many NGOs are anxious not to be seen to be associated with any military forces including, and perhaps particularly, NATO forces which are not blue-hatted. Médecins Sans Frontières, the large French NGO, has been particularly vocal in this regard on a matter of principle, but others, including British NGOs, feel similarly. The Principles of Good Humanitarian Donorship address this issue directly in relation to impartiality and neutrality. The Department also addressed this issue in its 2006 humanitarian policy paper *Saving Lives, Relieving Suffering, Protecting Dignity*.[74] This recognises that 'new dilemmas have emerged in crises such as Kosovo, Afghanistan and Iraq where third party military intervention has taken place and military forces have been involved also in relief and reconstruction work'. It recognises that military forces will, in some situations, have an obligation to meet the basic material needs of people but that delivering humanitarian assistance remains controversial. It goes on to note that UN guidance makes it clear that drawing on military capabilities for tasks with humanitarian objectives should be a strategy of 'last resort' and that decisions to use the military should be at the request of the civilian authorities who should resume primacy for the delivery of humanitarian assistance as quickly as possible. It goes on to state that the Department will 'look at the case for the deployment of military capabilities in different contexts, considering the implications for the protection of civilians, security of aid workers and the cost effectiveness of using military rather than civilian assets'.

Following his visit to Darfur, the Rt Hon Hilary Benn MP, then Secretary of State for International Development, made a speech in December 2004 at the Overseas Development Institute in London on the need for reform of the international humanitarian system. He criticised the international community's response to the Darfur crisis and argued for six specific proposals for change:

i. to improve leadership at country level with serious humanitarian crises; the UN should provide humanitarian co-ordinators with emergency powers to direct other UN agencies;
ii. humanitarian co-ordinators should have lead responsibility for needs assessment, planning, and resource allocation, supported by a better resourced OCHA. Based on a Common Humanitarian Action Plan donors should put their funds through the Co-ordinator;
iii. OCHA should set benchmarks for the scale and speed of response against which agencies can be held accountable;
iv. the establishment of a substantial new humanitarian fund under the control of the UN Secretary-General and administered by OCHA, from which co-ordinators can draw, accompanied by credible performance measurement and monitoring;
v. to balance the often unequal allocation of funds between different crises ECHO (the world's second largest humanitarian donor) should be the financier of 'last resort', focusing on the 'forgotten crises';
vi. disaster risk reduction should be built into development planning. The Department would make an allocation for disaster risk reduction investment equal to 10 per cent of its response to each natural disaster, to prepare for and mitigate the impact of future disasters.

Benn went on to address the issue of conflict. In relation to the 'responsibility to protect', he argued that the Security Council had a duty to respond swiftly when a government is unwilling or unable to prevent a humanitarian catastrophe. He cited the experience of the Rwandan genocide when the Security Council withdrew its peacekeepers from the country. He also cited the inadequacy of MONUC (UN Mission to the

Democratic Republic of Congo) to deliver peace and security in DRC, a country the size of Western Europe, and a country that 'has not had a functioning state for decades and has been mired in ethnic conflict across the region'. Finally he argued for more international and regional capacity to prevent conflict and for further action to control the flow of small arms and light weapons, including an Arms Trade Treaty.

Since then the UN, under the leadership of the Secretary-General, has taken a number of important steps to strengthen the humanitarian aid system and its own capacity to help prevent and manage conflict. In 2005 the World Summit recognised for the first time that states had a responsibility to protect their people, but the international community also had the responsibility to support states in protecting their populations, including in certain extreme circumstances the responsibility to intervene, including by the use of military support as a last resort. The World Summit also agreed that a Peacebuilding Commission should be established (it was formed in December 2006) to address critical weaknesses in the international response to conflict. The role of the UN at country level is being reformed, and Humanitarian Co-ordinators have been appointed in some countries with direct responsibility to OCHA. A Central Emergency Respond Fund (CERF), originally proposed by Benn, was also agreed at the World Summit, established with donor funding to enable the international system to respond quickly and more effectively to humanitarian crises when they occur, and also to provide additional funding for those crises that are under-funded. The aim was to secure annual funding of $500 million which, according to OCHA, is only 4 per cent of the $12 billion spent annually by the international community. In 2006 $300 million was pledged, with 60 per cent committed for rapid response to emergencies and nearly 30 per cent to under-funded ongoing crises. In addition, Common Funds have been created in certain countries, under the control of the Humanitarian Co-ordinator, to which donors are also being encouraged to contribute. The Department initially contributed £50 million to the CERF and has provided additional funding to country Common Funds.

Against this background the Coalition government invited Lord (Paddy) Ashdown to chair a group to undertake the first external, independent, Humanitarian Emergency Response Review, and to which Secretary of State Andrew Mitchell quickly responded,[75] accepting all its main recommendations, setting out specific policy and operational commitments. Lord Ashdown's report acknowledged that the Department has been widely praised for its leading role within the international humanitarian community as a policymaker, a funder and deliverer of aid; 'But being good is not going to be good enough given the challenges ahead.' The report predicted that the scale, frequency and severity of rapid-onset disasters will continue to grow in the coming years, not least in terms of climate-related disasters.

The report, in arguing for new ways to meet the new challenges, identified seven threads to a new approach: a more anticipatory approach with a greater use of science; the creation of resilience at the heart of the approach both to longer-term development and emergency response; improved strategic, political and operational leadership of the international humanitarian system; innovation to become more efficient and effective; greater transparency and accountability; the creation of new partnerships, including with emerging world powers and the private sector; strengthening the humanitarian space to give humanitarian workers greater access and protection, reasserting the core humanitarian principles of humanity, impartiality and neutrality, assessing people on the basis of need, regardless of their gender, religion, ethnicity or political allegiance.

In accepting the recommendations the Department acknowledged the most far-reaching would be to integrate effectively its longer-term development work with humanitarian responses to achieve greater capacity of countries to withstand a range of shocks, particularly in fragile and conflict-affected situations.

# 7
# Aid Channels

## Introduction

The purpose of this chapter is to provide an understanding of how the Department has chosen particular channels of aid in order to pursue its basic mission of helping to reduce poverty in the poorest countries, and the political and commercial considerations it has had to take account of. This is in the context of an evolving international aid architecture since the 1960s. In doing this it hopes to avoid reinforcing the traditional dichotomy between bilateral aid (that which the Department retains more or less direct management of) and multilateral aid (that which it provides through individual multilateral development institutions which have management responsibility for the funds they receive). Over time some of the key distinctions between bilateral and multilateral aid have been eroded with greater co-ordination between development partners and with a greater sense of common purpose within an agreed country-level framework.

## The official international aid architecture

The United Nations plays a crucial over-arching role in international affairs, including development. It was founded on the three inter-related pillars of development, human rights and security, though in earlier times its development work was often seen as quite distinct. The UN is a convenor of all its member states to discuss and agree the important policy issues and concerns relating to all its three pillars. UN texts are renowned for the agonisingly long time it takes to prepare and agree them, for their diplomatic and diluted language necessary to reach a consensus, and for their often limited readership. Cynics will say that the only people who really care about them are the international professionals (UN and diplomatic mission staff and delegates from capitals who, after long-night sessions, retreat home with relief to re-enter the real world). Others, who believe in the power of the UN over time to effect change, might refer one back to the UN's founding Charter and the Universal Declaration of Human Rights, and more recently to the series of Summit meetings of the 1990s and the World Summits of 2000 and 2005 committing all member states to the Millennium Development Goals which in recent years provided frameworks and targets for reducing poverty.

The UN's presence in-country is the Resident Representative, who is the main interface with the government regarding issues relating to each of the UN's three pillars, manages the UN Development Programme (UNDP) and has a co-ordinating role with respect to the work of its Specialized Agencies and other UN organisations working in the country. UNDP was created as the central co-ordinating and funding agency for the provision of technical co-operation to developing countries. It manages its own programmes of technical co-operation and uses the Specialized Agencies of the UN to manage programmes and projects on its behalf. The UNDP is funded by annual voluntary contributions from UN member states.

The UN has a number of Specialized Agencies, as explained in Chapter Three. They carry out both worldwide regulatory and advisory functions and provide technical co-operation to developing countries. Member states which are members of these Specialized Agencies make an annual assessment of their contribution. The DAC estimates what proportion of these assessed contributions relate to technical co-operation activities and should therefore count as oda. For many Specialized Agencies (such as FAO and WHO) this represents the bulk of their work, but for some it accounts for only a small proportion of their activities (for example, UNESCO, for which less than 10 per cent has counted as oda). Other agencies such as UNICEF, UNHCR and WFP rely on voluntary contributions for their programmes.

The Bretton Woods institutions – the International Bank for Reconstruction and Development (IBRD) and the International Monetary Fund (IMF) – were established after the Second World War, though the IMF is not regarded as a development finance institution. They have their own governance arrangements still heavily weighted in favour of the major OECD countries, though this is being increasingly questioned by the stronger emerging economies, particularly in the context of the current global financial crisis. The World Bank, together with its International Finance Corporation subsidiary, were capitalised by its members to enable them to borrow funds in the marketplace in order to lend on quasi-market terms to its members, but in practice to middle-income developing countries. The capital base comprises two components: paid-in capital (some 5 per cent) and callable capital. The former requires member governments to make a capital subscription from their budgets; the latter is an obligation to pay should the World Bank ever need to call upon it. The fact that the rich OECD countries were, at least until the present financial crisis, deemed creditworthy has meant that the World Bank could raise capital in the marketplace on the strength of its callable as well as its subscribed capital. Members have provided subscribed and callable capital, in general, according to their relative economic strength (that is, their national income). The capital base of the World Bank has been enhanced periodically to enable it to borrow larger amounts to lend to the middle-income developing countries that were judged able to borrow funds on quasi-market terms for their development. The International Finance Corporation, a subsidiary of the World Bank, was established in 1960 to provide equity and loan finance to help develop private-sector business, mainly in the middle-income countries. Its capital structure is similar to that of its parent IBRD.

In 1960 the International Development Association (IDA) was created as the 'soft window' lending arm of the World Bank to provide highly concessional long-term credits (that is, loans), with a zero rate of interest, to the poorer developing countries. It was created despite efforts much earlier by the UN to create a similar but more far-reaching organisation (see Chapter Two). The funds for the IDA are provided by donor governments in the form of grants through three-yearly replenishments. These pledges by member donor governments are provided in the form of unrecallable promissory notes deposited with their central banks over the three-year period and called down by the IDA as they are needed to be disbursed. The fact that donor country grants finance repayable loans has, over time, resulted in the IDA creating a pool of funds to supplement successive replenishments. For project lending disbursements are generally over an 8 to 10-year period, and for non-project (structural adjustment) lending, over 3 to 5 years. The three-yearly replenishments are negotiated between member (donor) governments. In addition to OECD donor governments, in recent years the stronger developing countries have become members of the IDA and have contributed to IDA replenishments. The negotiations have two dimensions: one concerns the overall level of the replenishment which raises issues related to the role of the IDA in the international aid system and its relative effectiveness in promoting development; the other concerns the relative contribution which donors are prepared to make. The starting point for the latter is their relative economic strength (for Britain some 6–7 per cent) but individual donors may take a more positive or negative view of the IDA's potential contribution to development, and will have regard to their actual and prospective total aid budgets and their own priorities for its use. The World Bank is not only the single largest provider of concessional credits to the poorer countries but it plays a crucial role in terms of both research and policy analysis at a global and country level, and co-ordinating donor efforts.

The World Bank Group (including the IDA) is by far the largest international financial development institution. For each of the four main regions of the developing world international financial institutions analogous to the World Bank have been created: the African Development Bank (the AfDB, based originally in Abidjan, but now in Tunis); the Asian Development Bank (the ADB, based in Manila); the Caribbean Development Bank (the CDB, based in Bridgetown) and the Inter-American Development Bank (the IADB, based in Washington). Like the World Bank, each has its own hard and soft windows and is financed in the same ways. They are financed by replenishments every three years to allow them to provide highly concessional long-term credits to its poorer regional members. The donor member governments provide the bulk of the contributions to the soft windows. The same issues arise as with the IDA, though geo-political and effectiveness issues are more to the fore. For example, Japan is well disposed towards contributing towards the finances of the ADB while the USA has been more sympathetic towards the IADB. Following the collapse of the Soviet Union, the European Bank for Reconstruction and Development (EBRD) was created, with its headquarters in London. It does not have a soft window (though it is able to provide some technical assistance) and its remit is to support the transition process towards market economies and help develop the private sector in the transition countries of the region.

The third and growing component of the multilateral aid system, though it is not multilateral in the full meaning of the word, are the European Union's aid programmes managed by the European Commission. These comprise two main elements: the European Development Fund, which provides aid to the African, Caribbean and Pacific (ACP) countries, financed by grant contributions from EU member states pledged every five years, analogous to the IDA; and the EC budget which provides development aid to other countries, notably in Asia, Latin America and the Mediterranean and, since the 1990s, to countries in East and Central Europe which have not already become members of the EU. In addition, the EC budget provides substantial humanitarian assistance and regular food aid through the European Community Humanitarian Office (ECHO). The EC budget is funded by member states, in general, according to their relative economic strength within the EU (about 17 per cent in the case of Britain). The EU and its member states now account for about 50 per cent of all oda.

A further component of the international architecture is the Commonwealth. It provides a unique forum for both developed and developing countries to discuss international issues of mutual concern, including development. Such discussions feed through into wider international discussion in the UN and into other aspects of the international aid architecture. The Commonwealth Secretariat, based in London, services the Commonwealth (including the bi-annual Commonwealth Heads of Government Meeting [CHOGM]), and administers certain modest development programmes, mainly the Commonwealth Fund for Technical Co-operation (CFTC).

In recent years various global funds have been established with an international governance structure. These include the Global Fund for AIDS, Tuberculosis and Malaria (GFATM), the Global Alliance on Vaccines and Immunisation (GAVI), UNITAID (International Drug Purchase Facility) and the Education for All Fast Track Initiative. Each was established to address particular development issues. The motivation behind the creation of global funds has been three-fold: a measure of frustration by some with traditional multilateral channels' ability to adequately address key areas of concern; a desire to tap new sources of funding, particularly the large private Foundations (notably the Bill & Melinda Gates Foundation) and the private business sector; and to broaden the governance structure, for example by including representatives of developing countries, NGOs and the private sector as well as the major donors.

The Rt Hon Gordon Brown MP, as Chancellor of the Exchequer, launched his own funding initiative known as the International Finance Facility (IFF), intended to raise additional concessional funds to help meet the MDGs by 2015. Its purpose was to mobilise funds over the intervening period beyond that which donors collectively were prepared to make available through their aid budgets by issuing bonds in the marketplace guaranteed by donor governments. After 2015, donors would meet the cost of repaying investors as the bonds matured. This initiative has been the subject of considerable debate within the development community. Some are concerned that there will remain much to be done after 2015, whether or not some or all of the MDGs are met, and that it would be inappropriate to mortgage future aid budgets in this way: better to provide additional development finance directly by increasing aid budgets further in the short term. Donors already meeting the 0.7 per cent UN aid target could be expected to be particularly vocal in this regard. Initially the Department resisted the scheme for fear it would mortgage its future aid budgets. However, eventually Clare Short accepted the idea. By 2009 the only example of this initiative bearing fruit was the International Fund for Immunisation (IFFIm) in support of GAVI, which the French supported in return for British support for their UNITAID initiative.

The final important component of the official international aid system is the aid provided bilaterally by donor governments. Donors, like the Department, provide financial aid to developing-country governments and others in the form of grants or concessional loans for agreed purposes. They also provide technical co-operation in the form of grants, the strict definition of which used to be assistance provided under a contract between the donor agency and the provider. Thus, technical co-operation may comprise the provision of consultancy and individual expert services together with associated equipment to a developing country or regional body; training in the donor or a third country; research and development carried out by an institution, usually but not necessarily, in the donor country concerned; and funding for civil society organisations (NGOs in old-speak) working in developing countries which again were in the past usually but not necessarily based in the donor country (see below for the Departments's more recent restructured definition of technical assistance).

## Policy choices

The Department, like other donors, makes choices regarding which of the components of the international aid system to use depending on its overall policy objectives, while having regard to political and commercial considerations. The overall stated mission of the Department over nearly five decades has been summarised as helping to reduce poverty in the poorest countries. It has therefore, in development policy terms, chosen those channels which were primarily focused on the poorer countries, and has pursued policies more directly intended to benefit poor people, and which it believes are effective in doing so. This has resulted amongst other things in it maintaining, whenever possible, substantial bilateral programmes focused primarily on its basic mission and which it understandably believes are well-managed, and supporting key multilateral institutions such as the IDA and the UN system, though not unconditionally.

There are several broad political considerations. Britain has a certain role and standing within the international community which it wishes to sustain and enhance. This argues for it participating actively and widely within the international aid system. In doing so the Department will tend to argue for reform and improvements in the way multilateral development institutions can help deliver its stated mission. It is inconceivable that Britain would cease to participate meaningfully in IDA. It has generally adhered to the principle of universality in its assistance to the UN as a permanent member of the Security Council, meaning that it should be a member of all UN bodies, though with the exception of UNESCO temporarily in the mid-1990s and the current Coalition government's intention to discontinue core support for those it regards as ineffective and therefore poor value for money. The Department has had no choice but to pay Britain's share of a growing EC budget for overseas aid, despite serious doubts about its geographical allocation and its effectiveness. Its ability to restrain the growth in EC budget aid has been constrained by the attitude of other member states and by the trade-offs made within the overall EC budget negotiated by the Treasury. Similarly, while the Department has had concerns about the effectiveness of the EDF there have been political constraints on the extent to which it was prepared to argue for lower quinquinial replenishments or for a smaller share of such replenishments: other EU member states, particularly France, and the European Commission have generally pressed for increasing its size.

At certain times the business community, through the DTI, has sought to influence the extent and nature of Britain's contributions to multilateral development institutions. Bilateral aid was, until 2000, largely tied to the procurement of British goods and services, with the exception of the provision for local costs. Procurement of goods and services from Britain by multilateral development institutions, which operate competitive bidding processes within member states, varies. In broad terms the proportion of offshore IDA procurement (that is, excluding local costs) from Britain has been in line with Britain's share of world trade in capital and intermediate goods. Not surprisingly its share of procurement by the ADB and IADB tends to be less than its world trade share, but rather better in the case of the AfDB. The

DTI generally favoured bilateral aid at least until it became untied, and logically favoured the minimum contribution to multilateral institutions consistent with retaining procurement access for British companies. Also logically, given that Britain's share of world trade exceeded its share of global GDP, it should have favoured a larger amount of relatively transparent and competitive multilateral aid-financed procurement.

## A case for bilateral aid

Donors have most control over their bilateral aid programmes. They can use their bilateral aid more directly to further their development policy objectives, provided they have the managerial and technical capacity for doing so, and to have regard to political and commercial considerations. For some donor countries geo-political considerations have been a major consideration (notably in the case of the US and Japan) while for others (notably Britain, France and, more recently, Portugal and Spain) history – their colonial past – has continued to be a major consideration in the geographical orientation of their bilateral aid. History has created both expectations, which these donors feel obliged to respond to, and comparative advantages which they believe they should exploit. Thus, Britain and France have focused bilateral aid on their poorer past colonies: not only are there expectations but they each better understand the institutions they helped create and the languages they bequeathed.

Britain had a substantial standing capacity in the form of scientific institutions and people with knowledge and experience of developing countries. In a world of tied aid the best way to ensure that this capacity was exploited and nurtured for the benefit of developing countries was to have a bilateral aid programme. The Department itself inherited a number of scientific institutions, and a substantial programme for supporting personnel working overseas in Britain's ex-colonies, particularly in Africa (see Chapter Three). There was also a wider group of British scientific institutions and universities already working on developing-country issues and many individuals interested in spending part of their careers working in developing countries, including some as volunteers. There is a large British NGO movement needing support for work in developing countries, for which the Department has over the past 30 years been an increasing source of funding, supplementing private donations. In addition, Britain had a well-developed consultancy industry also familiar with working in developing-country environments. Finally, the Department also inherited the CDC, with a wealth of experience in operating commercially in developing countries, which it wished to sustain and develop in the early decades through the provision of net funding from its bilateral aid programme.

Some of Britain's technical expertise might be used by the multilateral development institutions: individuals joined UN agencies and the World Bank and some scientific institutions and consultancy firms may be funded internationally. But it is improbable that the bulk of Britain's standing capacity would have been exploited in that way. The 1965 White Paper ('The Work of the New Ministry') stated that 'in our aid programme we shall give the highest priority to technical assistance which is not only in itself a vital contribution to all forms of development but is often a precondition of a successful programme of financial aid'.

In order to be effective in influencing policies and practices internationally, it is important to have one's voice grounded in the reality and experience of operating in the field through one's own bilateral programmes. Without bilateral operations a donor would carry much less credibility. A development agency such as the Department is also in a much stronger position to help shape wider international policies of its government that bear on development if the influence it seeks to have is based upon operational experience in the field.

In an ideal world much of the above may be unnecessary but we did and still do not live in an ideal world. The reader may suggest that much of this is an ex-post rationalisation for the Department having a substantial bilateral aid programme which its political masters would have wanted in any case, and which its staff wanted in order to enjoy a more varied and interesting career. During the 1997 Labour administration the Department took a more international approach to development assistance, but the increase in the size of its total aid budget has meant that it could also sustain a substantial and growing bilateral aid programme.

Given that the Department wished to maintain a substantial bilateral aid programme for sound development as well as for political and commercial reasons, did it target bilateral aid either in absolute terms or as a proportion of the total aid budget? None of the White Papers between 1965 and 2009 made any explicit reference to the intended future size of bilateral aid, nor did any ministerial speeches, though they did from time to time refer to the importance attached to having a substantial bilateral aid programme. The only formal policy statement bearing on the future level of bilateral aid was that made to Parliament in February 1980 following the Aid Policy Review carried out at the beginning of the Thatcher government (see Chapter Four). It said two things: first, that in future greater weight would be given to political and commercial considerations in the allocation of aid and, second, that careful scrutiny would be given to new multilateral aid commitments. The first by itself did not necessarily mean giving priority to bilateral aid given Britain's position internationally. The second, however, was a clear recognition that in the context of a smaller total aid programme in real terms and increasing levels of multilateral expenditure arising from past and largely inescapable commitments, bilateral aid should be protected to the strongest extent possible, and for political and commercial reasons. Even so, no specific target was set for bilateral aid; rather it was felt that it should not become just a residual difference between the total size of the aid budget and the sum of individual multilateral aid commitments determined largely by development considerations.

It might be argued that the commercial reasons for maintaining a substantial bilateral aid programme would better be expressed as domestic political considerations. The governments of the day believed in a liberal international trading regime and supported trade rounds intended to reduce restrictive tariffs and quotas. The government as a whole did not believe in subsidising uncompetitive exports. The bilateral aid procurement tying rules also provided for not buying uncompetitive British goods and services, though the preferred solution was to finance projects which required competitive British goods and services rather than, except exceptionally, financing projects requiring more competitive foreign goods and services. Thus a substantial tied bilateral aid programme was more a political sop to industry than a commercial instrument to promote British exports. The DTI's interest in a substantial bilateral aid programme derived in part from a desire to make its life easier with the industry lobby and in part to ensure that it could achieve a substantial allocation for the Aid and Trade Provision.

## Trends in bilateral and multilateral aid

Thus we might conclude that for nearly two decades the Department's policy was to target bilateral aid for political reasons, arguably beyond what might be the product of a series of development motivated decisions on the allocation of the total aid budget. Table 7.1 sets out, at five-yearly intervals, the way in which the aid budget expenditure has been allocated between some of its main aggregates over the period 1965–2005/6.

In the first full year the Department was open for business, bilateral aid expenditure accounted for 85 per cent of total expenditure. Nearly all expenditure arose from the commitments the Department inherited from other government departments (see Chapter Three). It also reflected the fact that at the time the Department was established

Table 7.1 Aid expenditure (£ million)

| | Total | Bilateral | | | Multilateral | | | | | | |
|---|---|---|---|---|---|---|---|---|---|---|---|
| | | Total | TC | Financial | Total | IFIs[a] | EC | UN | C'wealth | Research | GEA[b] |
| 1965 | 207 | 176 (85%) | 32 | 144 | 19 (15%) | 12 | – | 7 | – | – | – |
| 1970 | 214 | 195 (91%) | 46 | 149 | 20 (9%) | 8 | – | 12 | – | – | – |
| 1975 | 437 | 305 (70%) | 96 | 195 | 132 (30%) | 72 | 19 | 37 | 2 | 1 | – |
| 1980 | 941 | 678 (72%) | 253 | 424 | 264 (28%) | 87 | 120 | 48 | 8 | 6 | – |
| 1985 | 1266 | 772 (61%) | 314 | 458 | 494 (39%) | 162 | 234 | 84 | 8 | 6 | – |
| 1990/91 | 1694 | 1093 (65%) | 573 | 520 | 601 (35%) | 191 | 317 | 75 | 9 | 8 | – |
| 1995/96 | 2266 | 1159 (51%) | 703 | 500 | 1109 (49%) | 309 | 684 | 91 | 8 | 9 | 9 |
| 2000/1 | 2799 | 1511 (54%) | 801 | 710 | 1288 (46%) | 326 | 708 | 219 | 7 | 8 | 21 |
| 2005/6 | 4413 | 2738 (62%) | 1403 | 1337 | 1674 (38%) | 385 | 917 | 299 | 5 | 19 | 50 |

[a] International Financial Institutions.
[b] Global Environment Assistance.

in 1964 the multilateral aid system was still in its infancy: the IDA, established in 1960, was still gearing up its capacity to commit and spend funds. A decade later the international financial institutions (IFIs, mainly the IDA) were well-established, and Britain had joined the EU and was obliged to contribute towards European Commission (EC) aid programmes. But during this decade the real value of the Department's aid budget had fallen and as a result the amount available for bilateral aid fell to 70 per cent of the total. Over the next two decades a combination of the ever-increasing demands of Brussels, over which the Department was able to exercise little control, and for the most part a highly constrained aid budget, meant that by the mid-1990s bilateral aid accounted for only 50 per cent of total expenditure.

Britain's contribution to EC aid programmes went from nothing prior to entry into the EU in 1973 to nearly £700 million per year by the mid-1990s, or 30 per cent of the total aid budget. Only with the substantial increases in the Department's aid budget after 1997 has the proportion taken up by the EC declined to about 20 per cent, allowing bilateral aid to increase to 60 per cent of total aid expenditure.

The preceding paragraphs highlighted the impact of EC aid expenditure on bilateral aid at times when the total aid budget was being constrained. However, it is only to a somewhat lesser extent that is this true of multilateral aid generally. For both good development and political reasons the Department has wished to play a substantial role in the multilateral aid system, and thus protecting bilateral aid, other than by maintaining a growing aid programme, required some difficult decisions, particularly with regard to the IFIs which have represented the bulk of non-EC multilateral aid expenditure. But a policy decision to reduce the Department's percentage contribution to a new IFI replenishment takes several years to feed through into expenditure levels. During the Thatcher administration, when bilateral aid was being explicitly targeted, the Department did reduce its percentage contribution to new IDA replenishments, and it did cut some of its annual voluntary contributions to UN agencies, which eventually resulted in multilateral aid expenditure levels being lower than would otherwise have been the case. Instead of non-EC multilateral expenditure being some 25 per cent of total expenditure, it fell to about 20 per cent. For Britain to have fully protected its bilateral aid programme in the 1980s and 1990s it would have had to have opted out of the international aid system in a major way, which would have meant radically reducing its contribution to IDA to a much greater extent than it was prepared to do. This would not only have impacted upon IDA directly but also indirectly, unless other donors would have been prepared to increase significantly their percentage share of new IDA replenishments.

## Some bilateral aid priorities

It is now time to look more closely at the Department's bilateral aid programme in terms of particular instruments of development and political significance. Most of the reasons for having a bilateral aid programme given earlier fell under the heading of technical co-operation. More recently the Department's statistics have divided this into two categories. Technical co-operation now embraces only the provision and development of knowledge: personnel, training and scholarships, and research and development. 'Grants and other aid in-kind' includes support for the development work of British and other voluntary organisations; grants to the British Council and other UK institutions for development work; the Small Grants Scheme administered by UK Diplomatic Missions; funding for land and geological surveys; and the provision of books, equipment and other supplies.

It should be noted that for these purposes technical co-operation here includes the Department's aid administration costs. The reason for including these costs is twofold. First, the boundary between the Department's running costs and activities funded under technical co-operation has varied over time, partly as a result of policy and partly as a result of the more entrepreneurial staff of the Department using aid programme funds for which they were responsible to fund activities which should have more properly have been financed from running costs, the levels of which were separately agreed with the Treasury in order to contain civil service costs. Periodic corrections have resulted in changes in the boundary between technical co-operation expenditure and aid administration costs. Second, the boundary is somewhat arbitrary in development, if not public expenditure control, terms. Much of the work done by the Department is concerned with programme design and policy dialogue with developing countries. Sometimes this is carried out by external advisers and consultants funded under technical co-operation budgets, and sometimes by the staff of the Department, depending on the circumstances. In recent years the Treasury have accepted that the Department's aid administration costs may fall into two categories: running costs, broadly comparable with those of other government departments, and programme-funded administration costs, covering most but not all the costs of front-line staff in country offices.

In addition to technical co-operation programmes there were two bilateral financial aid priorities. First, the CDC, seen as an important element of bilateral aid, used to be funded in part from the aid programme through what was known as Exchequer Advances (see Chapter Eight). Second, one might include for current purposes the Aid and Trade Provision, which existed in the period 1977–97 and which formed an increasing part of the Department's bilateral aid programme for commercial rather than development reasons, which could only be provided from bilateral aid.

In 1979 the Joint Funding Scheme with British NGOs was introduced as a structured way of supporting their work in developing countries. Otherwise known as the 'pound for pound' scheme, the Department was ready to provide 50 per cent of the cost of agreed development projects, but 100 per cent of population-planning activities. For the large NGOs (OXFAM, CAFOD, SCF, Christian Aid and Action Aid) an annual block grant system was introduced in recognition of their substantial capacity for undertaking projects and their proven track record. They accounted for their expenditure on projects ex-post, no doubt providing lists of projects likely to prove most acceptable to the Department. The JFS grew exponentially in the 1980s and 1990s, to some extent as part of Chris Patten's (and then Lynda Chalker's) efforts to convince the NGOs that not all the Department did was motivated by short-term political and commercial considerations – an accusation levelled at the Department after the 1980 Aid Policy Statement to Parliament – and as part of a genuine belief that NGOs had an important role to play in helping to reduce poverty beyond the efforts or otherwise of governments. Under Clare Short, after 1997 the block-grant-funded NGOs were offered the prospect of a Programme Partnership Agreement (PPA) setting out a shared agenda of poverty reduction and an agreed strategy with each for contributing towards it. Subsequently PPAs were signed up with a growing number, and a wider range, of what now were to be called Civil Society Organisations (CSOs). For the other smaller CSOs a Challenge Fund was established (the CSCF) against which they could bid for individual projects to be funded against set criteria.

In 1977 the Aid and Trade Provision (ATP) was introduced in support of British industry against what was seen as the aggressive use of aid by other donors to support their exports. This is explained in some detail in Chapter Eight. The allocation of ATP grew substantially from about 5 per cent of total bilateral aid to about 10 per cent in the mid-1990s. At the same time the gross amount of new loans to the CDC was also growing (though the level of net lending declined to zero in the late 1990s) as part of a deliberate policy of allowing the CDC to grow its business, increasingly in support of the private sector in the poorer countries (see Chapter Eight).

The data provided below in Table 7.2 are based on the Department's recent redefinition of technical co-operation, though this has required some modest licence on the part of the author in interpreting the Department's statistics for earlier years. In the early years the Departmental expenditure was largely the result of inherited commitments and policy. Technical co-operation, despite its centrality to aid policy at the time, together with Exchequer Advances to the CDC, accounted for only about one-quarter of total bilateral aid expenditure, though by 1975 (a decade into the life of the Department) together they accounted for about one-third – predominantly technical co-operation expenditure.

By 1990/91, expenditure on these four activities (TC, the JFS, CDC and ATP) amounted to £704 million and accounted for 62 per cent of total gross bilateral aid expenditure. Technical co-operation alone accounted for £515 million or 47 per cent of bilateral aid. The growth of these four activities were a matter of policy but the fact that they accounted for such a high proportion of bilateral aid is also explained by the pressure on the total bilateral aid programme caused by the largely unavoidable growth in multilateral aid at a time when the total aid budget was being constrained. By 2010/11 the proportion of total bilateral aid accounted for by these activities was only 26 per cent. The ATP scheme had been terminated in 1997 and previous commitments had been fully spent, and CDC was now

*Table 7.2*   DFID: Gross bilateral aid expenditure

|  | Total Bilateral Aid | Technical Co-operation Scheme | Joint Funding | CDC | ATP | Total | % of Bilateral Aid |
|---|---|---|---|---|---|---|---|
| 1965 | 176 | 32 | – | 9 | – | 41 | 23 |
| 1970 | 195 | 46 | – | 9 | – | 55 | 28 |
| 1975 | 305 | 96 | – | 13 | – | 109 | 36 |
| 1980 | 678 | 246 | 2 | 20 | 30 | 296 | 44 |
| 1985 | 772 | 293 | 10 | 29 | 42 | 374 | 47 |
| 1990/91 | 1093 | 515 | 20 | 75 | 94 | 704 | 62 |
| 1995/96 | 1517 | 655 | 40 | 46 | 73 | 814 | 53 |
| 2000/01 | 1511 | 719 | 75 | – | 28 | 822 | 45 |
| 2005/06 | 2738 | 728 | 95 | – | – | 823 | 30 |
| 2010/11 | 4248 | 687 | 329 | – | – | 1116 | 26 |

[a] In 2010/11 includes all expenditure through UK CSOs.
*Source*: Departmental statistics.

fully self-financed. Though expenditure on technical co-operation and through CSOs had continued to increase, the total bilateral aid programme has been rising rapidly as the total aid budget increased.

The composition of technical co-operation under the old definition shown in Table 7.3 has varied considerably over time. The Department inherited the OSAS scheme (see Chapter Two), which supported British personnel working as public servants in the ex-colonies, and this was gradually replaced by a growing number of people contracted to the Department and working as advisers overseas (TCOs) and also by volunteers. Together with consultancies this has accounted for 40–60 per cent of all technical co-operation expenditure over the past 30 years. The fact that it continued to be such a high proportion of technical co-operation expenditure, however, is largely due to the inclusion since 1980 of the Department's aid administration costs for the reasons given above. Expenditure on education and training (excluding people employed in the education sector itself under contract to the Department) continued to grow over the years, to reach its peak in the early 1990s. The apparent decline since 1995/96 is partly the result of the Department handing over its grant-in-aid for the British Council to the FCO, though on condition that the Council continued its educational aid work, and partly by the decline in the Department's support for training in Britain. Meanwhile, support for research, which was always regarded as important but remained modest in bilateral aid expenditure terms for the first half of the Department's life, has increased dramatically over the past decade.

One might conclude the following from the above. Bilateral aid has always been regarded as a key element in the Department's work for both good development reasons and for political reasons. Because of Britain's multilateral obligations (a combination of political and development considerations) the bilateral aid programme was able to look after itself at times when the aid budget as a whole was growing. It only had to be targeted when the aid budget itself was being held back, but ironically could be protected at such times to only a very limited extent. Because of the priority given to technical co-operation, together with the other demands shown above, the proportion of bilateral aid that could be allocated to financial aid primarily for development purposes (that is, excluding ATP) became the residual element in the Department's bilateral country aid programmes. This resulted in severe pressure on financial aid for the poorer countries during the period 1979–97 and required difficult choices to be made between financing projects and sectors concerned directly with poverty reduction and providing much

Table 7.3  Technical co-operation expenditure (£ million) 1965–2005/06

| | Total Bilateral Aid | Total Technical Co-operation | Education & Training Students | British Council | Volunteers | Personnel Contract Staff | Consultancies | Total | Research | Other |
|---|---|---|---|---|---|---|---|---|---|---|
| 1965 | 176 | 32 | 4 | – | – | 22 | 2 | 24 | 2 | 1 |
| 1970 | 195 | 46 | 9 | 3 | 1 | 27 | 4 | 32 | – | 6 |
| 1975 | 305 | 96 | 16 | 11 | 1 | 42 | 10 | 53 | 9 | 8 |
| 1980 | 678 | 246 | 47 | 28 | 3 | 67 | 53 | 123 | 17 | 31 |
| 1985 | 772 | 293 | 66 | 38 | 7 | 57 | 74 | 128 | 19 | 31 |
| 1990/91 | 1093 | 515 | 116 | 46 | 15 | 80 | 123 | 218 | 41 | 94 |
| 1995/96 | 1517 | 655 | 109 | 34 | 24 | 74 | 203 | 301 | 60 | 151 |
| 2000/01 | 1511 | 779 | 37 | – | 28 | 140 | 286 | 454 | 108 | 105 |
| 2005/06 | 2738 | 823 | 18 | – | 28 | 493 | 521 | 179 | 105 | 105 |

needed programme/budgetary support for poorer countries, particularly in Africa, seeking to escape from economic and financial crises through economic and budgetary reform – without which they could not hope to resume growth and reduce poverty.

In 1991 Sir Douglas (now Lord) Hurd held an internal meeting with Lynda Chalker when he was Foreign Secretary to discuss aid priorities. He remarked that he understood the important role of technical co-operation in development; he recognised the need for programme/ budgetary support for countries committed to economic reform; and he accepted, though disliked, having to allocate part of bilateral aid for ATP. Could the Department, he then asked, any longer afford to finance major investment projects in developing countries from its bilateral aid programme? The answer, of course, was that for the most part it could not, and his conclusion was that these should be left to the multilateral development institutions which Britain funded.

## Key multilateral aid policy issues

### International financial institutions

The capital of each bank has been increased periodically through what is known as a General Capital Increase in order that the banks can increase the amount they can raise in the marketplace at any one time. However, the Department has increasingly taken the view that the level of new lending on quasi-market terms that the banks can make within their existing capital base is sufficient for the needs of their stronger regional members which could now increasingly borrow directly from the market. The IBRD in particular has the dual role of lending and research and policy advice, both of which, together with the role of the IMF, help middle-income countries access the world's capital markets. Nevertheless, a capital increase for the World Bank has recently been increased in the context of the post-2008 global financial crisis.

The triennial replenishments of the soft windows of the banks (the Funds) follow a regular pattern and in the case of IDA they are conducted by the IDA Deputies (senior officials from capitals). They start with a review of performance over the previous replenishment period; an assessment of the overall development financing needs of the recipient countries and the contribution that management believe the institutions should make; and a discussion of future key policy issues which the institution should adopt. This provides a framework for donor members to negotiate their respective contributions to a new replenishment within a target range and having regard to the level of 're-flows' generated by repayments of past credits by the recipient countries. Particularly in the case of the World Bank there will be a contribution from profits made on its lending to the middle-income countries. The relative contributions of donors will be determined in negotiation having regard to their shareholding in the bank, their relative economic strength within the donor community, and their own aid budget priorities.

The Department has always regarded the role of the World Bank Group, and particularly the IDA, as far more important than that of the RDBs in terms of its capacity for research and policy analysis, its overall policy direction, and the size and effectiveness of its lending operations. Britain provided 13.5 per cent of the IDA's initial capital of $969 million in 1960.

It is not intended to provide here a detailed account of each IDA replenishment and the Department's role. Rather it might be more helpful to identify three broad phases in IDA's role and policy evolution that not entirely surprisingly mirrors to a large extent that of the Department itself. In the 1960s and 1970s the IDA was concerned to establish itself as the premier development lending institution to the poorest countries. It was project-focused, lending initially in the traditional infrastructure sectors of power and communications and then increasingly in education and health. By the mid-1970s it was beginning also to concentrate on improving the livelihoods of the poor, particularly in the rural areas, something the Department's 1975 White Paper ('More Help for the Poorest') strongly welcomed. Its lending was increasingly in the context of sectoral analysis and policies developed with the countries concerned.

With a growing aid budget in the late 1970s the Department co-financed a wide range of projects with the IDA, including integrated rural development programmes. This was considered to be both a useful way of managing its larger bilateral aid budget and having a closer insight into the IDA's operations in the field. The enthusiasm of London departments for the former sometimes got ahead of that of staff in the regional offices who voiced doubts about the knowledge base for such activities (for example, the Tabora Rural Development project in Tanzania and the Tana River Basin Development project in Kenya).

Nevertheless, the IDA was by now well established as the leading international financial development institution and played a key co-ordinating role between individual developing countries and their development partners. For the IDA 6 replenishment in 1979 the Department provided 10.1 per cent of new donor funding, well above its relative economic strength among sectors of the larger donor community that were now members of the IDA. Up until this point, successive IDA replenishments, including new donor funds, had grown substantially in real terms, reflecting the IDA's growing role and standing in the international aid system.

The second phase of the IDA's work might be identified as being in relation to structural adjustment lending in the 1980s and 1990s, which is covered more generally in Chapter Five. It was, as said then, a controversial period in which the so-called Washington Consensus was always rather less of a consensus than some might have wished. The Department believed, with some justification, that it played a bridging role between the hawks (including the US) and the doves (notably the Nordics inside the Board and of course the NGOs). Japan was on the hawkish side in terms of economic policy but rather more dovish when it came to the politics of the extent of the policy intervention that was entailed. The Department backed the Washington Consensus in terms of the macroeconomic management reforms that were required but argued additionally for a greater concern about the quality of public expenditure rather than focusing solely on the total level of spending. The Department also urged the World Bank, as well as the IMF, to engage in a stronger dialogue with NGOs which were particularly critical of structural adjustment programmes and the level of conditionality associated with them.

During this second phase, however, despite the Department's overall support for the role of the IDA, it adopted a less generous stance towards its replenishments. It was a period when the size of the bilateral aid programme was being targeted because of the Department's constrained aid budget and unavoidable increasing commitments to EC aid programmes. Thus, for IDA 7 and subsequent replenishments before 1997, the Department argued for a share of IDA resources equal to its relative economic strength, which was about 6–7 per cent. Given the continuing problems with the US, which only became more difficult as the perceived economic and political governance shortcomings of developing countries were being highlighted, total IDA replenishments languished in real terms.

The third phase can be summarised as the period of Poverty Reduction Strategies (PRS) and pursuit of the Millennium Development Goals (MDGs), the former in theory and increasingly in practice becoming the property of governments rather than donors, and the latter being aspirations or better, signed up to by all members of the UN at the two World Summits in 2000 and 2005. While ownership has come to centre stage the issues over which conditionality were fought have not disappeared and, for the Department, have re-surfaced in recent years with changes in political leadership and the continued campaign against conditionality by the NGOs. It was accepted that achievement of the MDGs depended crucially on stronger economic growth and therefore a sound macro-economic framework within which the IDA and others could operate. Nevertheless as the PRS/MDG Consensus has replaced the Washington Consensus donor countries have an international development institution which, under the leadership of James Wolfensohn and again under its later Presidents, they can more readily and collectively support.

It was in the context of this third phase, for which Clare Short had been a strong advocate internationally, and with her ambitions for furthering improvements in the way the World Bank operated, that she approached the IDA 13 replenishment. It was an important part of her own poverty reduction strategy that the international aid system as a whole should become a more effective instrument and partner with those countries committed to the MDGs. She therefore decided to offer a quantum leap in Britain's contribution to the IDA by putting £1 billion on the table, which in the event put Britain's share back up to 10 per cent. This was on the understanding that the goal of the IDA was poverty reduction; a focus on the poorest countries with a commitment and capacity to reform; and stronger co-ordination with the rest of the donor community. There was however one important policy issue to be resolved at IDA 13, namely the extent to which the IDA should provide grants instead of concessional loans, a satisfactory resolution of which she made conditional upon Britain's higher contribution.

The issue of grants, in addition to technical assistance activities, had come up in IDA 12 and had been accepted in principle for post-conflict countries that were in arrears to the IDA and therefore not eligible for new credits. At IDA 13 negotiations the US proposed that in a post-HIPC world IDA should be able to provide up to 50 per cent in the form of grants. Despite the obvious political appeal it was feared that over time this would reduce the effective role of the IDA by reducing the volume of future re-flows – some believing this was the motivation behind the US proposal. The Meltzer Report to the US Administration had earlier recommended that the IMF should no longer have a role in the poorer countries and that the IDA should make grants, not loans that would not be repaid. The Department argued strongly against, and EU members collectively proposed grants accounting for 5–10 per cent of IDA expenditure for specific purposes: for post-conflict countries, for investment in global goods (notably combating HIV-AIDS) and regional issues. In the event a compromise was reached that up to 20 per cent of IDA expenditure could be provided as grants for these specific purposes.

Although Japan, a large provider of bilateral aid loans, supported Britain, the US pointed out that, perversely, those donors that had themselves much earlier moved to providing bilateral aid only in the form of grants were now the most opposed to the IDA doing likewise.

In IDA 14 the Department took a 13.8 per cent share and the grant debate was settled by reference to an individual country's debt sustainability framework and without a formal percentage limit. As it happens grants have been about 20 per cent of total IDA commitments. However Britain and Sweden also led a concerted move to have the World Bank undertake a fundamental review of conditionality, largely as a result of an NGO-orchestrated campaign to seek to abolish it. The Department's £1.4 billion commitment to IDA 14 was partially conditional upon first undertaking such a review (£50 million) and, second, adopting and implementing the conclusions of the Board of Directors (a further £50 million).

The review noted the significant change in conditionality over time for policy-based lending from an emphasis on macro-economic adjustment and growth to the more recent attention to complex institutional changes such as public sector financial management and social sector reforms. It argued that conditionality related to sensitive policy areas such as privatisation and trade liberalisation had declined and now focused on long-term institutional issues. There was a clearer distinction between 'triggers' or prior conditions for lending (the number of which had reduced) and 'benchmarks' describing the government programme (which had increased). It proposed five principles of donor good practice: reinforcing country ownership; an accountability framework with policy actions and outcome indicators; a customised framework to country circumstances not to be used to leverage additional reforms outside the government's agenda; conditions for disbursement limited only to those critical for achieving results; and conducting transparent reviews conducive to predictable and performance-based financial support. The World Bank is being held to these principles but the challenges remain: for example, the principle of ownership may be at variance with the need to ensure aid is effective. The review did not satisfy the NGOs, who continued to press for further change. This debate will not go away.

The IDA 15 negotiations were completed at the end of 2007, with the Department taking a 14 per cent share, for the first time exceeding that of the US. The main policy issues highlighted during the negotiations were aid architecture (with the World Bank being a platform on which others could operate); country-level aid effectiveness (meaning further decentralisation of the World Bank's operations and more transparency in its analysis and operations locally); and fragile states (which resulted in exceptional levels of assistance being agreed over a longer timeframe to help ensure their recovery from conflict).

Whereas the process by which the Department has managed its affairs in relation to the RDBs is similar to that described above, its policies towards them were rather different and, of course, influenced by regional considerations. Although the 2000 White Paper refers positively to the RDBs as having an understanding of the development issues of the regional member countries and the loyalty of those members, in general the Department has considered the RDBs to be less effective instruments for development than the IDA. This in particular influenced the Department's willingness to contribute towards their soft windows. It took a particularly negative view towards the IADB's soft window (the Fund for Special Operations) on the grounds of need. In the case of the ADF it might have been more positive if its allocations for the Indian sub-continent were larger (India itself being excluded), and whereas Africa was a priority for the Department it did not regard the AfDF as effectively managed. These attitudes towards the RDBs were reinforced in the case of the ADF and the AfDF by the fact that in the field they were largely invisible. Like the World Bank, their operations were heavily concentrated at Headquarters, but unlike the World Bank they did not have an important aid co-ordinating role, something which to varying degrees they resented and blamed the donors for. Policy towards the AfDF changed with the 2005 Commission for Africa Report which proposed that the AfDB should become a premier development institution in Africa. For the 2004 replenishment the Department offered £200 million and in the 2007 replenishment it doubled its contribution to over £400 million and became its largest contributor, for the first time overtaking France. This was more an act of political faith than an objective assessment of its effectiveness. The appointment of Donald Kaberuka, former Finance Minister of Rwanda, as its new President, rather than other contenders, was an important factor in this decision.

### European Bank for Reconstruction and Development (EBRD)

The EBRD was created in 1991 to promote the transition to open-market-based economies in Central and Eastern Europe, and countries of the former Soviet Union, committed to the principles of multi-party democracy, pluralism, and market economics. At least 60 per cent of its lending would be to promote the private sector and leverage in other private direct foreign investment. The British government made a successful bid to have it located in London: apart from the emphasising the obvious attractions of London as a financial centre the government offered

£40 million towards its establishment costs. This provided the Department with a mixture of frustration and amusement, and revealed a rather different approach to taxpayers' money by itself and the first French President of the Bank, Jacques Attali. The latter had ambitions for a rather more prestigious headquarters than the Department had bargained for. At one point Attali identified the new Grand Buildings off Trafalgar Square, but in the event another company already had an option on Grand Buildings and the Bank was established in the City at only a slightly lower cost. The Japanese Finance Minister of the day remarked in private that he did not understand why a Frenchman should wish to be looked down upon by Lord Nelson's statue in Trafalgar Square!

The EBRD was established with a capital base of €20 billion, 26 per cent of which was paid-in. Britain's share was 8.5 per cent, with €447 million being paid in between 1991 and 2009. The EC is uniquely also a member of the EBRD. The Bank has limited technical assistance funds of its own as it can only use net income for these purposes after its reserves reach a certain level. In 1998 the Bank made a substantial net loss following Russia's financial crisis but since then it has re-established positive net reserves. It has been a successful institution in promoting the transition process and attracting other private investment, and developed a strategy for graduation for the first eight countries that joined the EU. It re-engaged with Russia after the 1998 crisis and is focused increasingly in the Western Balkans, Central Asia, South Caucasus and Ukraine.

### European community aid programmes

When Britain joined the EU in 1973 the Department's concern was to have the poorer Commonwealth countries (including its remaining Dependencies) benefit from EC aid programmes, and in particular from an enlarged European Development Fund (EDF). The existing EDF under previous Yaoundé Conventions, which were aid and trade agreements, benefited Francophone Africa and the remaining French and Dutch overseas dependencies in the Pacific and Caribbean. Britain succeeded in having the African, Caribbean and Pacific countries of the Commonwealth (excluding South Africa) and its remaining Dependencies included in the first Lomé Convention of 1976 which provided for an enlarged EDF. It also, importantly, provided for preferential trade access for sugar and bananas, which was crucial economically for the Caribbean and Mauritius. Britain's contribution was about 15 per cent, with expenditure building up over the 1970s and beyond. Successive Lomé (later Cotonou) aid and trade agreements have been negotiated ever since, though the trade benefits have been gradually eroded with wider trade liberalisation measures.

Having secured the first Lomé Agreement, the Department's priority was to improve the direction and management of the EDF. Geographically the EDF favoured the Francophone African countries because they were already the established beneficiaries and France was determined that they should not suffer from EDF enlargement. The Department took the view, more strongly than some other member states, that EDF country allocations should be a function of relative poverty and population size, and not history and political importance. This was to be a long and continuing struggle. As regards the management of EDF funds, the Department soon discovered that the ways of the European Commission, and some of the member states, were rather different from its own approach to aid management. There was the added complication that the Commission felt that once member states had helped set the broad policy framework as part of the periodic negotiations with the ACP countries it should be left to get on with the job of aid management.

The Department's concerns were two-fold. Having decided the total size of the EDF and its allocation between ACP countries, an indicative country programme (that is, a list of prospective projects) had to be agreed. In the early days the EC made a (literally) flying visit to each country and returned with a list of projects agreed with the government, which member states were expected to endorse in what was called the EDF Committee and which were then set in stone. The Department argued that such indicative programmes should be subject to greater analysis of the country's development plans and priorities and co-ordination with the aid programmes of other donors, particularly those of member states. Put more crudely, the Department did not want to become committed to a wish list of projects that might bear little relationship to what it believed should be the development priorities of the government concerned, especially to some projects which it knew to be of dubious value. Particularly at a time when the Department, and others, were giving increasing priority to rural development and basic human needs it disliked indicative programmes dominated by large urban physical and social infrastructure projects.

By today's reckoning the Department's early approach to achieving a more effective EDF was rather old-fashioned; it also had little impact. It therefore decided to take a more strategic approach, including establishing a dialogue with, and seconding staff to, the Commission; encouraging member states to become more involved in the programming process rather than focusing upon individual projects; and encouraging project and programme ex-post evaluations. It also recognised the importance of encouraging the Commission, alongside member states, to engage in the broader development dialogue between the donor community and developing-country governments.

This was to become of crucial importance in the 1980s when a large number of ACP countries in Africa (and which now included the Lusaphone countries – Angola and Mozambique) were in economic crisis and in need of the help of the IMF and the World Bank. The key policy issue for the EDF was the willingness or otherwise to provide non-project (programme/budgetary) aid for ACP countries embarking upon economic reform. This was accepted in principle and became a growing component of the indicative country programmes in practice. For the Department it was essential that the EU and Commission were prepared to act alongside other donors and accept the lead role of the Washington institutions. For Brussels this was a sensitive issue: the EDF was seen as a contract between the ACP countries and member states, not an instrument to be used at the say-so of those in Washington. However, despite the initial misgivings, relatively rapid disbursing of non-project aid was provided in co-ordination with others in support of economic reform programmes that remained on track, thanks in large part to the influence of one senior French Commission official, Bernard Pettit. Macro-economic management and also good governance became issues in later Lomé/Cotonou Agreements and other regional protocols, providing a clearer basis on which the Commission could act.

In the early days the European Community's budgetised aid programmes were focused geographically on the Mediterranean and Asia/Latin America, and also provided for the EU's substantial food aid/humanitarian assistance programmes administered by the European Commission Humanitarian Aid Office (ECHO – see Chapter Six). With regard to the two regional programmes, the first has always been substantial for political reasons. The Department's policy over the years has been to limit its growth because of the relative wealth of most of the countries in the region, and to encourage a larger relative allocation for Egypt as the most populous and poorest country: this policy has been of limited success on either count. As to the Asia/Latin America programme, the Department has sought to increase the share going to Asia and in particular the Indian sub-continent and limit aid to the middle-income countries of Latin America, regarded as politically and commercially important by other member states. The Department succeeded, after a lot of effort, in increasing the share going to Asia to 60 per cent of the total, which can be held to be a modest success in the circumstances.

After the collapse of the Soviet Union and its Eastern European satellites after the late 1980s the EU began substantial programmes of technical assistance to the countries of Eastern and Central Europe (PHARE) and of the former Soviet Union, including Russia itself (TACIS). Their objective has been to help these countries make the transition to market economies and effective democracies. These programmes grew in size and absorbed an increasing part of the Department's 'attributed' expenditure (that is, Britain's share of the EU budget provided as external assistance which is attributed to the Department – see Chapter Ten) until a growing number became members of the EU. In addition to technical assistance, in the 1990s a number of countries in Eastern and Central Europe were seeking financial support for their balance of payments. Because of the immediate and substantial impact of such help were it provided directly from the budget, commercial banks were encouraged to lend funds against an EU guarantee. The Treasury, supported by the Department, argued for, and secured, a Loans Guarantee Fund by which about 15 per cent of the value of each loan guaranteed had to be provided from the budget and placed in the Fund against the possibility of default. Britain's share of this EU budget expenditure was attributed to the Department's aid budget, but it was better than taking an upfront hit of Britain's share of 100 per cent of EU budget loans.

The last quarter of a century saw some important developments in European Community aid policies and programmes. But despite much talk about the need for harmonisation and co-ordination of EU-wide development activities, and the importance of consistency in its external policies more generally, it seemed to many, including the Department, that little progress was being made. However, in 2000 the Council of the EU and the Commission issued a Joint Declaration on the European Community's Development Policy. For the first time poverty eradication was established as the central objective of its external development programmes. It identified six priority areas for action: links between trade and development; regional integration and co-operation; support for sound macro-economic policies and the promotion of equitable access to social services; transport infrastructure; food security and sustainable rural development; and institutional capacity building. Furthermore, the Commission would expect to be the lead donor in only one or two of these areas in any one country. Human rights, gender, the environment, good governance, conflict prevention and crisis management would be cross-cutting themes, to be mainstreamed in all aid programming.

The declaration also stated that 'the least developed countries and other low income countries will be given priority, in an approach which will take account of their efforts to reduce poverty, their needs, their performance and their capacity to absorb aid . . . To ensure consistency, the objectives of Community development policy will be taken into greater account in the conduct of other common policies'.

In 2005 the Declaration and its implementation was reviewed and the European Consensus on Development was agreed by the then 25 Heads of State and the European Commission in December 2005. It was the first time that a common vision for development had been adopted to steer both member states' own development efforts and the Commission's development programmes. Poverty eradication remained centre stage 'in the context of sustainable development, including pursuit of the MDGs', with priority given to the Least Developed Countries and particularly Africa. Finally, the Consensus importantly included the need for a strong coherence among EU policies, particularly in the areas of trade and security policy.

Like UN documents, the Consensus text is somewhat longer than it might be (some 52 pages), and it contains a section on the importance of aid to middle-income countries in order to help them meet the MDGs. But there was a clear if general statement on policy coherence in relation to the Doha Round, EU/ACP Economic Partnership Agreements, and to security, including a statement that the EU 'strongly supports the responsibility to protect'.

The Department has over the last decade or so taken a more strategic and broader, and perhaps a more realistic, approach to its relationship with the Commission and member states. It has recognised that the EU provides over half of all oda and is very conscious of the fact that it absorbed some 25 per cent of its aid budget. The Department has enjoyed not only an intellectual leadership in pressing for a more coherent set of EU policies, it has also had the advantage of a government-wide commitment to international development policies. The EU committed itself collectively to achieving the 0.7 per cent UN aid target by 2015 and an interim target of 0.56 per cent of GNI by 2010. These targets were more firmly embedded in EU policy than the pledges hurriedly agreed for the UN Financing for Development Summit in Mexico in 2002. However, it was a collective commitment not binding on individual states and because of the financial problems facing many members there has already been a lot of backsliding, making these targets improbable.

### United Nations

The potentially important role of the UN as a global organisation was emphasised earlier. The Department inherited from the Foreign Office in 1964 the responsibility for financing the UN's main development functions (UNDP, most of the Specialized Agencies, funded from assessed contributions, and its other development and humanitarian organisations, notably UNICEF and UNHCR, funded by voluntary annual or ad hoc contributions). The FCO has continued to be responsible for, and fund, Britain's wider relations with the UN and therefore plays the key policy co-ordinating role in wider UN fora.

The Department also inherited the principle of universality, meaning that Britain should be a member of all the UN's Specialized Agencies. However, at the end of 1995 Britain ceased to be a member of UNESCO because the latter's stance towards developing countries' state-controlled media and information sources was deemed incompatible with its efforts to improve governance and make the media more independent and accountable. Britain's assessed contribution to UNESCO came from the Department's aid budget despite only a small proportion counting as oda. As well, in 1995 the Department gave notice of its intention to leave UNIDO because it believed it to be largely ineffective, and because of its policy of supporting industrialisation in developing countries for its own sake, including supporting state-owned enterprises rather than encouraging a larger role for the private sector. Both decisions reflected a view that Britain could not effect sufficient reform from within. However, the new Labour government of 1997 reversed both of these decisions, with rejoining UNESCO being one of its manifesto commitments. But Clare Short soon became a less than enthusiastic supporter of the work of UNESCO, though at the Education for All Summit in 2000 she supported giving UNESCO a key role of monitoring follow-up action as a means of giving it a stronger focus on the relevant MDGs. In the case of the FAO the Department considered leaving, but decided against it, during the long period when Jacques Diouf was President. It was a time when the FAO was thought to be run as a personal fiefdom and was largely ineffective. Efforts to have a more effective leadership were undermined by the African members being unwilling to vote for change for fear that this was a vote of no confidence in an African leader and for what this might mean for future FAO work in their countries. Nevertheless the FAO's focus on agriculture, and therefore potentially on poverty reduction, made it politically too difficult to leave. As noted above, under the Coalition government the Department has taken a more robust view of the effectiveness or otherwise of a number of UN bodies.

In the 1970s the Department continued to be a supporter of the role of UNDP as the central co-ordinator of the UN's technical co-operation activities. UNDP used its own funds, contributed annually by member states, to finance not only activities managed directly by itself but also projects undertaken by the Specialized Agencies, particularly the FAO and WHO. The Department's policy was to discourage the Specialized Agencies from setting up their own separate Funds to undertake activities beyond what their income from assessed contributions would allow. Thus, it tended to provide contributions to UNDP annually in excess of what is might otherwise have judged to be appropriate purely on the grounds of aid effectiveness. However, when the spending cuts of 1979/80 came and the government wanted to protect bilateral aid, one of the few significant and immediate multilateral aid expenditure reductions that could be made was the annual voluntary contributions to UNDP. The Department reduced its annual contribution from £30 million in 1979 to £20 million in 1980, and it did not reach its former level in cash terms until the 1990s. Whether or not there was any causality, the fact is that over time some of the Specialized Agencies did establish separate Funds, arguing that funding from UNDP was insufficient and of course less predictable.

Since 1997 the Department has taken a more strategic approach, together with the FCO, to strengthening the role of the UN and its individual organisations in international development and in helping to achieve the MDGs. In 1999 it published one of its Institutional Strategy Papers relating to the UN. This recognised the particularly important role that the UN has made in efforts to prevent or reduce conflicts; in building global consensus on key issues; and in implementing development programmes. Its stated aims were for the UN to provide a lead on poverty elimination and sustainable development; work better together as a system and with others (particularly the World Bank); and to develop more cost-effective and focused development programmes. It supported the UN Secretary-General's process of institutional change launched in 1997 and gave particular emphasis to results-based budgeting, the review of agency mandates and field-level co-ordination, and improving the international response to complex crisis situations. It also had the aspiration of breaking down 'the opaque and sterile debates common in the UN but especially in economic and social fora'. It pointed out that support from the Department's aid budget alone to support the work of UN agencies amounted to some £145 million of core funding and a similar sum for additional voluntary funding for specific objectives and co-financing of projects in the field.

In the following year, 2000, the Department published a further Institutional Strategy Paper relating to its work with the UN.[76] It reflected the Department's long-held concerns about UNDP but held out the prospect of a stronger future relationship based on a shared approach to change and UNDP's future role. The Department wanted UNDP to give more emphasis to its role in co-ordinating the development efforts of the UN agencies and thereby facilitating a more effective UN development effort. This was consistent with the UN Secretary-General's reform process which established the UN Development Group, with the Head of UNDP chairing the Executive Committee comprising the Heads of all the UN's Funds and Programmes. At field level it supported the strengthening of the role of the UNDP Resident Representative as the Resident Co-ordinator responsible for the UN Development Assistance Framework (UNDAF) process intended to provide a common planning framework for assistance from all the UN agencies in support of agreed national development goals, and in particular helping to achieve the MDGs, and where necessary taking on the role of Humanitarian Co-ordinator. The Department shared the new Administrator's ambitions to transform UNDP into a more effective and efficient organisation through a greater focus of activities in which it had a comparative advantage and strengthening its ability to measure results and performance. On this basis the Department provided a multi-year commitment of £35 million per annum over the following three years as core funding, with continuing non-core support for specific activities which in 1999/2000 amounted to about £5m.

## The Commonwealth

The importance of the Commonwealth as a club of member states bridging a North/South divide, particularly in UN fora, has already been referred to. The Heads of Government meetings (CHOGMs) every two years, and the Ministers of Finance annual meeting in the run-up to the Annual Meetings of the IMF/World Bank in Washington have been useful occasions for policy dialogue on a range of political, economic and social issues. Britain launched its early debt initiative at the Finance Ministers' meetings in Toronto and Trinidad in the late 1980s. Perhaps the most notable achievement of CHOGM, and currently the most ironic, was to agree the Harare Declaration on good governance at its meeting in Zimbabwe in 1995. Cynics might say that it should not be surprising that (elected) governments should, among other things, condemn military coups. But the Harare Declaration represented an important statement that the Commonwealth as a whole believed in democratic forms of government, accountable to their people. This was most recently re-affirmed at the 2007 CHOGM in Kampala. The Heads of Government reiterated their 'commitment to the Commonwealth's fundamental political values of: tolerance; respect; international peace and security; democracy; good governance; human rights; gender equality; rule of law; the independence of the judiciary; freedom of expression; a political culture that promotes transparency and accountability; and sustainable development'.

The Commonwealth Fund for Technical Co-operation (CFTC) is the main development aid instrument of the Commonwealth, managed by the Secretariat in London. Its purpose has been to provide technical co-operation to its poorer members using the expertise available to it from around the Commonwealth (in part a form of South–South technical co-operation). The Department has historically agreed to provide 30 per cent of the finance for the CFTC but no more, leaving it to other contributors to effectively determine its absolute size. This has meant that the CFTC has had only a limited budget (some £20 million annually) to provide assistance to a wide range of countries. Not surprisingly it has been regarded as not very effective: indeed, under the Coalition government it has been put on notice that unless it can achieve better value for money Britain's response will be reconsidered in two years' time.

## Conclusions

The Department has chosen its aid channels for a mix of development and political reasons, including what it has seen as its own comparative advantage. One advantage has been that, uniquely among major donor governments, the Department has had responsibility for both multilateral and bilateral aid. A strong bilateral aid programme has fed into its policies towards the multilateral development institutions, though perhaps not always as effectively as it might have done. Its early comparative advantage as a bilateral aid donor was its knowledge and understanding of its Commonwealth partners and its technical co-operation programmes which continued to support the institutions of its ex-colonies, though with less impact upon institution-building than might have been expected of them. The Department targeted bilateral aid at times of aid-budget constraints, but it demonstrated why for both development and political reasons such a policy was likely to be largely ineffective.

The Department has been a long-time supporter of the multilateral development institutions. It has tended to see the World Bank as the central multilateral development institution rather than the UN, and has been obliged to accept the growing ambitions of Brussels. Since 1997 it has taken a more strategic approach towards the international aid system as a whole, including the multilateral development institutions.

It has taken a more coherent approach to the EC programmes with some success and it has put its weight behind UN reform, recognising that the UN potentially has an important central role to play particularly, but not only, in conflict prevention and resolution. In doing so the Department has set itself a more ambitious agenda. Attributing results to itself will be less important than having achieved a measure of success by collective action with others. In this regard the Department has moved on from developing its own more systematic approach to assessing the effectiveness of multilateral development institutions in recent years to joining with other donor governments to form joint assessments of performance, though the Multilateral Aid Review under the Coalition government was a largely independent exercise.

The global funds have sought to provide governance structures involving a wide range of stakeholders, each targeted at one or more of the MDGs. Their management appears to have been deliberately economical: the Global Fund only advertised for a senior management team in January 2008, having already secured financial commitments of $11 billion. They wished to avoid their initiatives being supply-led; rather funding programmes are demand-led locally. But the lure of large sums of earmarked money risks distorting priorities. Whether most of the funds they mobilise are truly additional is hard to judge, though in the case of the Department with a time-bound commitment to making progress towards the 0.7 per cent UN aid target they are unlikely to be. To achieve real world outcomes their funding needs to be additional to what cash-strapped recipient governments would otherwise have been able to allocate in their budgets, but not overwhelm poorly resourced health management and delivery systems.

In the 1960s and 1970s bilateral donors and the multilateral development institutions had quite separate if complementary roles, particularly when the focus was on individual investment projects, and some bilateral donors, notably the Department, had a comparative advantage in the provision of technical co-operation. As the focus changed over time to jointly supporting developing countries' policies and programmes with an increasingly shared objective of poverty reduction their distinctive characteristics lessened. This is widely held to be a good thing, and if other bilateral donors could further untie their procurement this trend would be reinforced. The fact that most agencies have had a multi-sectoral remit has also been a positive factor in achieving a more integrated approach. It will be imperative that the more sectorally focused global funds, with their substantial resources, do not undermine this.

# 8
# Associated Bodies

## Introduction

The Department inherited a large number of valuable associated bodies concerned wholly or partly with overseas development. Several of them were the sole responsibility of the Department's Minister: the Commonwealth Development Corporation (CDC), the Crown Agents, and a number of scientific units. The British Council, responsible for cultural diplomacy, was, and is, sponsored by the Foreign and Commonwealth Office (FCO), but because of its development role, particularly in the field of English language teaching, it was until 1997 jointly the responsibility of the FCO and the Department which also provided grants-in-aid and had a seat on its Board.

In addition to these, a number of scientific institutions in Britain had overseas units that worked on overseas development issues and were provided with core funding by the Department: the Hydraulics Research Station, the Institute of Hydrology, the Transport and Road Research Laboratory, British Geological Surveys and the Building Research Establishment. It also had a close association with a number of other institutions such as the Centre for Tropical Veterinary Medicine, part of Edinburgh University, the Institute for Tropical Medicine and Hygiene within the University of London, the Liverpool School for Tropical Medicine, the Institute for Development Studies and the Overseas Development Institute, to which it also provided funding.

This latter group of institutions were for the most part originally provided with ongoing funding on a three-year rolling programme basis and most had steering committees related to their overseas work consisting of staff from the institutions concerned and from the Department. Over the years, as the Department moved away generally from providing core programme funding to supporting specific time-bound projects of research its links with these organisations became more distant.

The rest of this chapter traces the history of those institutions for which the Department had statutory responsibility either solely or, in the case of the British Council, joint responsibility with the FCO. As will be seen, the Department's stewardship of these institutions evolved over time and eventually led, with the exception of the CDC, to their termination. That said, the Department retains a working association with most of them to varying degrees.

## The British Council

In 1934 there emerged from the Foreign Office a British Committee for Relations with other Countries with the aim of promoting

> a wider appreciation of British culture and civilisation by encouraging the study and use of the English language and thereby to extend a knowledge of British literature and of British contributions to music and the fine arts, the sciences, philosophic thought and political practice; encouraging both cultural and educational interchanges between the United Kingdom and other countries; strengthening the bonds of the British cultural traditions throughout the self-governing Dominions; and ensuring continuity of British education in the colonies.[77]

The word 'Committee' was soon replaced by the word 'Council' and in 1936 its title was officially shortened to 'The British Council'.

In 1940 the Council was granted a charter and after the war it was decided that the cost of the Council's work in the colonies should be borne on the vote of the Colonial Office, which preferred the Council to concentrate on the sciences and promoting good race relations, by making no ethnic distinctions in its work, rather than on more aesthetic activities. Much of the work of the Council in what became the developing world, particularly the Commonwealth, was in the field of English-language teaching and helping to manage the increasing flow of overseas students to Britain, only a small proportion of which the Council funded itself.

The Brogheda Report[78] concluded that the Council had a key role in supporting the policies of the three overseas departments (FO, CRO and CO) and that it should shift its pattern of activities to be 'more in line with the Government's political, strategic and commercial needs'.

This meant a shift of emphasis from cultural to educational activities, in particular the teaching of English; and a greater focus on the developing world, including in particular the Indian sub-continent. In 1954 the new Director-General, Sir Paul Sinker, began implementing the recommendations of the Brogheda Report and set up a further official committee to report on the teaching of English overseas (the TEO report).[79] This concluded that English, as either a first or second language, would be a worldwide language within a generation; English-language services were in great demand but the problem was the supply. The Council should increase the resources devoted to teacher training in both English as a foreign language (EFL) and as a second language (ESL); to increasing the supply of textbooks; and to provide educational advice overseas. In 1957 Dr Charles Hill was appointed Chancellor of the Duchy of Lancaster and produced his own report (the Hill Report) which was published as a White Paper.[80] It recommended as 'urgently necessary' an extension of the Council's overseas offices and an increase in the teaching of English. In 1958 the Commonwealth Scholarship Fellowship Plan was agreed, with Britain funding 50 per cent of the cost. To this day the Department funds Commonwealth developing-country students and the FCO funds those from developed countries.

By the 1960s the Council was established as Britain's provider of educational services in the developing world, particularly but not only in the field of English-language teaching (ELT). It was financed by the three overseas departments either in the form of annual grants-in-aid or by reimbursement of the costs of undertaking specific programmes overseas. In 1960/61 grants-in-aid from the three overseas departments amounted to nearly £6 million, compared to £3 million five years earlier, and £1 million was provided as agency expenditure. This arrangement suited the three overseas departments which had policy responsibility in these areas but little or no implementation capacity.

It was with some alarm that the Council learned of the machinery of government changes that were now envisaged: namely the creation of the Department for Technical Co-operation (DTC) which would implement the policies of the overseas departments in respect of overseas aid. They sought reassurances that a DTC would not take over their role: they obtained a general reassurance but no firm commitment that a newly created DTC would not want to review existing funding arrangements. In its 1960/61 Annual Report the Council 'welcomed the creation of the DTC and looked forward to close collaboration with the new department, especially in the field of educational aid'. No immediate changes in the role of the Council were made and in the following year the Council stated that 'its educational work in developing countries is complementary to technical co-operation'.

When Sir Dennis (later Lord) Vosper became the Minister for the DTC in 1961 he was also made responsible for co-ordinating the Overseas Information Services, and carried out his own review which he put to Cabinet in a paper that was not to be published. He was said to be impressed by the work of the Council. He argued for greater priority to be given to ELT, scholarships, visits and libraries. He also recognised the importance of maintaining the Council's efforts in Europe at a time when General de Gaulle had just said '*non*' to Britain joining the Common Market.

When the Department was established three years later the Council stated somewhat more confidently, in its 1964/65 Annual Report, that they had made proposals 'to bring the new Ministry into still closer touch with the education work in developing countries, the aim being to ensure that the Council contributes to the total British effort in the field of education assistance as effectively as possible'. In return the 1965 White Paper, 'The Work of the New Ministry', said that 'we are working in close harmony with the British Council, whose contribution is of major importance to English language teaching, the supply of teachers, the provision of books, the development of public libraries, and training and student welfare'.

At the time when the DTC and then the Department were being framed, there were a number of internal reviews bearing on their relationship with the Council. The Leach/Phillips Report noted that English language services accounted for about half of the Council's work, relatively focused in geographical terms, whilst the work of the DTC was widely spread in terms of geography and activity. It proposed a geographical split of responsibilities. For educational aid purposes the DTC would focus on sub-Saharan Africa, the Caribbean and those countries of South East Asia where the Council were not involved in recruitment of teachers, and the Council on other Commonwealth developing countries including the Indian sub-continent, as well as the developed world (OECD, in current parlance). When the Department was set up there was a tripartite meeting of the Treasury, the Foreign Office and the Department to consider future relationships. The Council proposed that the Foreign Office should retain overall responsibility for the Council but the Department should have a greater measure of control over educational aid. The Director-General of the Council judged that such an arrangement would best protect the interests of the Council as the provider of educational aid. The result was that a further inter-departmental review was set up. It found it difficult to distinguish meaningfully between the educational work of the Council overseas, intended to promote a wider knowledge of Britain, and the activities of the Department in this field. Looking at the Council's total activities, at one extreme the Council did aid-like work and at the other extreme it promoted drama, music and the visual arts. In between it funded libraries and dealt with the welfare of overseas students studying in Britain, only some of whom were funded by the Department. The Committee examined the Council's total expenditure provision for 1965/66 and, with some heroic judgements, concluded that 64 per cent was primarily for the three overseas departments and 36 per cent was for the new Department. It recommended that this formula should govern the financing of the Council's core activities (as distinct from agency work), until there was a substantial deviation from it in practice.

The Council complained that the demand for its educational aid services in the developing world was growing and its resources underutilised, while the Department continued to encroach on its traditional activities. The Mark/Phillips Report of 1970 further reviewed relationships between the Council and the Department. It recommended that the two bodies should consult more on educational aid policies; in-country, Council staff should administer educational aid for the Department; the Council should be the Department's adviser on all ELT projects. In effect the Council would be the Department's education advisers.

At this point it is worth looking at the way funding for the Council evolved over the decade 1960/61 to 1969/70 following the changes in the machinery of government and the Council's relationship with Whitehall.

The figures for the early years reflect the work done for the three overseas departments in their respective overseas countries or territories and their eventual merger into a single Foreign and Commonwealth Office. The DTC provided only modest funding for specific activities during its

*Table 8.1*　Sources of British Council income (£ million)

|                        | 1960/61 | 1962/63 | 1964/65 | 1966/67 | 1969/70 |
|------------------------|---------|---------|---------|---------|---------|
| Foreign Office         | 3.4     | 3.9     | 5.4     | 4.5     | –       |
| C/W Services Grant     | 1.5     | 2.7     | 3.9     | 2.2     | 8.0     |
| Colonial Services Grant| 0.9     | 0.5     | 0.3     | 0.3     | –       |
| DTC/Department         | –       | 0.2     | 0.4     | 3.9     | 4.6     |
| Earned Revenue         | 0.6     | 0.6     | 0.7     | 0.8     | 1.0     |
| Total Income           | 6.4     | 8.0     | 10.7    | 11.7    | 13.6    |

short life, and with effect from 1966/7 the Department provided 36 per cent of the Council's grant-in-aid, which for the most part reduced the amounts the other departments had to provide, and validated the conclusions of the interdepartmental review.

The next important event to impact on the Council was the oil price increase in 1973 which gave a number of oil-rich developing countries large sums of money to invest both overseas and at home. The Department responded by proposing 'Pay-TC', that is, rich countries, not just oil exporters, paying all or part of the costs of technical co-operation activities which it provided. It was suggested that the Council should follow suit and offer, and as necessary compete for, educational work in the Middle East, though the Treasury were initially nervous of this lest the Council lost money in doing so. Paid educational services were not a new concept for the Council and in the event it won substantial educational contracts in the Middle East let by the countries themselves, and succeeded in winning contracts for educational projects funded by the World Bank. It later branched out further and began managing projects for the Department in the health and agricultural sectors, notably in India. All this provided additional self-generated revenue to sustain a level of activity for the Council beyond that which government was prepared to finance by way of grants-in-aid.

The next external review announced to Parliament in January 1976 by the then Foreign Secretary, the Rt Hon James Callaghan MP, was to prove much more controversial. The Council were arguably saved by the 1978/79 'winter of discontent' which preoccupied Callaghan, by then Prime Minister, and the subsequent change of government in May 1979, though some in the Council thought the Report's conclusions to be so radical as to be of no real threat, only an extremely tedious and time-consuming process to have to be submitted to. It was part of a review of overseas representation undertaken by the Central Policy Review Staff (the Think Tank) of the Cabinet Office headed by Sir Kenneth Berrill. In this task he was supported by two people drawn from the FCO and the Department and some then Young Turks including Dr (now Baroness) Tessa Blackstone. It produced some very radical proposals for change, not all of which need detain us here. However the general thrust of the Berrill Report[81] can be illustrated by the following extract: '. . . In today's world a country's power and influence are basically determined by its economic performance. Inevitably therefore the UK's ability to influence events in the world has declined and there is very little that diplomatic activity and international public relations can do to disguise the fact'. For the Council the Report concluded that 'the present arrangements for the Government's overseas educational and cultural activities should be radically re-examined and we put forward two options, of which we think there is much to be said for the first (that is, the abolition of the Council) with responsibility for all educational aid administration being transferred to the Department'.

The second option was the retention of a separate British Council in the UK, incorporating the Technical Education and Training Overseas Countries (TETOC) and the Inter-University Council (IUC) and undertaking all *educational* recruitment and placement for the Ministry for Overseas Development (ODM), the incorporation of British Council representations overseas into diplomatic posts except in a few special cases, and considerable reductions in the numbers of educational and cultural staff overseas and in London.

The House of Commons' Select Committee on Defence and External Affairs rejected the main findings and recommendations of the CRPS. Eventually, in August 1978, the government published a White Paper.[82] Of the educational and cultural work of the Council it stated that it played a 'distinctive and valuable role in projecting Britain abroad, in furthering relationships with other countries and in stimulating the use of the English language . . .' (para 55)

> The Government do not accept the CPRS recommendation for the abolition of the Council. But they consider that closer co-ordination is required with the Foreign and Commonwealth Office, and also with the Ministry of Overseas Development and the Education Departments. It is particularly important that the Council's valuable contribution in the field of educational aid should be implemented fully within the scope of aid policies determined by Ministers. (para 56)

The White Paper went on to state that further reviews would be carried out. Para 59 states that Government 'see a continuing role for the British Council and the Inter-University Council (IUC) but they are considering the rationalisation of the activities of these bodies and of the Technical Education Organisation for Overseas Countries (TETOC) and of their relationship to the Education Departments and the Ministry of Overseas Development'. Some in the Council believed this to be more threatening than the Berrill Report itself: the latter was seen as too bizarre to worry about while the White Paper bore directly on the reality of the situation.

As part of the government's determination to cut public expenditure it reviewed all its Non-Deparmental Public Bodies (NDPBs) including the Council. This report[83] concluded that TETOC should be merged with the Council by March 1981 and cease to exist as a separate body. It also said that the purposes for which the IUC had been set up – to help in the creation of universities in the emergent Commonwealth countries – had been largely completed. A final decision on the future of the IUC would be taken once Ministers had decided on the future of the Council: in the event both bodies were merged into the Council in the course of 1981, with implications for the Department's funding.

Meanwhile the Board appointed Lord Seebohm to undertake what was the first external and thorough review of the Council's governance, financial management and organisation. He was assisted by Lord Chorley and a team primarily drawn from the private sector and the Civil Service Department. He reported in March 1981. His main conclusions of concern to the Department were:

1. the Department exercised too close a supervision of the Council's aid financed activities;
2. the banding system for countries which determined the proportion of the grants-in-aid provided by FCO and the Department should be reviewed, not least because once there was no agency expenditure in a country on behalf of the Department its contribution to the grant-in-aid in respect of that country should cease, with no necessary compensating increase by the FCO;
3. the Board should be reduced in size and with only two from government (the FCO and the Department);
4. that Paid Educational Services in the form of major management contracts exposed the Council to financial and reputational risk, and should only be encouraged where they contributed positively to the Council's main objective and not just to make money.

The Seebohm Report[84] was generally well received within the Council and many of its detailed recommendations were implemented over time. The Department were surprised at the report's criticisms of their relationship with the Council. The Department had said in evidence to the Enquiry that they were ready to relax their controls if there were a closer identity of view on overall aid policy and if the Board included members with relevant experience and expertise in relation to development issues. In response to item 2) above, the Department defended the banding system by saying that if the Council ceased development activities in a country and wished to remain there the logic was that the FCO should provide more money. Some changes to the size and composition of the Board were made but for more radical reform to achieve a much smaller and effective Board the Council had to wait another 15 years for Baroness Helena Kennedy to arrive as its Chairperson.

In 1983 the Department undertook a review of its manpower development aid. The outcome of this review were recommendations to focus manpower aid more on strengthening institutional capacities, providing training more directly related to projects, and giving more attention to the monitoring and evaluation of projects rather than just focusing on design and appraisal. This required the Council to respond by moving away from the management and administration of country-level training programmes; what were known as Technical Co-operation Training Programmes (TCTP) based on 'key sheets', drawn up in consultation with the Council, which listed training priorities for the developing country concerned. Instead, the Council was given the opportunity of managing educational projects and managing training more generally which comprised one element in more comprehensive institution-based development projects. But it was not until 1989/90 that the Department signed a new Memorandum of Understanding with the Council, which replaced the previous arrangement for providing an aid administration grant; and introduced a stronger and more accountable contractual relationship between the two parties for the management of aid activities. While the integration of more training into specific projects continued through the 1980s, the number of aid-financed training places in Britain continued to rise. In 1965 there had been some 6,000 aid-funded students in Britain; by 1984/85 that number was 10,000, and by the end of the decade it was about 13,000.

During this period the Council not only moved into the business of managing education projects for the Department, it also sought business from other aid agencies and diversified into other sectors, such as health project management. This brought criticisms from private sector consultancy firms that the Council had a favoured inside track with the Department, and allegations that the Council was able to subsidise the cost of its project management activities by the use of its grants-in-aid. The Council's financial management accounting was able to demonstrate to the Department at least that the latter was unfounded, though the Council had an undoubted advantage by having a government-funded presence on the ground, albeit for other purposes. The former was by definition more difficult to refute.

In the event, further changes in aid management by the Department provoked protests from both the Council and private management consultants. By the mid-1990s the Department was moving away from discreet projects to sector-wide approaches to providing aid, particularly in the education and health sectors. In itself this need not have been a threat to the Council and others, but increasingly the Department felt that better longer-term outcomes would be achieved by the ministries in recipient countries taking more direct responsibility for their own sector development programmes, including arranging for the provision of technical assistance and training, an increasing proportion of which could be provided locally. Thus the demand for the intermediary project management function was considerably reduced.

The Department's formal relationship with the Council ended in 1997, as explained in Chapter Four, when Clare Short handed over some £30 million to the FCO and gave it sole responsibility for the Council. Nevertheless, the Department has retained a working relationship with the Council in individual developing countries.

## The Commonwealth Development Corporation (CDC)

The early history of the Colonial Development Corporation and its contribution to colonial development was recounted in brief in Chapter Two. No sooner than it was established, however, the territories it was investing in were moving towards political independence. Its legislation was amended in the 1950s to allow the CDC to continue to manage its existing investments in an independent member of the Commonwealth, and in 1963 it was renamed the Commonwealth Development Corporation and permitted to make new investments in these countries, subject to ministerial approval on a case-by-case basis. In 1969 the CDC were allowed to invest beyond the Commonwealth on the same basis.

The rationale for the CDC under the 1945 Labour administration had been that there was a gap between what the public sector should do and what the private sector was prepared to do. This notion was challenged in the early 1950s by Treasury ministers who, seeing CDC make substantial earlier losses, suggested that it should be run down and its investments disposed of. However, the CDC's first two Chairmen had themselves been substantial political figures and their Lordships had already created a head of political steam in Parliament behind the work of the Corporation. Conservative ministers soon concluded that whatever their economic inclinations it would be politically impossible to persuade Parliament to kill off this relatively new and promising entity.

The CDC was financed for the first 35 years by annual Exchequer Advances, a quaint term which will be retained here, but which only means loans. They were made with relatively long maturities (repayment periods) and, prior to the formation of the Department, at rates of interest equivalent to the old Public Works Loans Board (PWLB) rates. As the CDC was required to break even one year with another the rate it charged on its loan investments needed to cover its management costs and provisions for bad debt. It had not been set up with any equity in its balance sheet to withstand adverse fluctuations in its fortunes. Nevertheless, after an unhappy start with some unwise and hasty investments in uncertain tropical agricultural environments it more than broke even in 1955 – something it has done since in all but three years.

After the formation of the Department the terms on which Exchequer Advances were made gradually became more favourable. Interest was waived on advances (which were drawn down in relation to specific investments) during the commissioning period. Later, in the 1970s, interest rates on Advances were softened and were well below the PWLB rates. From 1974, Advances for investments in the renewable natural resources sector were provided at 3 per cent and for other purposes at 5.75 per cent. By 1980 the bulk of Advances were being provided at the lower rate and in 1987 a unified rate of 3.5 per cent was introduced. This move to concessional rates of interest on the funds the CDC received was crucial to the future level of the CDC's activities, and to a strengthening of its balance sheet in the absence of any formal equity injection by government. The margin between what CDC borrowed and lent at increased from about 1 per cent in 1975 to 3.5 per cent a decade later. The success of the CDC's investments meant that it soon began to generate substantial surpluses which it could re-invest. The original rationale for the low rate of interest for renewable natural resources investments was that they were particularly risky and they yielded wider socio-economic benefits. The rationale for a unified low rate of interest was that it enabled the CDC to focus on the poorer, riskier and difficult markets and sectors, and was a substitute for providing the CDC with equity, something the Treasury continued to oppose. It also enabled the CDC to increase its future level of activity without an equivalent increase in the level of Advances. In this regard it should be noted that  while the repayment of Advances accrued to the Department, interest payments went to the Treasury's Consolidated Fund.

Having become responsible for CDC, the Department evolved a basic control framework for managing its relationship. It set strategic targets for future new investments, and required ten-year forward projections of activity, including that to be financed by self-generated funds, and periodic production of management accounts. It also required the CDC to develop investment appraisal systems that not only assessed financial viability but also the expected economic rate of return. The latter reflected the Department's cost benefit analysis approach to its own project-aid investments, considered particularly important in circumstances where distorted market prices did not reflect the economic costs of inputs and the economic benefits of outputs. This control framework centred around Quinquennial Reviews conducted jointly by the two parties, which also took a five-year forward look at the likely level of CDC activity and how it might be financed, including the level of Exchequer Advances that it might bid for annually. In all this the CDC Board remained responsible for individual investment decisions and managing CDC finances.

The early strategic targets related to the proportion of new investments to be made in the poorer (low-income) countries and in the renewable natural resources (RNR) sector. The former was 67 per cent in the 1970s, reduced to 50 per cent in the early 1980s in part in recognition of the problems facing the CDC in operating successfully in these markets at a time of economic crises and indebtedness. The latter was also 67 per cent in the 1970s and 50 per cent in the early 1980s, recognising the difficulties that the CDC was experiencing in finding commercially viable opportunities in agriculture, particularly in Africa. But the CDC exceeded its target for the poor countries by a comfortable margin throughout. A specific target for investments in the Commonwealth was only introduced in 1985 (67 per cent), reflecting its traditional area of business. As ministerial approval for operations outside the Commonwealth increased, a formal target for the Commonwealth was judged politically appropriate. During the period 1948–60 the CDC's investment portfolio averaged £65 million and for 1961–70, £138 million. Helped by the lower rate of interest charged on new Advances, this increased further to £217 million for the period 1971–75, and at the end of 1980 total outstanding investments had reached £351 million. Of this, 39 per cent was invested in basic infrastructure (including public housing), 41 per cent in RNR, and 20 per cent in the industrial and commercial sectors. By now its operating surplus before tax and interest payments was around £30 million annually.

The 1981 Quinquennial Review concluded that the CDC 'had the capacity to continue to play a distinctive development role and possessed in particular the special skills needed for the development of the renewable natural resources'. It reduced the targets for the poorer countries and for the RNR sector to 50 per cent, as noted above. However, the Review took place at a time when the aid programme was being substantially cut in real terms, and because of growing multilateral aid commitments the bilateral programmes were expected to be put under severe pressure. As a result financing options were put to ministers which included CDC borrowing funds in the marketplace, in order that it could continue to expand its activities at a time when advances from the aid programme could not be expected to grow significantly. This option was agreed and the 1982 CDC Act increased the statutory borrowing limit and provided for commercial borrowing of up to £50 million.

The conclusions of the Review were announced to Parliament in December 1981 and the CDC was the subject of attention by the Select Committee on Foreign Affairs' Subcommittee on Overseas Development in its 1982–83 Session Report, to which the government responded in April 1983.[85] The Subcommittee had urged that CDC's success in increasing its self-generated funds and its new ability to borrow commercially should not result in a reduction in the Department's Advances, to which the response was that the former would still count against the Public Sector Borrowing Requirement (PSBR). The Subcommittee also recommended that net Advances to CDC should never be negative, to which the response was that this would only be 'a product of exceptional circumstances'. It also recommended that there should be a strong case before the Minister agreed to add another non-Commonwealth country to the CDC's schedule: the government agreed to this but noted that only one of the five countries added to the CDC's remit since 1979 was outside the Commonwealth. The government disagreed with the Subcommittee's recommendation that the CDC should be exempt from UK tax, something no doubt suggested by the CDC which from time to time pointed out that overall it was a net contributor to the Exchequer. Finally, the Subcommittee recommended that the CDC's investments in the poorer countries should in future be as high a percentage of total investments as in the last five years (that is, 81 per cent), but the government stood by its reduced target of 50 per cent while pointing out that this was a minimum that it expected to be exceeded.

The CDC geared itself up in terms of prospective new investments to take advantage of the new commercial borrowing facility only to find itself thwarted by what became known as the Treasury's 'least cost rule' (see below). Instead, the Treasury agreed that the CDC could borrow £15 million annually for two years (1983/84–1984/85) from the National Loans Fund. The 1986 CDC Act enabled the CDC to borrow through an overseas subsidiary, the aim of which was to provide the CDC with a source of finance which did not count against the government's PSBR. Borrowing offshore for lending offshore was held not to have any UK macro-economic effects and therefore need not count against the PSBR. However the market for borrowing in this way was limited.

As it transpired, economic conditions in the CDC's markets were such that it was finding new viable investment less easy to bring to fruition, and the level of new investments fell to only £67 million in 1987 from its peak of £109 million in 1984. As a result the CDC took the opportunity to repay its NLF loans while still accepting Advances from the Departments which bore a much lower rate of interest. The Department defended this to the National Audit Office (NAO) by pointing out that it created space for the CDC to increase its investment levels in future years.

The 1986 Review envisaged CDC's new investments rising to £180 million annually over the coming five years. In addition to new Advances, it was envisaged that this would be financed by an increasing level of self-generated funds (its operating surplus was now about £50 million annually) and commercial borrowing. The Review agreed revised strategic targets of 60 per cent for the poorer countries (something the CDC was already achieving) and only 40 pper cent for the RNR sector. It also agreed that the CDC would invest increasingly in the private sector and more in the form of equity, something still in short supply in the poorer countries. By the end of 1986 the CDC's total investment portfolio was £670 million, of which only 16 per cent was in the form of equity or quasi-equity. By 1990 the latter had reached 19 per cent and the CDC was co-investing considerably with the IFC, the European Investment Bank, and its sister organisations in Europe (DEC in Germany, FMO in the Netherlands, IFU in Denmark and Caisse Centrale in France).

In 1986 the new Minister for Overseas Development, the Rt Hon Chris Patten MP, chose to enter into robust correspondence with the Chief Secretary to the Treasury to obtain his agreement for the CDC to borrow commercially on the London market as envisaged in the Quinquennial Review. He contested the Treasury's application of the 'least cost rule' which requires a brief explanation. As a matter of principle the Treasury did not like any public body to borrow directly in the market unless it could do so on terms at least as favourable as that available to government itself. This rule had been developed by a senior official in the Treasury who was later to become the Department's Permanent Secretary, Timothy Lankester. The Bank of England backed the Treasury, arguing that were the CDC to borrow in the market at a rate higher than government it would undermine the government's own creditworthiness in the marketplace and make it more expensive for it to borrow. To those not expert in these matters this was hard to credit, but the Treasury would not yield and Chris Patten had to accept defeat.

In 1990/91 the Monopolies and Mergers Commission (MMC – now the Competition Commission) decided to undertake an 'effectiveness, efficiency and economy' review of the CDC. As to why the MMC should want to do this, it should be explained that part of its remit under the 1980 Competition Act was periodically to review the operations of statutory bodies and nationalised industries. The NAO's 1989 Report on the Department's sponsorship of the CDC, while generally favourable, had noted that the Department had not undertaken a formal and sufficiently thorough Financial Management Survey of the CDC as required by the programme of work in respect of all Non-departmental Public Bodies announced by the Prime Minister in 1984 and to be completed by 1987.

This was the first thorough external review of the CDC in its history, with the MMC examining the papers and accounts, and taking written and oral evidence. Its report in 1992 gave the CDC an extraordinarily clean bill of health, and concluded that the CDC's 'activities are a highly effective form of aid' and that its 'strengths fit well with the trend in international thinking on development assistance'.

The internal Quinquennial Review that followed in 1993 took the Commission's report as its baseline and concluded that the CDC had a distinctive and important contribution to make to the development of the private sector. It confirmed its then current mandate, which was to 'invest in viable projects which cannot attract sufficient private funds', recognising that it 'can moderate risk that thereby attracts partners'. Ministers endorsed these conclusions and agreed that the CDC should further increase its proportion of new investments in the poorest countries, in the private sector, and in the form of equity. The target for investing in the renewable natural resources sector was abolished and, for the first time, a target rate of return on capital employed (of 8 per cent) was introduced. As part of the 1993 Public Expenditure Survey outcome the Treasury agreed that, in future, interest on outstanding Exchequer Advances, which they received, could be forgone. With this the Department introduced a net nil funding regime, meaning that new Exchequer Advances each year would in future equal the CDC's annual debt servicing of past loans, making the CDC no longer a direct burden on the current aid budget. By this time the CDC operating surplus was heading towards £100 million annually and the overall effect of the new funding arrangements meant that the CDC would be able to grow its investments by some 10 per cent per annum without having a net call on the Department's budget. Indeed, in 1994 the CDC made new investments totalling £240 million, with 22 per cent in the form of equity, and reporting an overall rate of return on capital employed of 7.9 per cent.

The next review set the CDC on a course that was intended to lead to partial privatisation. Although its aim was still to attract private direct investment rather than to substitute for it, the formal requirement to avoid competing with private investors was dropped. In future the CDC would invest only in the private sector except where investments in the public sector were intended to help facilitate privatisation, and new investments would be largely in the form of equity or quasi-equity products. At least 70 per cent of new investments were to be in the poorest countries, and 50 per cent in Africa and South Asia. A new set of Business Principles would be developed demonstrating the highest standards of corporate governance, including ethical, environmental, health and safety, and social policies.

At the Commonwealth Heads of Government Meeting in November 1997, held in Edinburgh, the new Prime Minister, The Rt Hon Tony Blair MP, announced that the CDC would become a public-private partnership. He described the CDC as 'an under-utilised resource and that it should have a larger role in mobilising new private finance for the poorer countries'. The CDC's unique character was to be preserved by government retaining a minority shareholding while it could 'look to maximising its success in creating and growing long term sustainable businesses, achieving attractive returns for shareholders and implementing ethical best practice'. Clare Short, as the Secretary of State for International Development since May 1997, had quickly become convinced that making the CDC a public-private partnership was the way to go. It is somewhat ironic that this was left to a minister regarded by most as being left of centre to have the necessary vision and robustness to still the critics to take such an initiative.

The CDC began to prepare itself more fully for the future it corporately relished, though some of the longer-serving members of staff and retirees were apprehensive lest the development mission was diluted. In 1998 risk capital represented over 60 per cent of new investments compared to 30 per cent the year before and the organisation was being re-oriented towards its future business. An enabling Bill was introduced in Parliament in 1998 after a considerable struggle, as always, to obtain a slot in the government's legislative timetable, to give effect to the

Prime Minister's announcement. The 1999 CDC Act provided for a CDC Group PLC wholly owned by government but with a view to introducing private capital in due course. The Act also provided for the Department to convert some £755 million of outstanding Exchequer Advances to equity in the CDC.

Earlier, preliminary testing of the market for private capital was encouraging though it was recognised that the past level of returns on capital did not provide a strong track record of delivering the sort of returns a private sector investor would expect, particularly in the risky markets in which CDC operated. Once the Act was in place, further testing of the market took place and it eventually became clear that, in the near future, given the lack of a track record, investors were likely to want an unacceptably large discount to net asset value to come on board. The Department and the CDC therefore agreed to move to a hitherto unplanned 'Plan B'. This was to explore the feasibility of privatising the management of the CDC's funds while retaining ownership of those funds in the public sector. The arrangements for this were developed and ministers agreed that CDC Group PLC would remain wholly owned by government and that a new management company called Actis would be created with the management partners owning 60 per cent and government 40 per cent, though 80 per cent of its economic value would accrue to government were Actis sold. At this point it should be noted that the government had established the Shareholder Executive, with staff drawn from the public and private sectors to advise departments on their management of such bodies, and they assisted the Department in developing this model. For the purposes of valuing Actis, an independent committee of the CDC Board was established with the help of external financial advisers. This was based on the understanding that Actis would manage 95 per cent of CDC funds for the first five years provided it could use them.

The 'old' business of the CDC was divided into two parts. The outstanding loans to the public sector of £165 million became directly owned by the Department by requiring the CDC to issue a debenture to government of a like amount. These were then managed by Actis with a view to securing repayment. However, a substantial part of these loans was forgiven under various debt relief initiatives, notably HIPC. The so-called legacy business (equity and loans to individual private sector companies) was also managed down by Actis on behalf of CDC, the proceeds being returned to them. This left the CDC with a portfolio of managed funds which it would seek to grow with a restructured and strong balance sheet. New targets were set for CDC investments; 70 per cent of new investments should be in the poorer countries with a per capita income of less than $1,750 (based on 2003 World Bank data) which included all lower-income countries and those below the mean for lower middle-income countries; and 50 per cent in Africa and South Asia.

These changes were announced to Parliament in January 2004 and then put into effect. The CDC's mission was 'to generate wealth, broadly shared, in emerging markets, particularly in poorer countries, by providing capital for investment in sustainable and responsibly managed private sector businesses'. The total value of the CDC's portfolio doubled from £1 billion at the end of 2003 to £2 billion at the end of 2006, with total returns in 2006 after tax of £375 million, representing 21 per cent of total average net assets for the year. The CDC's targets for the poorer countries and for Africa and South Asia have been met.

The CDC began with two equity fund managers: Actis Capital and Aureas Capital, the latter having started earlier, focused on small and medium-sized businesses in East Africa, and as a joint venture with Norfund, Norway's sovereign wealth fund. Outside of Actis and Aureas, the CDC started its new life with £50 million of 'reserved capital' to allow them to develop relationships with two or three other fund managers, and therefore be in a stronger position at the end of the first five years. However, by the end of 2007 the CDC already had 47 per cent of its funds with 42 other fund managers. This unexpected development came about for a combination of reasons: the amount of cash generated for the CDC from realisations has been more than double that projected; Actis succeeded in attracting more third party funds than had been anticipated; and the deal flow within funds has not been quite as fast as envisaged. This left the CDC with a growing amount of cash to re-invest with other fund managers.

At the same time the CDC developed a strong code of Ethical Business Principles which fund managers and third party funds had to buy into. In turn, fund managers require the individual business in which they invest to adopt and implement the same code. The CDC also reports on its development impact through its investments, including encouraging local private equity fund managers, particularly in countries where equity markets remain nascent and equity funds remain scarce. Following a review in 2008, it was agreed that more ambitious investment targets should be set for the period 2009–13, with 75 per cent of new investments being in low-income countries and 50 per cent of new investments being in sub-Saharan Africa.

However, a further review was conducted by the Department and the CDC under Andrew Mitchell as the Coalition government's first

Secretary of State for International Development. The new CDC 2011 business plan[86] contained an introduction by the Secretary of State which stated: 'So – if you're in the business of helping reduce poverty, you have to believe in economic development and growth. Growth that is broad-based, inclusive and sustainable; in which all people benefit from the proceeds of prosperity; and in which even the poorest have access to the opportunities and markets that it creates.' The CDC's mission was stated as: 'To be a pioneering investor, stimulating the private sector and demonstrating the power of enterprise and private capital to reduce poverty in the poorest places of the world.' The key policy implications of this were:

1. the use of a wider range of instruments including debt, guarantees and direct equity investmnents, in addition to externally managed private equity funds; and
2. future investments would only be made in Sub-Saharan Africa and South Asia.

## Crown agents

The origins of the Crown Agents are to be found in the mid-18th century, and a century later were largely in a form that is recognisable today. That said, its legal form has undergone three phases over the last 150 years. The Crown Agents emerged as an entity by a series of administrative acts and remained unincorporated until it became a statutory corporation under the 1979 Crown Agents Act. This second phase lasted less than two decades until the 1995 Act paved the way for it to be privatised under the ownership of a Foundation.

The first Crown Agent was appointed by the Treasury in 1749 for Nova Scotia, with the sole purpose of accounting for parliamentary grants made to the territory. Subsequent appointments were made by the Treasury in respect of colonial territories in receipt of grants until 1810, when each territory, as the Principal, formally appointed the Crown Agent, but on the firm recommendation of the Secretary of State for the Colonies. By this time the Crown Agents were offering other services to their territories in the fields of procurement and finance, including the raising of loans on the London market. Following a colonial review, in 1833 two Crown Agents were appointed as Joint Agents General for Crown Colonies covering 13 territories, though they carved up the territories between them, rather than acting as a unified organisation (albeit with two heads) until 1858 when a further reorganisation took place. Finally, in 1863 they became the Crown Agents for the Colonies, a name that continued for nearly a century. Prior to this reorganisation the Crown Agents had been prohibited from providing services to territories with 'responsible government' which, as noted in Chapter Two, meant that they could only operate in countries eligible for, though not necessarily in receipt of, parliamentary grants. In 1874 a revision to colonial regulations prohibited local merchants from procuring imported goods for colonial territories without responsible government, thus giving the Crown Agents a monopoly in those territories. At about the same time colonies with responsible government began using the Crown Agents' services at their own discretion. In 1880 the Treasury, with remarkable prescience, but to no effect, became concerned that they might have a contingent liability should the Crown Agents make a trading loss, or act in a way that gave a territory's government a claim on them, and transferred responsibility for the Crown Agents to the Secretary of State for the Colonies. However, the only connection between the Crown Agents and Her Majesty's Government should be through the Secretary of State's responsibility generally for the good governance of the colonies, in the belief that this would avoid any contingent liability.

After the Second World War, Crown Agents' business thrived with the colonies wanting to make good years of neglect of their infrastructure, and the Agents further developed their consultancy role in engineering design in sectors such as railways, roads, power and telecommunications to complement their procurement services. As they became more profitable during this period they adopted a policy of holding a reserve of £250,000, distributing any surplus to their Principals. In 1954 their name was changed to Crown Agents for Oversea Governments and Administrations to reflect the fact that they were now working for the governments of independent countries and their parastatal organisations and local municipalities. The number of staff they employed grew from 800 in 1945 to 1,400 in 1955. But this period of prosperity was increasingly overshadowed by the rapid contraction of the British Empire, and the growing uncertainty this created. In particular, when Ghana became independent in 1957 President Nkrumah immediately discontinued Crown Agents' services. The 1960 independence of Nigeria (a country for which they did a lot of business) was another case in point, though in fact Crown Agents continued to do some business there.[87]

The decline in their largely captive market and the deterioration in their profitability (reserves were down to £180,000 by 1960) led the Crown Agents to consider ways of diversifying their business activities and operating on their own account rather than as agents for others. This was despite the fact that in 1964 general responsibility for the Crown Agents was transferred to the new Minister for Overseas Development and they became responsible for procurement of goods and many services under the aid programme and for the management of aid loan and grant accounts. In many respects, however, this was not new business and the future scale and direction of British aid was itself uncertain. Diversification into own-account business meant taking on financial and operating risks with which they were unfamiliar and did not have the capital base with which to withstand fluctuations in cash flow. The Crown Agents believed they were encouraged in this by being told by the government in 1962 that they were 'on their own'. So began a short but disastrous period in an otherwise long and distinguished history of service to others 'oversea', though its clients abroad never suffered.

It is not intended to dwell unduly on the short period 1967–74 when the Crown Agents launched out on their own account into secondary banking and property development, and which resulted in their having to approach the government in December 1974 for a recoverable grant of £85 million in order to meet their liabilities. It was the first time in their history that they had sought and received any government funding. But it is necessary to cover this period and the resulting Enquiries to understand why the Crown Agents became incorporated in 1980. In 1963 the Crown Agents began acting as a bank (that is, a deposit-taker) rather than acting as an agent for investing Principals' funds, and later other banks approached the Crown Agents to deposit short-term funds with them. In 1967/68 the Crown Agents began investing in secondary banks and, jointly with others, in properties, including overseas, using Principals' funds or money borrowed in the market, and taking on foreign currency risk. The problem was that the Crown Agents did not have an appropriate level of reserves for these sorts of financial activities, though they hoped to generate them through the success of the business, which initially they did. From 1972 to the first half of 1973 was a period of expansion generally in secondary banks and the property market, but by the end of 1973 the British economy was suffering from the sharp rise in oil prices, the 'three-day week' and a hike in interest rates. By 1974 many property developers, and the secondary banks that had financed them, were in further difficulty, and with them the Crown Agents. By mid-1974 Crown Agents were estimated to have assets of £273m at book, but not market value, and short-term liabilities of £289 million.

Later in the year the newly appointed Chairman informed the Department of the full extent of the Crown Agents' liquidity and solvency problems. He expected the end of year accounts to show negative net reserves of £55 million with interest payments to be made on borrowings of £11 million in the first half of 1975. He asked for a recoverable grant of £85 million to provide a capital reserve of £30 million. In October the Department issued a letter instructing the Board to pay due regard to best banking practices, not to engage in transactions which might embarrass the government or conflict with the interests of their principals, and not to engage further in the property market. In December the Department informed Parliament that subject to its approval a recoverable grant of £85 million would be made. These funds would, until required, be invested in government-guaranteed debt and local authority deposits. In February 1975 a further instruction was issued that Crown Agents should make an orderly and phased withdrawal from property and secondary banking and for realisations to be put into a separate account.

By 1971 there had already been concern with the direction which the Crown Agents were heading and an Advisory Committee was set up in August 1971, chaired by Sir Matthew Stevenson.[88] Its terms of reference were to consider 'whether there was any changes in the status, functions and financial operations of the Crown Agents, including particularly their relationship to HMG'.

The Committee reported in March 1972. It noted that the Crown Agents' consultations with the Department were informal and that the usual apparatus for governance and accountability was missing. For example, there were no prescribed limits to Crown Agents' activities or borrowings, nor a Board of Directors of a usual kind accountable to shareholders. It concluded that the Department was not well placed to make good these deficiencies but that HMG was ultimately liable in respect of any Crown Agents' losses. Nevertheless, subject to withdrawing immunity from tax, and appropriate changes in organisation and status, the Crown Agents' activities should be allowed to continue. On the issue of status, the Committee reflected on four options: a nationalised corporation; private sector status with HMG minority shareholding; a limited company with HMG the majority shareholder and Principals as minority shareholders; and a limited company wholly owned by HMG. The first made HMG wholly liable and probably not liked by Principals; the second was attractive but unlikely; the third was difficult to achieve; and the fourth (like the first) would require legislation. The Committee concluded that its preference was for option two (a public-private partnership in today's parlance) and that becoming a nationalised corporation was 'at best a last resort'.

In April 1975 the Department appointed a further Committee of Enquiry under Judge Faye[89] 'to enquire into the circumstances which led the Crown Agents requesting financial assistance from the Government'. This was a more thorough investigation into the events of 1967–74. Its main conclusions were 'that the expansion of own account business had been unwise in nature and degree; there had been a lack of expertise and management procedures combined with folly and too much euphoria; and a lack of transparency and low ethical standards'.

These two reports were not published until December 1977, alongside a statement by the Minister for Overseas Development. This statement rehearsed the history and explained the steps to be taken to make the Crown Agents more accountable, including for the first time submitting to the Department quarterly management accounts and 'reporting any particular matters of special interest'. It concluded by stating that the Crown Agents had now been put on 'a different and better footing', and that the government now had 'confidence in the Board of the Crown Agents and in their traditional activities now and in the future on behalf of their overseas Principals. It stands behind the Crown Agents'. It promised to bring forward legislation based on the White Paper of 1976.[90] The White Paper rehearsed the past and proposed legislation that would make the Crown Agents a statutory corporation with defined areas of activities, with a Board appointed by the Minister. Subsequent debates in Parliament led, with a resolution of both Houses of Parliament of 28 February 1978, to a Tribunal being established by the Home Secretary of the day, the Rt Hon Merlyn Rees MP. It was chaired by Sir David Powell Croom-Johnson DSC VRD, with the following terms of reference: 'to enquire to what extent there were lapses from accepted standards of commercial or professional conduct or of public administration in relation to the operations of the Crown Agents as financiers on own account in the years 1967–74'. The report of the Tribunal was finally published in May 1982.[91] In brief, it blamed the Crown Agents for not being equipped to undertake what it did, and the government for having a contingent liability but no formal constitutional relationship with the Crown Agents. It criticised government (the Department, Treasury and the Bank of England) for not heeding the early warning signals about own account operations, and for each of them not having a clear sense of their own responsibilities resulting in 'many papers passing to and fro, which only concealed the fact that nothing was being achieved . . . nobody took the lead'.

The Crown Agents Act 1979 provided for the Crown Agents for Oversea Governments and Administrations as a statutory corporation (vesting day was 31 March 1980) with the financial aim of 'breaking even, taking one year with another'. It provided for the Crown Agents to act as agents for any scheduled authority or body which in summary was any public sector body, international organisation or charity (but not the for-profit private sector), whether overseas or in the UK in relation to a defined number of activities. It also provided for them to carry on business on their own account in relation to the above scheduled authority or body for a more limited set of activities set out in the Act which were mainly of a consultancy nature but which also allowed them to purchase and sell on goods and provide short-term credit. The Minister was given the power, amongst other things, to appoint the Chairman and members of the Board. Finally, it provided for a commencing capital debt to be repaid over time, as determined by the Minister. This was set at £30 million, which was eventually repaid with interest.

In addition, the Act provided for the creation of a Crown Agents Holding and Realisation Board (CAHRB), separate from the Crown Agents but administered by them, to hold certain unrealised assets (that is, those acquired during the period 1967–74 in respect of property and secondary banks) and to seek to realise them over time. The liability of the unincorporated Crown Agents to repay the £175 million of recoverable grants paid to them by government ceased the day before incorporation. In addition to the original grant of £85 million, a further grant of £90 million had been provided in February 1978 as part of a financial restructuring of the Crown Agents. Realisations by the Board were to be paid to government. Thus was finally laid to rest a turbulent period in the Crown Agents' history, and a new constitutional, accountability and business framework established.

From now on the fortunes of the Crown Agents would depend not on empire but rather on their ability to maintain, and attract new, business from around the world. They did at the time, however, have one captive market in the form of the Department's bilateral aid programme. Financial aid loan and grant accounts in the name of recipient governments were managed by the Crown Agents, which had a history in the services provided to colonial territories in respect of parliamentary grants. All capital and intermediate goods imports financed by Britain's tied aid programme were procured by them on behalf of recipient governments, for which they arranged for inspection, insurance and shipment. They had earlier recruited a large number of staff (mainly teachers) on behalf of developing-country governments, whose services were in part funded from the aid programme. Finally, they also continued to manage the payment of overseas pensions on behalf of the Department. However, soon after incorporation the Department relocated most of its service department to East Kilbride, together with Crown Agents' pensions staff. The Department then took pensions work in-house, together with most of the Crown Agents' staff, not least to help meet its civil service relocation targets.

If one accepted Britain's commitment to the 0.7 per cent UN aid target at face value one might have thought the Crown Agents had a bright future. However, over the next 17 years not only did the overall size of the aid programme largely stagnate but significant changes in its direction and management had a serious adverse impact on the level of Crown Agents' business. First, multilateral aid, particularly that going through European Union aid programmes, increased as a proportion of total aid, resulting in a real decline in bilateral aid. Second, as the Department shifted from project to programme (budgetary) aid during the 1980s and 1990s, which was increasingly provided as direct financial support to the budgets of recipient governments, the proportion of bilateral financial aid that became untied increased (see Chapter Eight), and as a result Crown Agents' procurement business for the Department fell substantially. In addition the Department began using other procurement agents, albeit in a small way.

Partly as a response to this, the Crown Agents sought to diversify their aid procurement business and also to develop further their consultancy work. They provided services to the World Bank, to the European Commission aid programmes and to other bilateral donors. They were particularly successful in providing procurement services in respect of Japanese non-project (programme) grant aid in sub-Saharan Africa. Japan was under pressure both to participate in the international aid effort to support reforming African countries and for that aid to be untied. Eager to show that such aid was untied in fact and not just in name, and that it could be properly accounted for, they found the Crown Agents' reputation for impartiality, and probity, as a public sector institution, particularly useful. During this period, however, they also lost very substantial fund management business from Brunei (some £5 billion in 1983) and from Hong Kong (some £1 billion, much later) which they had to adjust to. The then Sultan of Brunei had wanted British Gurkhas to remain in the country after independence in 1984, but when the British government refused he withdrew from the Crown Agents' fund management services. Though Prime Minister Thatcher changed her mind on the Gurkhas, the Sultan did not reverse his decision in respect of Crown Agents. One result of this was that Crown Agents had to look much harder at what services they provided were profitable and which were not, now that a degree of cross-subsidy from a lucrative fund management contract was no longer available. Finally, in their traditional markets, developing-country governments were being encouraged to privatise many public utility operations to which Crown Agents provided services. Once privatised, the Crown Agents, under their Act, were precluded from doing business for them and the Board sought a change in the Act to allow them to continue to do so. However, it was unlikely that legislative time would be found for this and the Department did not press it.

As the Crown Agents continued to adjust to a changing market and seek changes to their legislation, the government continued to look for candidates for privatisation. The Department were asked to examine the prospects for privatising Crown Agents, to which the Board was itself receptive to as being one way of securing its future in a changing world. External consultants were employed to advise: they looked at various options and recommended a trade sale for which they believed there would be interest among the private sector. However, by this time the Japanese government was an important customer, and both the Crown Agents and the Department were concerned that a trade sale to the private sector would undermine its confidence in Crown Agents and lead to the Japanese government withdrawing its business: there was already pressure from Japanese trading houses not to use Crown Agents for aid procurement. If so, a trade sale was likely to fail, not least because those that had indicated an interest in a purchase did not obviously have the reputation for probity that would have been required. It was concluded, therefore, that privatisation should take the form of creating a Foundation (a company limited by guarantee). While Crown Agents would continue to offer its services with the intention of being profitable, such profits would not be distributed to a shareholder. Any surplus would either be used to develop Crown Agents' services or be applied to development causes. This concept was put in a paper to the Japanese government which indicated that it would provide a satisfactory basis for them to continue to use Crown Agents' services. At the same time a number of public, private and international organisations were approached to sound out interest in their being associated with such a Foundation, to which there was a generally positive response. When the Foundation was established, government provided a loan of £5.5 million in order to strengthen its initial balance sheet: £2.5 million to be repaid according to a fixed schedule over eight years from 31 December 1997 bearing an interest rate of 5 per cent, and £3 million to be repaid once its Reserves had reached £21.9 million, carrying an interest rate of 2.25 per cent. In both cases there was provision for the interest rate to be varied if the level of Reserves changed. The terms of these loans required 'state aids' approval by the European Commission.

The Crown Agents Act (1996) provided enabling legislation which paved the way for the Crown Agents to become a Foundation in the private sector as a company limited by guarantee. Debate in Parliament during the passage of the Bill made it clear that this option for privatisation had considerable support. The change took place in March 1997 in the run-up to the May General Election with the support of the then Labour Shadow Minister, Clare Short. The Crown Agents for Oversea Governments and Administrations Ltd became a wholly owned subsidiary of the Foundation and its main operating company. This recognised the international nature of Crown Agents' activities and its unique client base among governments, ministries and other public sector bodies, international funding agencies and emerging private sector entities. The new constitution was designed to ensure that the Crown Agents continued to adhere to the highest standards of integrity and impartiality while providing services on commercial terms. The initial members of the Foundation reflected this status, Sir David Rowe-Ham CBE became the first President of the Foundation and the late Mr D. H. Probert CBE continued as the first Chairman of its operating company.

The Crown Agents have been right to emphasise its role in development, despite operating on a commercial basis. It has used its traditional strengths to continue to provide key expertise in both development and humanitarian operations, the latter mainly, but by no means exclusively, for the Department. Its consultancy services have been particularly important in helping to reform and strengthen countries' revenue services and debt monitoring and management, particularly in Africa. Part of its operating surpluses, after meeting its repayment obligations to government, have been remitted to the Foundation for development activities in the field of human resource development.

### Scientific Units (Natural Resources Institute)

The Scientific Units which the Department inherited had a long and distinguished history, dating back to colonial days. The Imperial Institute was founded in 1887 from which eventually evolved the

Tropical Products Institute (TPI) in 1957, and which later absorbed the Tropical Stored Products Centre created in 1964. The Centre for Overseas Pest Research (COPR) was formed in 1971, based largely on the Anti-Locust Research Centre (ALCR), which had its origins in the Imperial Bureau of Entomology established in 1912, the Colonial (later Tropical) Pesticides Research Unit (1948) and the Tropical Pesticides Research Headquarters and Information Unit (1964), previously the Tropical Pesticides Research Committee (1955). The Land Resources Development Centre (LRDC) (1978), previously the Land Resources Division, grew out of the Directorate of Colonial Surveys, established in 1946, which later was restyled as the Directorate of Overseas Surveys (DOS). For a further understanding of the genealogy of these institutions see the chart reproduced at Figure 8.1.

These institutions and their predecessors provided advice to the Colonial Office and to the colonial territories, and later to independent Commonwealth and other countries. In this they were assisted by a number of colourful characters, including Harold St John Kilby (1885–1960), father of the defector and spy Kim Philby, who journeyed across the 'Empty Quarter' of Saudi Arabia by camel collecting insect specimens and plotting locust movements; Sir Boris Uvarov (1889–1970)[92], an eminent entomologist who spent his life tracking and studying locusts; and Sir Wilfred Thesiger (1910–2003),[93] who also travelled the Empty Quarter with Bedouin tribesmen to map the desert area and locate locust outbreaks. Others, some of whom were only slightly less colourful, joined the colonial service as agriculturalists and surveyors and later returned to Britain to join either one of the Units or the Department itself as professional advisers.

After 1964 each of the Units was headed by a Director responsible through the Department's senior management to the Minister. Each had a Steering Committee chaired by the Director responsible for advising on its three-year rolling work programme which was funded from the aid budget. In addition the Units undertook specific aid-funded projects in individual developing countries funded by the Department's geographical departments, and later to a lesser extent by other donors, mainly the World Bank and the European Commission. The Units also provided important specialist advice to the Department's own cadre of professional advisers. With the early focus by the Department on rural development, the Units' scientific expertise and experience was in considerable demand.

However the 1980s saw a threatened reversal of the Units' fortunes. The aid programme as a whole was being reduced and within it, despite

178

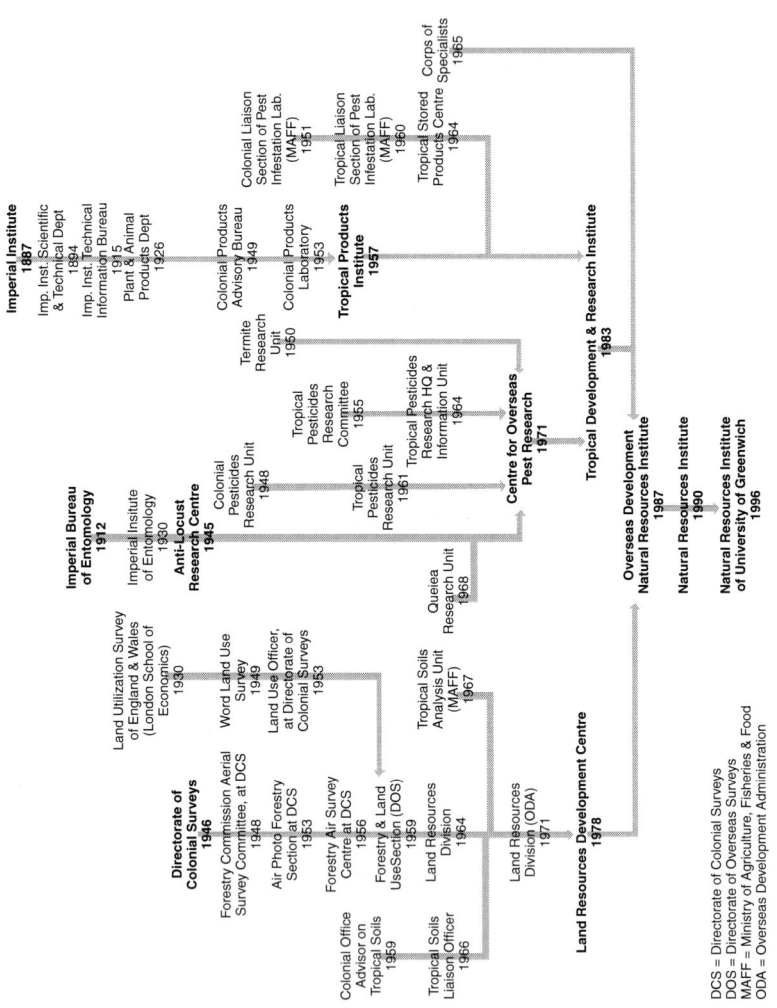

*Figure 8.1* Organogram of scientific units

DCS = Directorate of Colonial Surveys
DOS = Directorate of Overseas Surveys
MAFF = Ministry of Agriculture, Fisheries & Food
ODA = Overseas Development Administration

the government's wishes to the contrary, the share of bilateral aid was set to fall; and the 1981 Aid Policy Review provided for an uncertain framework against which to judge what emphasis would be given to rural development. At the same time the new Thatcher government embarked upon a series of initiatives with a view to making government more efficient, and less costly. Sir Derek Raynor (of Marks and Spencer) was recruited to undertake a series of efficiency scrutinies of Civil Service functions. The second of these focused on NDPBs. For the Department this meant a review of its Scientific Units in the context of a prospective fall in the Department's demand for their services. The main recommendations of the review were, in summary: TPI and COPR should be amalgamated to form the Tropical Development and Research Institute (TDRI) with some reductions in staff, mainly in the support areas; a material reduction in the staffing of LRDC; and the activities of DOS should be absorbed by the Ordnance Survey, with some functions going to LRDC. The Units that would form TDRI would be brought together and relocated outside central London. In future the Department should commission work with clearly specified objectives and costings and be ready to invite bids from the private sector. These recommendations, which were accepted by ministers, were greeted with considerable dismay by staff.

The House of Commons' Select Committee on Foreign Affairs' Subcommittee on Overseas Development examined these proposals and in their report (Fourth Report 1982/83 Session) were generally critical of what was proposed. The Government's response[94] pointed out that TDRI had become effective as of 1 April 1983 with the same scientific capacity as before, and that it was reviewing relocation on a single site which would strengthen management and reduce costs. Over seven years TDRI would reduce staff by 25 per cent by greater focus and economies in support services. It defended the need to reduce the scale of LRDC operations, involving staff reductions of about 45 per cent, and to merge the DOS with Ordnance Survey which would lead to a 60 per cent reduction in staff because of the declining demand for its services and the capacity of the private sector to undertake such work. It also defended the adoption of the 'Rothschild' principles for commissioning work which would result in programmes of research better reflecting the needs of developing countries. Finally, the government denied that Sir Derek Raynor's review had failed to look at the benefits of the work of the Units but accepted that a declining bilateral aid programme required it to look at the future standing capacity that it should retain.

In doing all this it acknowledged the deservedly high international reputation which the Units enjoyed.

The Department's relocation study for the Units concluded that both TDRI and LRDC should go to the Royal Naval Dockyard at Chatham. They were to be amalgamated and re-named the Overseas Natural Resources Institute (ONRI), shortly afterwards to become NRI. The redevelopment of the old Dockyard site was only just beginning and NRI would be its first occupant. The move was completed in 1990. The initial cost estimate soon escalated dramatically to almost £44 million and in order to finance it the Department, with Treasury agreement, embarked upon a private finance initiative (PFI). Lloyds Project Leasing Ltd were the effective owners and developers of the Dockyard with a 125-year lease from English Estates (later English Partnerships). The Department entered into a finance leasing arrangement taking an under-lease for 25 years and borrowing £44 million from Lloyds, to be serviced by annual nominal interest payments and a final bullet payment of the £44 million in 2014. PFIs were designed to bring in private capital for projects the government did not wish to find the up-front costs for, provided the higher cost of private capital could be expected to be offset by the benefits of private sector management, though this was not a strong consideration in this case. In 1994 the Department sub-let 20 per cent of the space at Chatham to the University of Greenwich which then, in an expansionary mode, wished to create a campus in Chatham.

Soon after the creation of NRI the government launched its Next Steps initiative, designed literally to be its next step in streamlining the work of the Civil Service. Each ministry was required to examine the scope for hiving off executive, as distinct from policy, functions into separate 'Next Steps Agencies' and giving them greater financial and management autonomy. The obvious candidate for the Department to offer was NRI, which became a Next Steps Agency in 1991. NRI in 1991 was already a separately managed institution; now its Director became the Accounting Officer formally responsible directly to the Minister, and also answerable to Parliament (the Public Accounts Committee) for NRI's good management. In fact the Department's Deputy Secretary chaired an advisory committee for NRI on which the Director sat. The financial arrangements were such that NRI was now allowed to grow provided it could secure income for its services, whether from the Department or from other agencies. The NRI secured income from the Department partly by bidding for, and winning, certain research programmes within the Renewable Natural Resources Research Strategy (known as the Yellow Brick because of its colour and size) and by competing for other project business from the Department's bilateral country programme managers.

The Cabinet Office then undertook a 'prior options' review to consider the future of the government's research establishments, with privatisation being one option. The Department, seeing the writing on the wall, proposed the privatisation of NRI. In preparation for privatisation a review of NRI's prospects was carried out, as a result of which it was concluded that the Institute's focus should be narrowed and that staffing should be reduced by some 120 people. This was achieved during 1994/95 almost entirely by voluntary redundancies. An Information Memorandum was prepared by NRI and the Department which showed, amongst other things, that 85 per cent of the Institute's income came from the Department (43 per cent research strategy programmes; 15 per cent advice and support services; and 27 per cent country programme activities) and 15 per cent from work for other agencies. On this basis bids were sought and a consortium of universities led by the University of Greenwich was declared the preferred bidder. In the event NRI was sold for £1 plus its audited net current assets at the end of the financial year (£1.935 million), effective from 1 April 1996. Within a year of privatisation Greenwich approached the Department to complain that the Information Memorandum had been misleading in terms of the volume of work NRI could expect to obtain from the Department: country programme managers in particular seemed to have reduced the volume of business they awarded to the Institute. It was suggested by Greenwich that they should not pay the remainder (some £1.3 million) of the value of net current assets still due. In the event the Department took administrative action to enhance some of the ongoing research work being undertaken by NRI and Greenwich met its obligation in full under the sale agreement. NRI has retained its international reputation for its research and problem-solving work in relation to development in the poorer countries, though it receives limited support from the Department.

## Comment

Each of the four associated bodies – and here the Scientific Units score as one, as indeed they became NRI – had quite different relationships with the Department. In one case, the British Council, the lead sponsor department was the FCO and thus the Department never felt fully liable for the overall performance of the Council against its corporate objectives.

As regards the other three, the Department's governance relationship after the incorporation of Crown Agents broadly matched the nature of their activities and the perceived financial risk. The two statutory corporations (the CDC and Crown Agents) had Acts of Parliament that circumscribed their activities in broad terms and set financial parameters and objectives. Each had their own Cadbury-style Board, that is, non-executives being in the majority and one of them being Chairman, and all appointed by the Department. NRI, like the Crown Agents prior to incorporation in 1980, was created by a series of administrative acts and was essentially seen as an extension of the Department. Indeed, in terms of governance, it was treated for most of its life as just that. The Director of NRI was responsible to a senior manager in the Department and it was subject to similar running-cost controls as the Department itself. Only later did NRI become a Next Steps Agency and receive more managerial and financial autonomy.

Prior to the financial difficulties of the 1970s there was no formal governance relationship between the Department and the Crown Agents, and after incorporation in 1980 the oversight arrangements by the Department were light and unobtrusive. The CAHRB got on with the task of trying to realise the assets ill-advisedly acquired and which led to such financial difficulties, and repaying the Treasury as and when it did so. The Crown Agents' ongoing activities, formally constrained by legislation, did not subsequently require any injection of funds by the Department except on privatisation. The main area of risk was Crown Agents' deposit-taking (that is, banking) function, which was undertaken on behalf of its Principals by Crown Agents Financial Services Ltd (CAFSL). Although exempt from the Banking Act as a statutory corporation, the Department arranged for the Bank of England to supervise CAFSL as though it were not exempt. This provided the Department and the Treasury with the assurance that these services were carried out without undue risk.

It was the CDC that was subject to greatest scrutiny and strategic guidance, though without interfering with the day-to-day management of the organisation or with individual investment decisions, except where there were strong political considerations. Ironically, because of policy reasons the Department wanted the CDC to focus mainly on the poorest and often most difficult markets, it was inviting for the CDC to invest in more risky assets. Furthermore, the Department increasingly criticised the CDC for engaging in what was in effect sovereign risk bank lending to public sector organisations and set targets, albeit not always quantified, for investing in the private sector, and in the form of equity without, in the Board's view, an appropriately strong balance sheet.

The governance relationship with each of these four bodies involved very few people within the Department. Their broader relationship with the Department depended upon the nature of their activities. The work of NRI and its predecessors was probably seen as the most integral to the objectives and operations of the Department, though tensions arose from time to time over the issue of competition. Whereas their up-stream research was generally respected by their peers in the Department, bilateral aid departments were increasingly encouraged, to ensure value for money by seeking competitive bids for commissioned work. Thus NRI's down-stream, consultancy-type activities were increasingly subject to competition. Furthermore, as socio-economic factors became to be seen as important as pure science in developing and managing renewable natural resource-based projects, NRI was thought not to be responding sufficiently to what the market was now demanding.

The Crown Agents have been widely respected for their service functions, without which the management of much of the bilateral aid programme in the past would have been more burdensome and risk-prone. And for a long period, when infrastructure projects were in their heyday, Crown Agents were the Department's advisers on telecommunications projects. Beyond that, few in the Department fully understood the development motivation of Crown Agents staff.

The relationship with the British Council has been both more complex and ambiguous. Except for those in the field, the Council was often viewed as engaged in cultural diplomacy, not development. For many who joined the Council quite the opposite was the case, and the withdrawal of the Department as a co-sponsor of the Council after 1997 was greeted with dismay. In fact the Department's disengagement did not itself affect the relationship in the field. For those working overseas there was generally close collaboration between the staff of the Department and the Council. The tensions that arose were two-fold. In the early days Council staff were the Department's ELT advisers and were thought by some to be their education advisers more generally. Over time, as the relationship evolved and the Department increased the number of its own Education Advisers, professional tensions arose until it was accepted by the 1990s that the Department looked to its own professional staff for advice as to who may, in certain areas such as ELT, a declining area of activity, turn to the Council. The other area of tension was during the period that the Council sought to diversity its activities into sectors beyond education and were thought by the Department to be seeking an inside track rather than bidding in open competition with others.

Perhaps the least amount of collaboration in the field took place between the Department and the CDC. There was some contact professionally between agriculturalists in both bodies, but for the most part they were seen to be pursuing different sorts of activities. As private sector issues rose up the development agenda the Department's staff in the field were encouraged to consult private business, and therefore also the CDC, about the business environment and incentives or otherwise for foreign investment. Occasionally the CDC would ask country offices to help fund large feasibility studies in the RNR field for which they could not afford the up-front costs: but the reply would normally be that it was not in accordance with agreed priorities, or that there were no uncommitted funds available in the timescale required.

One might conclude from this that the Department's associated bodies were indeed associated legally but only in varying degrees in terms of shared mission and activities. Today only the CDC remains a responsibility of the Department, and that is not for the want of trying at least partially to disengage. Clare Short disengaged with the British Council largely on the grounds that the grant-in-aid was not unambiguously driven by the objective of poverty reduction. NRI was sold because the Department no longer saw merit in ownership, only in using its services as and when it wished. The Crown Agents became an independent Foundation, partly because the Department no longer saw any advantage in having corporate responsibility for it but wished to continue to have access to its services, and partly because the Crown Agents realised that it needed to be released from its statutory constraints if it were to survive in a changing world – but that would have potentially involved greater risk for the Department. Just as governments have now realised that they do not need to own or even subsidise the commanding heights of their economies in order to extract the economic rent, so the Department has learned that ownership is not necessary in order to buy services. The trick has been to disengage in terms of ownership while still leaving an organisation in place to do business with as required.

# 9
# Commercial Issues: The Tying of Aid and the Aid and Trade Provision

## Introduction

Commercial considerations have been an ingredient in most donor country aid programmes since they began. They are best dealt with in two parts. First, most donors' bilateral aid programmes, albeit usually provided on highly concessional terms, have for the most part been tied to the procurement of goods and services from their own countries. However misplaced, donor governments believed that tied aid benefited the balance of payments and created employment. It has been generally believed that in political terms there would be stronger public support for aid if it were thought to be mutually beneficial.

The second commercial aspect of aid has been the credit race, in which OECD countries softened the terms of their export credits to win business in developing countries by using aid. Export credits were generally separate from a donor's aid programme and governed by an agreement which set common terms for such credits, including interest rates and maturities. This agreement is known as the 'Arrangement for officially supported export credits' (or the Consensus). The purpose of the Consensus was to achieve uniformity of export credit terms and avoid a credit race by which OECD countries subsidised their exports to developing countries on differential and competing terms. Export credits have been provided either by official bodies (as in the case of Germany, France and Japan) or by countries, such as Britain, guaranteeing the provision of loans by private banks at the agreed fixed rate of interest. Because banks used to finance such loans by short-term borrowings in the market at variable rates of interest the British government (through the Export Credits Guarantee Department – ECGD) established an interest rate stabilisation fund. The cost to the taxpayer of fixed rate export finance (FREF) peaked at some £370 million in 1981. Over time the Consensus was persuaded to set more commercial rates of interest and the banks went into the capital markets for cheaper, longer-term, finance: the result was a substantial decline in interest payments to the banks for export credit purposes.

However it proved difficult to retain two entirely separate sets of transactions: highly concessional tied aid on the one hand and standard export credit terms on the other. Donor countries began providing both mixed credits (a combination of aid and export credits) or tied aid on less concessional terms. The Consensus therefore agreed that if a country derogated from normal export credit terms it had to do so according to certain rules. Thus mixed credits had to have a minimum grant element of 25 per cent (based on DAC methodology – see Chapter Ten) but with the export credit deemed to have a zero grant element regardless of the prevailing agreed interest rate for such credits. Any such proposed derogation had to be pre-notified to other members of the Consensus, which gave others the opportunity to match a competitor's terms in what was called a 'common line' approach. Both mixed credits and other tied aid loan transactions were known as tied aid credits. All tied aid credits were in principle subject to the same prior notification procedures.

## The tying of bilateral aid to British procurement

The concept of mutual benefit from the giving of aid has a long history in the case of both Britain and other donor countries. As was noted in Chapter Two, the early attempts to help the Colonies in the 1920s, including the Colonial Development Fund Act of 1929, were motivated by the thought that this would help reduce unemployment at home. Subsequent CD&W Acts until 1959 contained no formal procurement restrictions and CD&W expenditure was available to finance the local costs of projects without limit. However restrictions on imports generally from outside the sterling area ensured that most offshore costs of projects financed exports from Britain. Not until the late 1950s, with the introduction of Exchequer loans under Section II of the 1959 CD&W Act and Commonwealth assistance loans under Section III of the ECGD Act, did Britain introduce the general presumption that imports by the colonies and independent Commonwealth countries financed under these Acts should be sourced from Britain. The then Chancellor's 'surplus capacity initiative' in the early 1960s was a more direct effort to promote British exports with the use of aid to the independent Commonwealth (see Chapter Three).

The Department inherited the presumption that its bilateral aid should be used to finance British goods and services, except for local costs. This reflected successive governments' abiding concern with the balance of payments and, as aid became more concessional, it was thought that in political terms also aid would be more readily acceptable domestically if it was seen to finance British goods and services. Successive statements, then and later, that Britain favoured an international agreement on the untying of aid reflected as much a calculation that Britain would, in balance of payments terms, be a net beneficiary, as it did any view that untied aid would be more beneficial to the recipient country.

After its creation the Department found itself subject to more formal tying rules than had obtained in the past. The use of aid for third party, foreign, imports became subject to scrutiny by the Board of Trade, later to become the Department for Trade and Industry (DTI). If Britain were 'uncompetitive' in the supply of certain goods and services there were two options; either the developing country or another donor might finance such imports, or if it were a relatively small element in a project a waiver might be granted so that British aid could fund them. The rules for such a waiver became progressively more elaborate and restrictive. In general the DTI were unimpressed with comparative delivery times and the importance of the recipient having standardised equipment which it could better operate and maintain. They also argued for a minimum 20 per cent price differential before agreeing that British aid should fund foreign goods. This led the Department generally to accept that aid should fund only British exports and when it did not there was often protracted correspondence within Whitehall on the issue of a waiver.

It was also the case that British goods provided under aid required a certificate from the supplier that the British content of its goods amounted to at least 80 per cent of their value. This particular requirement proved increasingly problematic; how did a supplier of widgets know what proportion of the value of the inputs it bought to manufacture them originated in Britain? And as Britain became part of an enlarged free trade area and a single market within the EU what was the relevance of this? Only very much later did the DTI accept that such calculations were both increasingly fictitious and irrelevant. Nevertheless, even in the early 1990s the DTI resisted the thought that the Department itself should be able to agree a waiver without DTI approval beyond the minimal sum of £20,000.

The Department, however, achieved a minor concession on untying in the run-up to the UNCTAD conference on the second Special

Programme of Action for the Least Developed Countries in Paris in 1990. Britain took a unilateral initiative to allow Least Developed Countries to procure goods and services financed by its bilateral aid from both Britain and other poor, low-income (not just Least Developed) countries. Although it was a minor concession for most Least Developed Countries it did mean it was more significant for Bangladesh which could use British aid for procurement of goods from India. It would seem that the DTI were not aware that Bangladesh fell within the UN category of Least Developed Countries at the time this concession was agreed. Equally, those in the Department responsible for managing bilateral aid to Bangladesh were for the most part unaware of this concession.

As regards the provision of local costs for projects, the Department only had to have the agreement of the Treasury. This reflected in part the DTI's particular concern that aid should not be seen to finance foreign goods lest it were thought that British industry was uncompetitive in certain areas, whereas the provision of local costs carried no such implication. The Treasury's early concern with the balance of payments led it to take a somewhat restrictive stance on the provision of local costs for aid-financed projects. Nevertheless, by the late 1970s it accepted that most poor countries (with the notable exception of India) needed local-cost finance for their public investments. Thus most aid agreements with countries in Africa, and Bangladesh in Asia, contained an acceptance that a significant proportion (up to 40–50 per cent) could be available for local costs. By the 1980s the Treasury accepted the view that with a floating currency the balance of payments tended towards a balance, and became less concerned with the provision of local costs. That said, the issue of local costs for India was a hard fought battle which was only conceded by other departments in the context of aid-debt forgiveness (see Chapter Five).

Technical co-operation was also generally tied to British consultants, the provision of British nationals as individual advisers, and training of developing country personnel in British institutions. Britain, like other donors, was conscious of the potential commercial advantage of such activities. Independent and professional British consultants would be more likely to design projects to British standards, and people trained in Britain would be more likely to favour British equipment after they returned home.

With the move to a single market within the EU the European Commission sought to argue that all bilateral aid provided by member states should be open to EU-wide procurement. As regards financial aid, the member states successfully resisted such moves, though the

Department itself would have been content. They had on their side the technicality that under financial aid it was the recipient-country institution that did the procurement, albeit closely supervised by the donor. However, by definition technical co-operation was procured by the donor. Within the EU this became subject to EU directives on procurement in a single market. These require member states to advertise EU-wide except for projects under about £90,000, which can be awarded without competition. It has also had the effect of considerably reducing the number of consultancy contracts for which the Department's spending divisions could successfully argue internally for a waiver of any competition on the grounds of urgency.

The provision of short-term programme aid for essential imports (capital and intermediate goods), which gradually evolved into longer-term sector-wide assistance programmes (SWAPS) and general budget support (see Chapter Five), presented new issues in relation to the tying of aid. Programme aid was given to countries in economic crisis, which agreed a programme of economic reform with the IMF. In most cases governments had introduced administered foreign exchange regimes in order to ration the limited amount of foreign currency available relative to demand. In this situation it was possible to identify specific end-users of foreign currency and their requirement for imports from Britain, and therefore tie the provision of programme aid to British exports. However one important objective of the economic reform programmes was progressively to restore a functioning foreign exchange market in which the exchange rate was determined by the supply of, and demand for, foreign currency. As such markets developed and rationing by governments declined it would have been counter-productive to seek to tie programme aid to the supply of particular British goods. The DTI reluctantly relaxed the tying rules in response to this. Initially it insisted that the recipient government obtain import documents showing that the value of imports of capital and intermediate goods from Britain at least equalled the amount of programme aid provided. Later it accepted that under the Special Programme for Africa, co-ordinated by the World Bank and to which Britain contributed with bilateral programme aid, an increasing percentage could be untied. It has to be said that in reality all programme aid to Africa was untied once foreign exchange markets were functioning again and by the early 1990s the percentage that remained formally tied was essentially a political fig-leaf for the DTI to satisfy its industry lobby. With the move to SWAPS and general budget support this element of the aid programme was both de facto and de jure provided as untied (that is, local cost) aid. Over time this meant that a large proportion of all financial aid had become untied. It made much easier Clare Short's case in 2000 for Britain unilaterally to untie all Britain's bilateral aid programmes.

The tying of aid by donors potentially reduces the real value of the aid provided – some studies have suggested by as much as 30 per cent.[95] However, much depends upon the way tied aid is managed by the donor and the freedom of action available to the recipient country. If a donor country makes a conscious effort to finance projects that require offshore inputs for which it is competitive the real value of tied aid may approach its nominal value. If on the other hand a donor country seeks to finance activities in which it lacks a competitive advantage the opposite will be the case. At the time that most of British financial aid was tied (except for local costs) there was the assumption that Britain's wide industrial base enabled it to finance most projects on a reasonably competitive basis. However the issue of developing country institutions standardising their plant and equipment from one or two sources made tying an important issue in itself. A responsible donor would avoid projects where tied aid would require the recipient to extend the range of plant and equipment it would have to manage in the future. Other donors might use tied aid to break into a new market not withstanding this consideration. An astute, price conscious recipient would seek to have donors finance projects with tied aid where they are competitive and whose plant and equipment they had already standardised on. The middle-income countries and others such as India which were much less dependent upon bilateral aid were in a stronger position in this regard. But some countries, heavily dependent upon aid and with only a limited number of donors, could not afford to be so discerning.

Before moving on to the Aid and Trade Provision (ATP), one should note two particular occasions when the use of bilateral aid was driven by commercial considerations. In the late 1970s the then Minister for Overseas Development, Judith Hart, agreed to bilateral aid being used to supply ships to India at a time when the shipbuilding industry in Britain was struggling to find sufficient exports to sustain output and employment. In the mid-1980s the Westland Helicopter Company was also struggling to find sufficient buyers to sustain its operations. The FCO/ODA were instructed to send telegrams to their Missions overseas to seek to identify potential buyers, supported by bilateral aid on the basis that the helicopters would not be for military purposes. Only India showed any interest, in relation to its development of offshore oil and natural gas supplies. Eventually India's offshore oil and natural gas corporation purchased a fleet of Westland helicopters for commercial use, financed by a substantial bilateral aid grant. Unfortunately the helicopters proved unsuitable and as a result of technical failures were grounded. The aid agreement between the Department and the government of India precluded their use for military purposes. Years later the Indian government decided to cannibalise the helicopters and sell them in the form of spare parts. They sought the agreement of the Department, recognising that they might be used by purchasers of the spare parts for military purposes. The Department eventually agreed that it would be unreasonable to object.

## The Aid and Trade Provision (ATP)

### Mixed credits

The ATP scheme was established in 1977 under the then Labour administration. Its introduction was a response to what the DTI saw as an aggressive use of aid by other donor countries to promote their exports, and it was abolished in 1997 by the incoming Labour administration at the insistence of Clare Short (see Chapter Four). Whereas most bilateral aid was provided on highly concessional terms on a stand-alone basis, some donors were providing an increasing amount of 'mixed credits' (or what the French called *credit mixte*). A mixed credit, as the name suggests, is a combination of an export credit on relatively hard terms and aid (on either highly concessional loan terms or in the form of a grant). The increasing use of this instrument by other OECD countries led British industry to complain that it was being put at a competitive disadvantage in terms of the export finance that was available to it via an ECGD-supported export credit. It also came at a time of renewed concern with the balance of payments for which the government was having to seek assistance from the IMF.

The original basis of the ATP was that a contingency provision should be available within the aid budget to enable the government to offer a mixed credit to match that of a competitor OECD country. Proposals for a mixed credit would be put forward by the DTI, usually on the basis of arguments by one or more British companies which were competing for business in a developing country, but were being disadvantaged by the (alleged) offer of a mixed credit by another OECD country. Such mixed credits usually carried a grant element of 25.1 per cent to keep within the rules of the Consensus (see above). In Britain's case this involved an export credit on standard terms amounting to 74.9 per cent of the export content of the contract being pursued, and an aid grant of 25.1 per cent. ATP began as a contingency provision, rather than a fixed allocation, within the aid budget, because of the uncertain demand for it given that it was intended to be only a matching facility. Initially ATP grants were, however, to be no more than 5 per cent of the bilateral aid programme. For the aid grant to count as official development assistance (oda) the project had, at least in theory, to be assessed as contributing towards the development of the developing country concerned.

Although Britain regarded itself as only matching the aggressive use of aid by others, some OECD countries did not see it in the same way. In particular, outside the francophone countries of Africa, France almost exclusively provided its financial aid in the form of mixed credits, which it argued were programmed with the developing country concerned in the same way as other donors' aid programmes. They regarded matching by Britain on an ad hoc basis as the aggressive use of aid; needless to say this was dismissed by the DTI with considerable derision. Japan presented a different challenge, which will be discussed below.

There were at least five players within Whitehall: the DTI, the ECGD (responsible to the DTI but with its own legislation and Accounting Officer), the Treasury, the FCO and the Department. At times other Whitehall departments that 'sponsored' particular sectors of British industry became involved.

The five Whitehall players each had their own role and motivation. The DTI's motivation was the promotion of British exports and its role was to listen to the case put forward by industry and make a proposal to an official inter-departmental committee on ATP (formally a subcommittee of the Joint Aid Policy Committee). A necessary condition for a mixed credit was that the ECGD regarded the country as sufficiently creditworthy to be 'on cover', that is, it was prepared to guarantee an export credit provided by a private bank. Within a short space of time this left few eligible poor countries: notably Botswana, Ghana and Kenya in Africa, and the countries of the Indian sub-continent – though, apart from India, ECGD cover was very restricted. ECGD cover for middle-income countries (such as China, Malaysia and Thailand in Asia, and Brazil and Mexico in South America) was more liberally available and these countries were of particular interest to British companies. The ECGD were also guardians in Whitehall of the Consensus rules.

The Treasury was concerned with value for money in its broadest sense. Its instincts were against subsidies, which is how it viewed ATP. It tended to argue against mixed credit proposals which would largely exhaust the ECGD cover limit for a country on the grounds that it was likely to crowd out other export credit business on standard terms. One might add that it also generally argued for lower ECGD cover limits for developing countries on account of the credit risk involved and because in the early days ECGD provided the banks with fixed rate export finance (FREF) which generally required a substantial government subsidy.

In 1982 the Treasury's Deputy Chief Economist, Ian Byatt, chaired a group of Whitehall economists, including from the Department, to produce a report on export subsidies. It concluded, in accordance with established economic theory, that it was better to leave other OECD countries to provide export subsidies in certain areas and for British industry to focus its export efforts elsewhere. Matching others' subsidies only made sense if they were temporary and as a result they could be persuaded to desist. This report was not published for several years though it became common knowledge and was rubbished by the DTI and industry as lacking any understanding of the real world.

The Treasury also sought to make the DTI put forward an economic case for each ATP proposal. This the DTI found difficult to do and to be fair to them it was in economic terms virtually impossible if one accepted the Byatt Report conclusions. However the Treasury also wished to see ATP used in markets in which it might enhance the prospects for future business on commercial terms rather than encourage countries to believe they could always expect ATP support in future. The FCO, on the other hand, generally supported proposals for the use of ATP.

The Department's role was to assess the 'developmental value' of any proposal and to seek to impose a budgetary discipline for ATP to avoid it taking up an increasing amount of bilateral aid. Both presented considerable challenges. The phrase 'developmental value', which gained currency, proved to be unfortunate. The DTI and industry thought it smacked of value judgements by do-gooders, and second-guessed what a sovereign developing country had decided to do in its own interests. In fact, the Department had a well-established investment appraisal methodology (see Chapter Five), consistent with that applied in principle to British public investments, accepted more or less within the international community, and by many developing country governments, or at least their professional staff.

The Department faced a number of difficulties in appraising potential ATP projects. First, it was commonly asked to make an assessment against a short deadline: DTI and industry tended to argue for the need for a rapid matching offer of mixed credit finance to be made, even though it was often difficult to establish whether or not a competitor had made a mixed credit offer. Furthermore, decisions by the developing country concerned in practice often took a very long time despite pressure by the DTI and British companies for an urgent decision.

The other main problem was access to adequate information. With some exceptions the Department did not have much first-hand knowledge of the country and sector concerned, and its investment options (that is, in the middle-income creditworthy countries). It was difficult to establish a dialogue with a developing country, unlike for other projects for which they were seeking aid as part of a regular, ongoing aid programme. The British company bidding for a contract had little information itself other than the estimated capital cost of the project. Thus in the early years of ATP the Department made hurried judgements on the basis of inadequate data.

The result was that the Department tended to approve ATP projects unless there were strong arguments to the contrary. On those occasions when the Department did feel it had a sufficient basis for opposing an ATP project proposal, either the project fell off the radar screen because of indecision by the developing country, or the DTI contested the Department's assessment. The latter often resulted in the case being referred to ministers. The Pergau Dam case will be discussed later, but other less notable cases arose from time to time when the Department was usually also over-ruled. Two cases are worth recording.

In the case of an Indonesian chemical plant project the Department's officials concluded that it had at best a 2 per cent rate of return, well below Indonesia's own hurdle rate for public investments of about 10 per cent. A ministerial meeting was called to discuss the matter, chaired by the then Lord Privy Seal at the FCO. The meeting was notable for one particular reason. The then Minister for Overseas Development, the Rt Hon Neil Martin MP (the first ODA Minister under Mrs Thatcher) said that he was an old-fashioned Tory who believed in the rule of law, and that under the Overseas Development Co-operation Act (1980) he was only empowered to approve funds for activities which he believed would promote the development of the country concerned and this proposal did not fall into that category. Nevertheless, the decision went against the Department, though the project never went ahead.

The other example worth recording was in relation to a proposed coal-fired thermal power station in Nigeria that was put forward by the DTI in the mid-1980s. The Department argued that the investment was inferior to capturing the gas being flared by Nigeria's oil industry and installing gas-fired turbines. This case was referred to ministers and eventually to the Prime Minister. Mrs Thatcher, much to the surprise of the Department, ruled in its favour and ATP support was not provided; though to what extent this was influenced by Nigeria being governed by a military dictatorship at the time is difficult to say.

The debate in Whitehall on ATP in the 1980s can best be described as guerrilla warfare. The Treasury contested most proposals on value for money grounds, often supported by the Department. This did not deter the DTI from pressing proposals, with the ECGD often being caught in the middle. The situation worsened as the DTI argued for initiating mixed credit offers to pre-empt the competition that it was convinced either would emerge or which had already given informal indications of support to the developing country. The Treasury fought such proposals: despite the Byatt Report it had concluded that the best way to contain the DTI's ambitions was to insist on only matching others, thereby containing to some extent the credit race. This led, on occasions, to a mixed credit being offered on the conditional basis that another country made such an offer. But this had the effect of encouraging the developing country to seek out other offers of mixed credits and exacerbating the credit race.

As explained above, the Consensus rules set the minimum level of concessionality for a tied aid credit (whether mixed credit or other tied aid finance) at 25 per cent. It also required a country offering a tied aid credit to give prior notification of its intention to do so. This was intended to help create transparency and allowed another country to indicate that it intended to match such an offer. Over-matching (that is, offering a tied aid credit with a higher concessionality) was not permitted. However, British industry, supported by the DTI, often argued that it had intelligence through its commercial contacts that a competitor country had made an informal offer despite it not having been pre-notified, and that therefore Britain should initiate its own offer. It was this that led to much further argument within Whitehall.

### Soft loans

By 1981 the DTI had become increasingly concerned with the 'threat' to British exports from Japanese aid loans, particularly in Asia. At this time Japan had committed itself to an expanding aid programme. Although some of its financial aid to the poorest countries, particularly in Africa, was on grant terms, the bulk of its aid was in the form of 'soft' aid loans. Most of these were tied to Japanese procurement, though during the 1980s Japan progressively provided an increasing proportion which was formally untied. This however did not impress a cynical DTI and British industry which were convinced that through informal means Japanese companies would continue to gain business. The DTI were particularly concerned about the growing volume of Japanese soft aid loans to countries such as Indonesia, Malaysia, Thailand and China. They felt that the mixed credit instrument available under ATP was not effective in matching Japanese soft aid loans which had a much longer maturity (25–30 years compared with a repayment period for a typical mixed credit of 7–10 years). There was also a concern that a typical Japanese aid loan in Asia nominated in yen carried an interest in the range of 1–3 per cent, which was little below what the Japanese government could itself borrow at.

In addition, there was evidence that some countries, particularly those accustomed to Japanese aid, preferred long-term soft loans rather than a mixed credit, with the same level of concessionality. Indonesia, for example, under a Presidential Decree, would only accept long-term concessional loan finance for its so-called priority projects. China also expressed a preference for long-term soft loans, though it later realised that mixed credits involved a subsidy in respect of the export credit element which was not reflected in the grant element calculation.

This led the DTI to propose a long-term soft loan facility under ATP to compete more effectively with the Japanese. Like the French, with their *credit mixte*, the Japanese complained that their soft aid loans were part of their normal aid budget and programmed in advance on a country basis. They did not resort to matching other donors' offers of aid.

Soft loans would be made available by British private banks backed by an ECGD guarantee. The novelty was two-fold. First, the loans would be repayable over 20 to 30 years and the interest would generally be 3 per cent, well below the internationally agreed export credit interest rate which the ECGD supported through its fixed-rate export finance scheme (say 7 per cent for purposes of illustration). The difference between 3 per cent and 7 per cent needed to come from the ATP budget. There were two options for doing this. First, the 4 per cent interest differential on the loan amount outstanding could be provided annually to the banks (via the ECGD) on the over the life of the loan (the interest top-up option). This would be relatively undemanding on the ATP budget in the short term but if the government were to continue making new soft loan commitments each year the amounts of interest subsidy required of ATP would progressively increase and the budget would be increasingly mortgaged for many years ahead.

The other option was to provide lump sum payments to the banks over the construction period of the project (and the draw-down period of the loan) which was the time over which exports were being realised. The banks would invest such funds to create a future stream of income equivalent to the interest rate subsidy required. This meant ATP payments typically over three to five years, depending upon the nature of the project. Clearly for any given ATP budget allocation many fewer soft loan commitments could be entered into in the short term.

The reader, like the author, might well take the view that the latter option was the responsible approach to the management of public expenditure. The Department certainly took that view, as did the Treasury until the last minute. The DTI were relaxed about which option should be adopted, provided that the ATP budget was appropriately enhanced. The soft loan scheme was being discussed in Whitehall during 1985 in the run-up to the Public Expenditure Survey (PES) which would agree the Department's aid budget for the three years 1986/87 to 1988/89. The Department was arguing for an increase in its total aid budget to pursue its basic mission, and that any increase in ATP to finance soft loans should be additional to that. While the Treasury was confident in containing the overall size of the aid budget for other purposes it realised that it would be politically difficult for it to avoid providing additional funds to finance ATP soft loans, and the DTI would resist a reduction in mixed credit activity to accommodate them within the existing ATP budget. On the eve of the PES settlement at official level the Treasury announced it had been converted to the first, pay as you go (interest top-up) option for soft loans. This required only a modest increase in ATP funds over the Survey period but stored up increasing problems for the future. The Treasury insisted that the soft loan scheme should be for only five years, before the end of which there should be a review, and that the annual commitment of soft loans could build up over the first three years to £250 million annually and remain at that level until 1990/91. It was also agreed that, in principle, soft loans would be available to all developing countries eligible for ATP support where there was ECGD medium-term cover, although it was recognised that Indonesia and China would be the main recipients. Soft loans were to be used instead of mixed credits only where they would be clearly more effective in winning contracts.

The author's professional experience of the Treasury is limited to the aid budget and related issues such as export credit and debt, albeit over many years. The decision by the Treasury was undoubtedly the most irresponsible approach to public expenditure the author has witnessed. The senior official in the Treasury who announced this about-turn was visibly uncomfortable with the message he had to relay, as indeed was the Department. It should be added that the Foreign Secretary, Sir Geoffrey (now Lord) Howe, and a former Chancellor of the Exchequer, wrote opposing the Treasury's decision, but to no avail.

The three priority target countries agreed for soft loans were China, Indonesia and India. Some form of government-to-government umbrella agreement was considered for each of these countries. For China, a £300 million soft loan agreement was signed in May 1986 and, in September 1988, an agreement for a further £300 million was signed, though this covered both soft loans and mixed credits. In July 1986 a £140 million soft loan agreement was signed for Indonesia and a further £100 million was agreed in 1988. The government also gave a commitment to the Government of India, to provide sufficient ATP, whether in soft loan or mixed credit form, to finance £300 million of UK business over five years: a formal agreement as such was not considered necessary.

The review of soft loans was carried out by a Whitehall committee of officials, chaired by the Department, which reported in August 1989. The budgeted costs for soft loans for the five years compared to actual expenditure at that time was as follows:

*Table 9.1*   Soft loan budgeted costs (£ million)

|          | 1986/87 | 1987/88 | 1988/89 | 1989/90 | 1990/91 |
|----------|---------|---------|---------|---------|---------|
| Budget   | 3       | 10      | 20      | 20      | 32      |
| Out-turn | –       | 7       | 7       |         |         |

At the time the Report was being drawn up £400 million of soft loans had been committed in the first three years of life of the scheme, against a forecast of £562 million and a total agreed for five years of £1062 million. Even without further new soft loan commitments beyond 1990/91 the original projections showed ATP interest payments peaking at £45 million in 1995/96 and still amounting to £20 million in 2005/06.

The Report calculated the present value subsidy cost to the government of mixed credits and soft loans, using the two alternative financing methods (annual interest top-up, and lump sum payments over the draw-down period of the loan). This showed that, for any particular grant element level, mixed credits were the most economical form of finance and for soft loans that the pay as you go (interest top-up) method for soft loans was more costly than the lump sum method. The Report accepted that there had been occasions when the availability of soft loans was decisive in winning export business. It concluded that if soft loan commitments were to continue beyond 1990/91 then:

i.  the presumption in favour of mixed credits should continue, with soft loan financing only being offered where it would clearly be more effective in securing business; and

ii. if support for soft loans were continued, the 'lump sum' method of financing them would be more economical, and would be a more responsible approach to managing public expenditure.

One advantage of the soft loans to China and Indonesia was that umbrella agreements were established and discussions were held about which projects might be financed. This resulted in a more orderly dialogue though, particularly in the case of China, the DTI became frustrated by an agreed list of possible projects which precluded them from pursuing other business opportunities.

**Restricting the international credit race and reform of ATP**

The gradual reform of ATP had politically to be pursued in parallel with internationally agreed disciplines. Discussions with the OECD were taken forward on two fronts, in the Consensus and the DAC. In 1983 the DAC agreed 'Guiding Principles on the use of Associated Financing'. Associated Financing was the polite term for mixed credits, or for more devious arrangements by which a country might offer an export credit for one project on the understanding that it would provide concessional aid for another.

The terms of the DAC Agreement were a mild approach to trying to secure a more effective use of aid. It encouraged sound projects, a higher grant element for poorer countries, limited use of aid in the stronger middle-income countries, and good value for money for the recipients. At a later date the Guidelines were strengthened to provide for consultations within the DAC concerning the development appraisal of individual projects, though this never became a strong feature in the efforts to achieve greater disciplines.

Within the Consensus a battle was fought to both increase the minimum level of concessionality from 25 per cent to 35 per cent, and to change the method of calculating the concessionality, both of which were agreed in 1987. The latter was aimed at those countries with low-interest currencies. Instead of using the DAC-standard 10 per cent discount rate the concessionality of each tied aid credit offer was to be calculated by reference to the cost of borrowing by the donor country concerned – the commercial interest reference rate (CIRR). It was aimed primarily at Japan, who complained that whereas the CIRR was typically the rate at which a donor government might borrow over five to 10 years their soft loans had a maturity of 20 to 30 years. The effect of this agreement was that the real cost of tied aid credit for countries such as Japan would become much greater. This undoubtedly encouraged

Japan formally to untie a larger proportion of its soft loans, though the DTI also challenged decisions by a developing country to award a contract to Japan under an untied soft loan when it thought it had evidence that a British bid was more competitive. In agreeing this change members of the DAC agreed not to seek to change the method of calculating the grant element for oda purposes.

The real breakthrough, internationally, came with the Helsinki Agreement, jointly negotiated in both the Consensus and the DAC and agreed at an OECD Ministerial meeting in 1992. The Agreement sought to achieve much harder-edged disciplines that would prevent a continued credit race in the stronger middle-income countries which diverted the use of oda from the poorer countries. It also sought to ensure a higher minimum level of grant element for tied aid credits in low-income countries.

The new disciplines applied to all tied aid credit transactions of special drawing rights of SDR2 million and above, and with a grant element of less than 80 per cent. The key provisions of the Agreement were:

i. except for the UN category of Least Developed Countries a tied aid credit shall not be extended to public or private projects that normally should be commercially viable if financed on market or Consensus terms;
ii. there shall be no tied aid credit to countries whose per capita income would make them ineligible for 17- or 20-year loans from the World Bank;
iii. the minimum grant element for a tied aid credit to a Least Developed Country shall be 50 per cent.

The first provision proved particularly difficult to negotiate, not least because different OECD countries even in 1992 still had rather varied views within their own economies as to which public investments should be commercially viable. There was little dissent from the idea that the telecommunications sector should be commercially viable and, with somewhat less enthusiasm, that the power sector should be likewise. There would be arguments in the future about other physical infrastructure projects. The Agreement states that the key tests for aid eligibility are:

- whether the project is financially non-viable, that is, does the project lack capacity with appropriate pricing determined on market principles, to generate cash flow sufficient to cover the project's operating costs and to service the capital employed, or

- whether it is reasonable to conclude, based on communication with other participants, that it is unlikely that the project can be financed on market or Arrangement terms.

The Agreement provided for consultation in such cases and the need for a common line to be adopted, which would also build up a body of experience over time. In the absence of a general agreement that a project should be eligible for aid, if a donor country still wished to make an offer it had to write a formal letter to the Secretary General of the OECD explaining that 'the over-riding non-trade related national interest that forms this action. The participants expect that such an occurrence will be unusual and infrequent'.

It should be appreciated that the intention was not to prevent poorer countries receiving aid for commercially viable projects: indeed it would have been perverse to do so. Poor countries could receive tied aid with a concessionality over 80 per cent for such projects or possibly aid on harder terms if that aid was untied. Making Least Developed Countries exempt was an unfortunate political necessity to achieve an agreement, though few such countries at that time would have been deemed sufficiently creditworthy to have been offered a mixed credit or tied aid on semi-concessional terms.

The second provision meant that developing countries with a per capita income of over $2465 in 1990 would be ineligible for such tied aid credits. This excluded the upper-middle-income countries such as Brazil, Malaysia and Mexico, which had often been seen as attractive and relatively creditworthy markets in which to pursue export business, if necessary on terms softened by aid which they did not need.

The Helsinki Agreement took a long time to negotiate as it went to the heart of the credit race. It proved rather more effective than some had dared to hope. Much of the credit race was by definition in the stronger markets (some of which were now ineligible for such support) and generally in sectors where it was now argued that investments should be commercially viable – even if the developing country wished to pursue a different policy. It substantially reduced the scope for offering tied aid credits on semi-concessional terms to win export business, and thereby reduced the diversion of aid budgets away from the poorest countries that needed it most.

The Helsinki Agreement paved the way for a Whitehall review of ATP in 1992. The Department, rather opportunistically, took the opportunity of the DTI having a perceived free-market minded Secretary of State during the Conservative administration between 1979 and 1997, namely the Rt Hon Peter Lilley MP. The review was initiated by the then Foreign Secretary, agreed by ministers including the Prime Minister, and conducted by an official committee chaired by the Department. It was the first comprehensive and thorough review since the ATP scheme was established 15 years earlier.

The review considered the benefits to the UK economy, and British industry in particular, and to developing countries against the costs, including the opportunity cost of using aid in this way rather than pursuing more directly the Department's stated mission. By 1991/92 the ATP budget was taking up nearly 10 per cent of the Department's total bilateral aid budget. The report considered three options: abolition of ATP; continuation of the scheme similar in scope to the existing one; and a scheme more closely focused on particular low-income countries. It recommended the last of these on the following basis:

Under option (iii) ATP would be focused on those lower income, but moderately creditworthy, countries which need concessional aid resources for their development and could use it effectively, and with which the UK has important political and economic relations. Government to government umbrella agreements, possibly specifying amounts (consistent with ECGD constraints), could provide the basis for managing ATP in each country. Ministers would keep under review those countries considered to be eligible for ATP. If ATP were made a more effective aid instrument, less significance need be attached to its domestic economic effects to justify its continuation.

The argument for this option is that because ATP represents an integral part of the overseas aid programme and is now a significant part of total bilateral aid, and because its costs cannot be justified solely in terms of the economic benefits to the UK, ATP expenditure should more effectively contribute towards other objectives of the aid programme in order to justify its continuation. This argues for focusing ATP on those lower-income, but moderately creditworthy, countries which need concessional aid resources for their development, can use it effectively, and with which the UK has important political and economic relations.

The report was considered by Ministers, and Lady Chalker, Minister of State for Overseas Development, made the following statement to Parliament in 1993 in answer to a Parliamentary Question from Lord Orr-Ewing:

The Government has concluded its review of the Aid and Trade Provision (ATP). It has decided that the scheme should continue. It will help finance sound projects that will contribute to sustainable development and which are of particular industrial and commercial importance to Britain. The ATP budget for 1993/94 of £110 million will be enhanced by £7 million subject to Parliamentary approval. The scheme will in future focus on creditworthy low income (income per head under $700) developing countries.

There will be a transitional period during which a few projects already at an advanced stage of consideration, which would not be eligible under the revised scheme, will exceptionally be taken forward. The selection of projects under the revised scheme will take account of the new OECD rules governing the use of tied aid which came into force in 1992. Specific measures to improve the effectiveness of ATP and achieve better value for money will be implemented immediately.

This revised scheme will provide a clearer framework for industry within which companies should be able to obtain an early indication of the prospects for ATP funding for individual projects.[96]

## The Pergau Dam Affair

This chapter would be incomplete without a reference to the Pergau Hydro-electric Dam Project in Malaysia, one of the largest projects for which ATP support was agreed. This is because it not only demonstrates the problems of managing ATP but most importantly because it is the only occasion when the use of aid funds has been challenged in the courts and declared to be illegal.

The issue arose in 1988 in the same way that most ATP projects began: a British firm was seeking a negotiated contract to build the Pergau Dam with the state-owned Malaysian electricity authority and sought ATP funds to soften its financing terms, initially through a mixed credit arrangement. The DTI supported the use of ATP and put the proposal to the Department in late 1988. However, it had earlier emerged that a Protocol had been signed in March 1988 between the then Secretary of State for Defence, Lord Younger, and the Malaysian government concerning potential defence contracts amounting to some £1 billion which also mentioned the giving of British aid of some £200 million.

This was drawn to the notice of the then Foreign Secretary, Sir Geoffrey (now Lord) Howe, who required such a link between arms sales and aid to be withdrawn. In June 1988 Lord Younger wrote to the Malaysian government explaining that there could be no link between arms sales and the provision of aid. However, this letter was delivered to the relevant Malaysian minister on 28 June by the British High Commissioner who simultaneously delivered a letter from himself which contained a general offer of ATP for other projects. A formal Memorandum of Understanding on arms sales between the British and Malaysian governments was signed subsequently, making no reference to aid.

The Department made a preliminary assessment of the Pergau Dam project and advised the DTI to take a cautious approach given the size of the project and because the economics might at best be marginal, and making it clear that further information would be necessary to undertake an appraisal. In January 1989 the British consortium (comprising Balfour Beatty and Cementation) put in a revised cost estimate of £316 million in cash prices with a UK content of £195 million. In March 1989 the Department sent an appraisal mission to Malaysia which lasted for only two days. An earlier report by the World Bank in 1987 had noted Pergau as a possible hydro-electric site but had concluded that Malaysia should concentrate on gas-fired electricity generation until the turn of the (20th) century. An earlier consultancy report by consultants Snowy Mountains Engineering Corporation had identified Pergau as a site for a 600 megawatt project at an estimate cost of £140–150 million at 1986 prices. In constant price terms the £316 million price tag was 50 per cent higher than the Snowy Mountains estimate, though there were thought to be some offsetting savings from lower transmission costs. The brief appraisal visit, which did not have access to Malaysia's own model for determining the least cost programme for future electricity generation development, concluded that the economics were marginal at the price estimated by the Consortium.

An oral report to this effect was made on the mission's return and conveyed to No. 10, as Prime Minister Thatcher was meeting the Malaysian Prime Minister in London the following day, 15 March 1989. At this meeting Thatcher made an oral offer of an ATP grant of £68.5 million, this being 35 per cent of the estimated UK content of the project.

On 31 March 1989 the Consortium informed the DTI and the Department that their price estimate had risen to £397 million. The DTI and the Department expected that this price might be reduced in subsequent negotiations between the contracting parties and therefore in April 1989 a formal offer of an ATP grant was made of £68.5 million based on the earlier price estimate, valid for six months. Further assessment by the Department concluded by February 1990 that the project was uneconomic at the higher price and would be a 'very bad buy' and a burden on Malaysian consumers. The Department concluded that Pergau should be deferred by nine years or possibly indefinitely. Nevertheless, the ATP offer was renewed in April 1990, still on the basis of the earlier price estimate of £316 million.

In October 1990 the ATP was not renewed pending a DTI/Department survey of the Malaysian power sector. As a result of this review, at which time the Department did have access to Malaysia's own corporate model for determining a least cost generation development programme, it concluded that Pergau would be an uneconomic investment until 2005 at the earliest, and if it did proceed in the immediate future it would cost Malaysia £100 million more in electricity costs over 35 years compared with a less expensive alternative (that is, gas turbines). Nevertheless, in December 1990 the Malaysian government confirmed that they would proceed with Pergau and issued a contract award letter to the Consortium in January 1991 setting a price ceiling of £417 million, which included an increase over £397 million to cover an increase in the ECGD's insurance premium and taxation of expatriate staff.

As was the case of negotiated contracts rather than competitive bidding situations the Department had earlier introduced price investigations to assess the reasonableness of a company's price, looking at how the price was constructed. For Pergau this was first done in May 1989 based on the earlier price of £316 million: the Department was satisfied that the pricing structure was reasonable and appropriate. In January 1991 a second price investigation was carried out which concluded that the revised price had been constructed reasonably, bearing in mind the risks involved in construction.

Faced with the letter of award of contract by Malaysia, the Permanent Secretary, Sir Tim Lankester, as the Department's Accounting Officer, had to decide what advice finally to put to Ministers. The Accounting Officer's Memorandum, amongst other things, required him to consider whether the proposed use of public funds voted by Parliament meets two important tests. First, that it would not be irregular or improper use of such funds (that is, it would not be illegal under the legislation under which ministers exercised their powers) and, second, that it would not constitute an imprudent and uneconomic use of public funds. On these matters the Accounting Officer consulted the Principal Finance Officer (that is, the author). On the second issue he advised that the project, at the price negotiated, was clearly uneconomic, and in terms of the Accounting Officer's Memorandum would be an imprudent and uneconomical use of aid funds. He advised that in his experience the Pergau project was a clear-cut case of bad value for money. Some projects were not readily subject to quantitative analysis and there might be a range of conflicting considerations, both quantitative and qualitative, that had to be brought to bear. In such cases, and where the balance of judgement was a marginal one, the Accounting Officer's advice not to proceed might be rejected by ministers without prudent and economical administration being called into question. Pergau, in his view, was not such a case. He advised the Accounting Officer to draw the relevant factors to the attention of the Minister, to refer to the possibility of criticism by the Public Accounts Committee, and to ensure that if his advice was overruled that the advice and its overruling were apparent clearly from the papers.

As to whether the use of aid funds would raise questions of impropriety and regularity (that is, be illegal) he advised that according to the methodology the Department had developed for assessing aid projects one might contest whether Pergau would contribute to the development of Malaysia because of cheaper alternatives, and therefore whether the financing of it would be ultra vires the 1980 Overseas Development and Co-operation Act. He believed, however, that it would be a difficult position to sustain in legal terms for a project which was likely to be successfully implemented and produce electricity for which there was expected to be demand. His view was that it would be important that the Secretary of State, in exercising his powers under the Act, had in his mind that the project would benefit Malaysia in terms set out in Section 1 of the Act (see Chapter 3). On this basis he would not advise that expenditure on Pergau infringed the requirements of propriety and regularity so long as Treasury authority was obtained and proper Estimates provision taken. This advice was tendered, it has to be said, without taking legal opinion.

In the light of this advice the Permanent Secretary advised the Minister, then the Rt Hon Lynda Chalker, in his minute of 5 February 1991, that the provision of aid funds for Pergau would not be consistent with his responsibility to ensure that aid funds were administered in a prudent and economical manner and that he would wish to have an instruction from the Minister or from the Secretary of State, then the Rt Hon Sir Douglas (now Lord) Hurd, if the Department were to incur expenditure on the project. This advice was also put to the Secretary of State in a minute of 7 February. The Secretary of State, after considering Sir Tim

Lankester's views and subsequent interdepartmental discussion, including consultation with the then Prime Minister, the Rt Hon John Major MP, in July 1991 decided that the project should go ahead, most importantly because of the commitment given by Thatcher when Prime Minister. The irony is that by this stage the DTI had come out in favour of gas turbines rather than build a dam, which they saw as primarily 'muck-shifting'.

The Secretary of State later set down his own reasons for his decision more fully to the Public Accounts and Foreign Affairs Select Committees that considered the matter. He had always viewed Pergau as a development project. He had felt strongly that the commitment of the then Prime Minister Thatcher, given in 1998, should be honoured. He was also conscious of Britain's commercial and political relations with Malaysia and in particular the importance of seeking to expand trade opportunities following the earlier Malaysian policy of buy British last, which was first invoked when Britain substantially increased fees for foreign students coming to Britain in the early 1980s, for which Malaysia was a major source.

Both Select Committees issued critical reports in 1994: the PAC[97] on issues of value for money, and the FAC[98] on wider issues including the (temporary) link between aid and arms that occurred in 1988. The PAC, while agreeing with the Accounting Officer's judgement, criticised the Department for its handling of the project, including its late and inadequate appraisal and agreeing to renew offers of ATP despite its growing concerns. It also strongly criticised the Department for changing the ATP support from a mixed credit to a long-term soft loan, with annual interest top-up payments over its life. The general policy with regard to the use of soft loans, reaffirmed in the 1992 Review, was that they should only be used where it was considered essential to secure the business (notably in Indonesia and China) because the public expenditure cost was higher in present value terms. In this case it was decided to offer a soft loan with a life of 15 years because the ATP budget could not absorb the upfront costs of a mixed credit. The extra present value cost was estimated to be up to £56 million. The PAC thought the Department should have approached the Treasury to find a way for the least cost option to be chosen. (In practice the Treasury would have been likely to ask the Department to find the funds from within its overall aid budget.) In Parliament the Opposition were critical and unhappy with the extent of ministerial disclosures in answers to Parliamentary Questions and in debates, which they regarded as insufficient.

The Foreign Affairs Select Committee focused first on the link created between aid and defence by the protocol signed by the Secretary of State for Defence. They criticised the lack of consultation with the

FCO in London, particularly on 'such a sensitive issue as a conditional link between development aid and defence sales which was contrary to stated Government policy'. They were also critical of the steps taken to break this link and concluded that the letters sent to the Malaysian government in 1998 had both the 'aim and effect . . . to assure the Malaysian Government that the arms deal and an aid package would nevertheless proceed in parallel'.

They recognised the 'moral obligation' created by the Prime Minister's offer made in 1998 (and the subsequent confirmation of that offer) but were critical of the consortium for pressing for such an offer based on misleading information on the expected price of the project.

On the ATP scheme more generally, they welcomed the decisions announced by ministers in 1993 following the Review of ATP, though they recommended that the income per head ceiling of $700 for countries to be eligible for ATP should be increased.

The NGO community were also heavily critical of Pergau and opposed the use of aid funds for it. The World Development Movement (WDM) decided to challenge it in the Courts and in June 1994 obtained leave to seek judicial review. The Court ruled that WDM had an interest in the outcome of its application which itself was a precedent given it had no direct financial or other material interest in Pergau proceeding – they were not just 'busy bodies or cranks'. The Court then ruled that the Secretary of State had acted illegally in terms of the 1980 Act:

> It was for the court to decide whether the conduct was or was not within the statutory purpose. If Parliament had intended to confer a power to disburse money for an unsound developmental purpose it could have been expected to say so expressly . . . Successive ministers, guidelines, governments and White Papers over the years and without exception have construed the power under the Act as relating to economically sound development . . . The fact that the dam met the need for electricity begged the question of where there was need for energy to be generated at substantially greater cost than by other means, and the Malaysian government's determination to go ahead with the scheme does not advance the argument. Accordingly, whereas here the contemplated development is on the evidence so economically unsound that there is no economic argument in its favour it is not . . . possible to draw any distinction between questions of propriety and regularity on the one hand and questions of economy and efficiency of public expenditure on the other.

The Secretary of State is . . . fully entitled when making decisions to take account of political and commercial considerations . . . had there in 1991 been a developmental promotion within Section 1 of the 1980 Act it would have been entirely proper for the Foreign Secretary to take account also of the impact which withdrawing the 1989 offer would have had . . . on political and commercial relations with Malaysia . . . but on the evidence before the Court . . . there was in July 1991 no such purpose within the Section. It follows that the July 1991 decision was . . . unlawful.

The government decided not to appeal against the Court's ruling but preferred to let the matter rest rather than continue to draw attention to it. However, in the *Public Law* journal of Spring 1996, Lord Irvine QC, then Shadow Attorney General, published an article, 'Judges and Decision Makers: the Theory and Practice of Wednesbury Review'. This was a wide-ranging review of the state of judicial review and the principle on which it is based. In the article Lord Irvine turned to the Pergau judgement and argued that while 'on the strong facts the Secretary of State might well have acted perversely had he decided that the development was sound, but in principle this primary factual judgement should have been for the decision-maker not the court . . . The soundness of development in the context of an overseas aid statute requires evaluation and that should be for the Secretary of State not the court'. The implication was that in his view an appeal might well have been successful.

WDM had also sought to have the aid programme compensated for past and future expenditure on Pergau but the court concluded that that was a matter for government. Having reviewed other ongoing ATP projects in the light of the Court's ruling the Department concluded that three other projects might be questioned under the new ATP guidelines introduced following the 1992 Review. This was confirmed by the Secretary of State during the Parliamentary debate of 13 December 1994. The government refused to provide additional aid in respect of past expenditure of £24 million but did agree to find expenditure from elsewhere for all four projects in 1994/95 and 1995/96 (£65.5 million), those being years for which the size of the aid programme had already been determined. It in fact came from the Treasury's Central Reserve to augment ECGD's budget. For a personal account of the Pergau dam affair see Sir Timothy Lancaster's own monograph.[99]

## Conclusion

The guerrilla warfare of the 1980s gave way to a relatively orderly and more responsible period after 1992, before ATP was finally abolished in 1997. The Helsinki Agreement proved far more effective than many expected in introducing discipline into the international credit race, particularly by largely excluding major sectors with substantial capital projects and increasing the cost of subsidising exports in the poorest countries. The Helsinki Agrement paved the way for Whitehall agreement on ATP that focused support on the poorest countries, together with more responsible project appraisal. By the time it was abolished in 1997 the worst excesses had been ended. The Pergau Dam affair had played an important part in all this.

# 10
# Aid Volume

## Introduction

This chapter seeks to demystify the term aid and to explain the internationally agreed UN targets for capital flows to developing countries. It will explain the definition of official development assistance (oda) which most people think of as aid, not least because the UN target for aid of 0.7 per cent of Gross National Product (GNP) (and since 2000 Gross National Income [GNI]) is set in terms of net oda. Important changes in the definition of oda, particularly over the last two decades, will also be traced. Britain's official net oda performance since the Department was created in 1964 will be set out, and compared with that of other DAC donors.

There are important differences between official capital flows to developing countries reported to, and published by, the DAC as oda and other official flows (oof), and the size of the aid budget and outturn expenditure announced to Parliament by the government, not only because the former is published on a calendar year basis while the latter is on a financial year basis (ending 31 March). These differences will be explained, as will the concept of Britain's Gross Public Expenditure on development (GPEX).

## UN targets for resource transfers to developing countries

### The 1 per cent target for total net resource flows

In 1960 the UN General Assembly launched the First Development Decade and in that context adopted a resolution that net total official and private resource transfers from the industrialised countries to the developing countries should be at least 1 per cent of their gross national income annually. In the five years prior to 1964 Britain's total net resource flows had exceeded this target but failed to meet it in the rest of the 1960s. In 1968 UNCTAD passed a further resolution that the 1 per cent target should relate to GNP at market prices and agreed by the DAC. GNP at market prices is in general higher than gross national income, which made the 1 per cent target more demanding.

### The UN 0.7 per cent aid target

In 1968 The Rt Hon L. E. Pearson, former Canadian Prime Minister, accepted an invitation from Robert McNamara, the then President of the World Bank, to chair a Commission on International Development. It reported in September 1969.[100] Its purpose was to review the experience of 20 years of development assistance, assess the results, clarify the errors, and propose policies which would work better in the future. Much of the Commission's work relating to development issues remains pertinent today, but the focus here is on its recommendations on future resource transfers to developing countries.

The Pearson Commission's first recommendation was that each industrialised country should as a minimum meet the already agreed 1 per cent target for total resource flows 'as rapidly as possible and in no case later than 1975'.

However the Commission realised that the 1 per cent target made no distinction between private flows on commercial terms and official flows whether on quasi-commercial or concessional terms. Official flows were within the control of donor governments, unlike private flows, and potentially more predictable. It argued that developing countries needed more concessional flows to avoid future debt problems. It noted however that oda (see below for definitions), having reached a peak for DAC countries as a whole of 0.51 per cent of GNP in 1961 had fallen back to only 0.39 per cent in 1968. The Commission recommended that each donor should reach net oda disbursements of 0.7 per cent of GNP 'by 1975 or shortly thereafter, but in no case later than 1980'.

As indicated in Chapter Five, in the 1960s the 1 per cent target had some academic backing based on the early growth models. Professor Hollis Chenery[101] calculated a savings gap for developing countries necessary to achieve 5 per cent growth in GDP of some $10 billion, roughly 1 per cent of OECD countries' GNP. The 0.7 per cent aid target had more to do with actual aid flows in the 1960s and what was considered to be politically feasible.

The relevance of the 0.7 per cvent target today is that it remains something the international community can use as a barometer of a political willingness to help developing countries make economic and social progress. Its weakness is that most development economists would today regard the original methodology for the 1 per cent target to be flawed, and that now it is linked to the size of rich countries' economies rather than to the current needs of poor countries.[102]

The Commission recognised that achieving a 0.7 per cent aid target would be demanding and identified four categories of donors:

   i. six donors – Germany, Canada, Sweden, Norway, Denmark and the Netherlands – which had plans for a substantial increase in oda and which with the exception of Germany could be expected to reach the 0.7 per cent target by 1975;
  ii. Japan, Australia and Switzerland, which would meet the target by 1975 if they sustained recent substantial increases in oda;
 iii. France, which then uniquely exceeded 0.7 per cent in 1968 (though this included aid to its overseas *'départements'* which were an integral part of France) and need only increase its oda by the same as its GNP growth; and
  iv. the United States, United Kingdom, Italy and Belgium, where 'more serious problems exist'; oda as a percentage of GNP had fallen in the 1960s and was now far below the target proposed for 1975. They 'will face considerable difficulties in meeting it. As a first step they should stem the decline in the proportion of GNP devoted to official aid'.

The Commission was also careful to emphasise that the proposed new aid target was not intended to crowd out or substitute for private flows – the 1 per cent target was only a minimum. Private flows can be influenced by donor governments by not seeking to impose balance of payments capital controls and by developing countries adopting policies that would encourage, rather than deter, them through their economic policies and administrative procedures. In the last analysis private flows depend on the prospects for adequate rates of return and the private sector's confidence in being able to remit funds as appropriate.

In the context of the Second Development Decade the UN General Assembly adopted the 0.7 per cent target for oda. All DAC countries, with the exception of the US, accepted the target in principle but not necessarily any timetable for meeting it. Since then there have been numerous UN meetings at which the target has been discussed. Developing countries have pressed for a timetable for achieving it.

On occasions this has been supported by some DAC members that had already achieved it or had stated plans for doing so. But other DAC members have opposed a timetable and no consensus for a timetable has ever emerged in a UN text.

Britain has always accepted the target in principle but has until recently opposed an internationally agreed timetable. It has however been ready to sign up to UN texts that referred to best endeavours, including for example at the Rio Earth Summit in 1992 to reaching the target 'as soon as possible'. While appearing positive and accepted by the G77 as the best consensus they could achieve, the Treasury were comfortable in the knowledge that this did not constrain any future Public Expenditure decisions. However, Britain has recently set its own timetable of reaching the 0.7 per cent oda target by 2013, something confirmed by the current Coalition government despite other cuts in public expenditure.

### Definition of official and private flows

Initially the Development Assistance Committee of the OECD defined oda transactions according to the following criteria: 1) it was to be an official flow of donor government funds to a developing country (that is, all countries which were neither members of the OECD nor the Soviet Union and its satellite countries of Central and Eastern Europe); 2) that they should be for development purposes; and 3) they should have a grant element (that is, a degree of concessionality) of at least 25 per cent.

Those official flows that do not count as oda either because they are not sufficiently concessional or are not provided explicitly for development purposes, were termed 'other official flows' (oof) and shown separately in DAC statistics. For Britain the latter have included the loans provided under Section III of the ECGD Act, Section II of the CD&W Acts, and most CDC loan investments (because they were not sufficiently concessional) plus interest stabilisation grants paid by the ECGD to private banks which were used to provide guaranteed export credits at subsidised fixed rates of interest to developing countries (as they were not specifically for development purposes).

Private flows are those capital transactions, with more than one year maturity, from a donor country to a developing country. They include all forms of investment including direct investment whether on equity or loan terms, bank lending and export credits. They exclude transfers to and by private individuals, except grants by private voluntary organisations for development and welfare purposes which in the statistical publications are shown separately.

The degree of softness of a loan is determined by calculating the present value of the future repayments of the loan and interest payments, using an annual discount rate of 10 per cent. This value is compared with the face value of the loan. The difference between these two values is defined by the DAC as the grant equivalent of the loan. The percentage ratio of the grant equivalent to the face value of the loan is called the grant element of the loan. To qualify as oda the grant element must be at least 25 per cent.

Thus, aid given as a grant by definition will have a grant element of 100 per cent. At the other end of the spectrum a loan provided at an interest rate of 10 per cent whatever the repayment period will have a grant element of zero. If a loan is provided at less than a 10 per cent rate of interest the grant element will be positive: it will be higher the lower the rate of interest and the longer the repayment period (a grace period before which any repayments need to be made would also add to the grant element). There is therefore scope for trading off the interest rate charged with the loan repayment period in order to achieve a particular grant element. The Department's typical loan terms in its early years for the poorer countries carried an interest rate of zero, repayable over 25 years with a seven-year grace period. This provided for a grant element of over 75 per cent. In the early 1980s the Department decided to provide all financial aid on grant terms. Technical co-operation has always been made available as grants.

The use of a 10 per cent discount is somewhat arbitrary and also anomalous. The grant element was intended primarily to reflect the burden on the donors' budgets. The discount rate therefore assumed that on average donors could borrow funds in the marketplace, if it needed to, at a 10 per cent rate of interest in nominal terms. Inflation was generally higher in the 1960s and 1970s than it is today and therefore nominal interest rates were also higher. The larger the grant element the larger was the expected burden over the life of the loan on the donor's budget: recall the point made in the 1965 White Paper that official flows that counted as aid should involve a sacrifice.

The use of a single nominal discount rate is anomalous because it applies to all loans regardless of the currency in which they are made. Bilateral donors usually make loans in their own currencies. Some donor countries had relatively high and persistent levels of inflation and therefore could only borrow at high levels of nominal interest rates in their own currencies. Thus if they could only borrow at, say, 12 per cent and gave a loan to a developing country at 10 per cent, although there was expected to be a burden on their budget, the grant element was still zero.

On the other hand, even in the 1980s some donors enjoyed low rates of inflation and could borrow over relatively long periods of time at lower nominal interest rates than 10 per cent. If they then provided a loan to a developing country at their own borrowing rate there would be a positive grant element based on the DAC 10 per cent discount rate (including possibly sufficient to give a grant element above 25 per cent) even though there would be no anticipated burden on their budgets. This situation prevailed for some donors (notably Japan) prior to the economic circumstances in recent years when most donors could borrow at well below a 10 per cent nominal interest rate (even those with their own debt problems). Efforts in the DAC to address this issue have been to no avail.

The main message is that oda required a degree of concessionality (grant element/budgetary burden), as measured by a methodology agreed by the DAC, whatever its deficiencies at the time and now. In today's relatively low inflation era, and improved capital markets allowing donor governments to borrow at fixed interest rates over longer periods of time, it can reasonably be said that the DAC methodology using a 10 per cent discount rate provides a grant element figure which overstates the true burden on virtually all donor budgets – though an aid grant unequivocally has a true grant element of 100 per cent. Finally, these calculations of grant element assume that the loan will be repaid on schedule.

Looked at from the developing countries' point of view the issue is rather different. Some, particularly the poorer countries and those with poor records of economic management and already high indebtedness, have found it difficult to borrow on the market at all. For them a donor loan, even with a low grant element, may seem very attractive. On the other hand, stronger and well-managed economies which can attract market funds at reasonable rates of interest will be less impressed with official loans bearing relatively low grant elements. For the recipient the relevant discount rate is not that decreed by the DAC but the rate of interest which at the margin it can borrow at in the international capital markets. Borrowing official aid loans at a low nominal rate of interest may seem attractive but if it comes from a donor with a low inflation rate and is denominated in the donor currency the borrower can expect that currency to appreciate over time, thereby increasing its repayment burden.

Oda is generally scored when expenditure is incurred, not at the time when a commitment is made. There is, however, one important exception to this. In the case of contributions to the soft windows of the World Bank (IDA) and the regional development banks, pledges are usually made for a three-year period. The Department deposits unrecallable promissory notes with the Bank of England which are encashed as needed by the banks. At the time the promissory notes are deposited they count as oda though public expenditure is only incurred by the Department when the notes are encashed, usually over several years.

It has been the usual practice for the Department's Finance Director to make deposits of notes of one-third annually of the amount pledged for each three-year period so that any one year's oda is not artificially distorted. However if there are significant changes in a donor's commitment to the banks this can have a distorting effect. For example in 1979 the Department increased its commitment to IDA and very large note deposits were made such that total oda by Britain for that year amounted to 0.51 per cent of GNP, though in public expenditure terms the figure was only about 0.41 per cent.

Advances by the Department to the CDC are an internal transaction and do not count as an official flow to developing countries. CDC investments in developing countries are counted as official flows when they are disbursed. The bulk of CDC loans were not sufficiently concessional to count as oda; rather they counted as another official flow (oof). It is however an anomaly that equity investments made by the CDC count as oda despite the fact that they were made in the expectation of earning a commercial return: this was as a result of an agreement in the DAC in the early 1980s that equity investments by an official body (not just the CDC) should be counted as oda.

The definitions of oda and oof otherwise remained largely unchanged until the early 1990s. Two developments led to change: one was the recognition of the debt problem facing developing countries, and the other was the collapse of the Soviet Union.

When the international community began to agree substantial levels of debt forgiveness for the poorer developing countries on the basis that they would never be able to repay all their export credit debts, there was pressure to count such debt forgiveness as oda provided, as was usually the case, it was in the context of an economic reform programme agreed with the international financial institutions (the IMF and the World Bank) designed to enhance long-term development prospects. The DAC agreed that such debt forgiveness under successive initiatives should count as oda. Initially debt relief counted as oda on an annual basis according to the reduction in the annual debt servicing that the agreement provided for. The interim debt relief provided prior to the Completion Point under the Highly Indebted

Poor Country (HIPC) initiative (see Chapter Five) was counted as oda on an annual basis. At Completion Point, when the stock of debt is irrevocably forgiven, it now counts as oda in that year. This explains significant annual variations in annual oda to individual countries in recent years. Similar treatment has applied to a limited number of other developing countries which have received substantial stock of debt reductions, notably Nigeria and Iraq. The recent complaint by NGOs that the present Coalition government is using this to exaggerate its oda performance is surprising given that this definition of oda has been in force for some time and they have been closely involved in debt forgiveness issues for many years.

The second major change in the definition of official flows occurred following the collapse of the Soviet Union. The Russian Federation, those countries that had been part of the Soviet Union, and its previous satellite countries in Eastern and Central Europe, were said to be Countries in Transition to a Market Economy. German unification put what was East Germany into the OECD. Yugoslavia, however, already had developing-country status, not least because it had been a longstanding and leading member of the Non-aligned Movement. Assistance to countries in transition was initially shown separately and did not count as oda even if it otherwise met with the oda criteria. However this classification was not sustainable and the DAC eventually agreed a two-part list of non-OECD countries, distinguished largely by the level of income per head using the World Bank's four-income per head categories.

All high-income countries (with an income per head of US$9206 and above in 2001) were placed in Part II, though this required a run of three consecutive years because of possible variations in annual national income. The Part II list therefore included a number of traditional developing countries and Slovenia which were in the high-income category. However, certain other transitional countries were also put in Part II even though their per capita incomes were in the middle-income category. The middle-income transition countries in Part II were Belarus, Bulgaria, the Czech Republic, Estonia, Latvia, Lithuania, Romania and the Slovak Republic.

The Part I list included non-high-income traditional developing countries plus Armenia, Azerbaijan, Croatia, Georgia, Kazakhstan, Kyrgzstan, Moldovia, Serbia and Montenegro, Tajikstan, Turkmanistan, Ukraine and Uzbekistan, all middle- or low-income countries.

All Part I countries became eligible for oda. Part II countries were eligible for what became official aid (oa), but which was otherwise defined in the same way as oda. However the DAC has now adopted a single list of countries (previously Part I) that are eligible for oda. From 2006 oa is no longer reported to and published by the DAC, though individual donor countries such as Britain have continued to show it in their own publications.

A new system of National Accounts (SNA 1993), co-sponsored by the OECD and other major international organisations, broadened the coverage of Gross National Product (GNP) and it was redefined as Gross National Income (GNI). The change in nomenclature for aid reporting did not take place until 2000 when all DAC donors would use the new system. GNI comprises the total value of goods and services produced within a country (that is, its Gross Domestic Product or GDP), together with income received from other countries (notably interest and dividends), less similar payments made to other countries.

## Britain's performance against the UN targets

Table 10.1 shows Britain's performance against the UN targets for net resource transfers to developing countries. It gives figures in absolute nominal (that is, cash) terms and as a percentage of GNI. Britain's performance against the 1 per cent UN target for net total flows has fluctuated very considerably. This is due largely to the fluctuations in net private flows which are the difference between two large numbers: the gross outflow of private flows and repayment of earlier flows, mainly bank lending to the stronger middle-income developing countries. Thus relatively small changes in either can cause relatively large changes in the net level of flows.

Britain exceeded the 1 per cent UN target in 25 of the 45 years between 1964 and 2008, but varying between very large net flows, particularly in the period 1976–81, and very low net flows in some other years, such as the second half of the 1960s and the first half of the 1970s when confidence by the private sector (particularly the private banks) in the economies of the developing countries was low.

Britain has never met the 0.7 per cent UN target for oda agreed to in 1970. Having reached 0.66 per cent in 1964, the year the Department was created, it generally languished in the period 1965 to 1985 between 0.33 per cent and 0.40 per cent. The exceptions were 1977–79 when the Labour government agreed a substantial real-terms increase in aid. The figure of 0.51 per cent for 1979, however, is largely explained by a high level of deposits of promissory notes with the Bank of England for IDA, compared to their encashment, as explained above. There then

*Table 10.1*  Britain's oda, oof and private flows to developing countries (1964–2010)

| | Official flows | | Private flows on | | | UK | | DAC average | |
| | oda | oof | Market terms | Voluntary grants | Total flows oda, oof and private | oda as a total as a % of GNI | oda as a total flows as a % of GNI | % of GNI | Flows as a % of GNI |
| | (1) | (2) | (3) | (4) | (5) | (6) | (7) | (8) | (9) |
|---|---|---|---|---|---|---|---|---|---|
| 1964 | 177 | | 157 | n/a | 334 | 0.66 | 1.25 | | |
| 1965 | 172 | | 200 | n/a | 372 | 0.60 | 1.31 | | |
| 1966 | 157 | 150 | 150 | n/a | 487 | 0.63 | 1.13 | | |
| 1967 | 173 | 6 | 118 | n/a | 297 | 0.44 | 0.74 | | |
| 1968 | 173 | 6 | 128 | n/a | 307 | 0.40 | 0.71 | | |
| 1969 | 180 | (1) | 299 | 14 | 478 | 0.39 | 1.04 | | |
| 1970 | 186 | 3 | 317 | 14 | 520 | 0.36 | 1.01 | 0.34 | 0.78 |
| 1971 | 231 | 5 | 297 | 19 | 552 | 0.40 | 0.96 | 0.35 | 0.80 |
| 1972 | 243 | 6 | 315 | 20 | 584 | 0.38 | 0.92 | 0.33 | 0.76 |
| 1973 | 246 | 25 | 307 | 23 | 601 | 0.34 | 0.82 | 0.30 | 0.79 |
| 1974 | 307 | 34 | 655 | 23 | 1020 | 0.40 | 1.25 | 0.34 | 0.65 |
| 1975 | 388 | 14 | 633 | 24 | 1059 | 0.39 | 1.00 | 0.36 | 1.17 |
| 1976 | 487 | 17 | 3882 | 29 | 4415 | 0.39 | 3.37 | 0.33 | 1.10 |
| 1977 | 638 | 57 | 3329 | 29 | 4053 | 0.44 | 2.71 | 0.33 | 1.09 |
| 1978 | 763 | 185 | 3887 | 29 | 4865 | 0.46 | 2.93 | 0.35 | 1.24 |
| 1979 | 1016 | 67 | 5226 | 51 | 6359 | 0.51 | 3.25 | 0.35 | 1.17 |

| | | | | | | | | | |
|---|---|---|---|---|---|---|---|---|---|
| 1980 | 797 | −71 | 4475 | 52 | 5253 | 0.35 | 2.32 | 0.38 | 1.04 |
| 1981 | 1081 | 173 | 4549 | 47 | 5850 | 0.43 | 2.34 | 0.35 | 1.25 |
| 1982 | 1028 | 89 | 2405 | 57 | 3579 | 0.37 | 1.29 | 0.38 | 1.15 |
| 1983 | 1061 | 137 | 2769 | 55 | 4022 | 0.35 | 1.33 | 0.36 | 0.91 |
| 1984 | 1070 | 350 | 2091 | 105 | 3615 | 0.33 | 1.13 | 0.35 | 0.99 |
| 1985 | 1180 | 299 | 292 | 130 | 1900 | 0.33 | 0.54 | 0.35 | 0.53 |
| 1986 | 1185 | 220 | 3024 | 130 | 4558 | 0.31 | 1.20 | 0.35 | 0.66 |
| 1987 | 1142 | 161 | 693 | 135 | 2131 | 0.28 | 0.51 | 0.35 | 0.55 |
| 1988 | 1485 | 181 | 607 | 134 | 2408 | 0.32 | 0.52 | 0.34 | 0.61 |
| 1989 | 1578 | 280 | 3756 | 160 | 5775 | 0.31 | 1.14 | 0.32 | 0.59 |
| 1990 | 1485 | 354 | 1652 | 184 | 3675 | 0.27 | 0.68 | 0.33 | 0.48 |
| 1991 | 1815 | 293 | 866 | 215 | 3188 | 0.32 | 0.56 | 0.33 | 0.55 |
| 1992 | 1848 | 170 | 3035 | 250 | 5303 | 0.31 | 0.89 | 0.33 | 0.63 |
| 1993 | 1945 | 87 | 3523 | 300 | 5855 | 0.31 | 0.94 | 0.30 | 0.73 |
| 1994 | 2089 | 22 | 5356 | 350 | 7816 | 0.31 | 1.15 | 0.30 | 0.83 |
| 1995 | 2029 | 135 | 5661 | 307 | 8132 | 0.29 | 1.15 | 0.27 | 0.75 |
| 1996 | 2050 | 52 | 11345 | 245 | 13692 | 0.27 | 1.83 | 0.25 | 0.88 |
| 1997 | 2096 | −69 | 8830 | 216 | 11073 | 0.26 | 1.39 | 0.22 | 0.86 |
| 1998 | 2332 | −33 | 4048 | 253 | 6600 | 0.27 | 0.83 | 0.23 | 0.81 |
| 1999 | 2118 | −15 | 7056 | 297 | 9456 | 0.24 | 1.05 | 0.24 | 0.80 |
| 2000 | 2974 | −47 | 1383 | 354 | 4664 | 0.32 | 0.50 | 0.22 | 0.54 |
| 2001 | 3179 | 2 | 3242 | 216 | 6639 | 0.32 | 0.67 | 0.22 | 0.46 |
| 2002 | 3281 | −3 | 1573 | 231 | 5083 | 0.31 | 0.49 | 0.23 | 0.35 |
| 2003 | 3847 | 30 | 7251 | 238 | 11367 | 0.34 | 1.01 | 0.25 | 0.39 |
| 2004 | 4302 | −85 | 12858 | 213 | 17288 | 0.36 | 1.45 | 0.26 | 0.52 |
| 2005 | 5923 | −54 | 19212 | 399 | 25473 | 0.47 | 2.03 | 0.33 | 0.93 |
| 2006 | 6770 | −102 | 7676 | 295 | 14640 | 0.51 | 1.11 | 0.31 | 0.89 |

*(continued)*

*Table 10.1* Continued

£ million (net)

| | Official flows | | Private flows on | | | UK | | DAC average | |
|---|---|---|---|---|---|---|---|---|---|
| | oda | oof | Market terms | Voluntary grants | Total flows oda, oof and private | oda as a total as a % of GNI | oda as a total flows as a % of GNI | % of GNI | Flows as a % of GNI |
| | (1) | (2) | (3) | (4) | (5) | (6) | (7) | (8) | (9) |
| 2007 | 4921 | –22 | 23909 | 334 | 29142 | 0.36 | 2.10 | 0.28 | 1.16 |
| 2008 | 6356 | –12 | 16524 | 256 | 23123 | 0.43 | 1.59 | 0.30 | n.a. |
| 2009 | 7223 | 195 | 8193 | 211 | 15821 | 0.51 | 1.11 | 0.31 | n.a. |
| 2010 | 8452 | –12 | 7930 | 228 | 16597 | 0.57 | 1.12 | 0.32 | n.a. |

followed a trend decline in Britain's oda performance to 0.24 per cent of GNI in 1999. Whilst the Labour government increased the size of the aid budget on coming into office in 1997, the Department initially made no new promissory note deposits for IDA, although encashment of notes was substantial, accounting for about 8 per cent of the Department's expenditure. Since that time an expanding aid budget, together with substantial debt relief which also counts as oda, has been reflected in an improvement in Britain's oda performance, reaching 0.57 per cent of GNI in 2010. Much of the increase in oda in the early years of the Labour government was due to substantial debt relief but since then it has been the result of very substantial increases in the Department's own budget. As Britain moves towards the 0.7 per cent aid target by 2013, debt forgiveness will play a much smaller part (only Sudan now remains a significant debtor) requiring further very substantial annual increases in the Department's aid budget.

In 2005, during the UK Presidency of the G8 and the EU, firm time-bound commitments were made to increase aid levels in the future. The G8 agreed to double aid worldwide by 2010 with half of the additional resources going to Africa. The EU member states agreed to double their collective effort to over US$80 billion in 2010 compared with 2003 levels, with at least half of the new funds going to Africa. In terms of aid as a percentage of GNI, they committed to collectively achieving 0.56 per cent. The UK Comprehensive Spending Review (2007) provided for total oda to increase to £9.1 billion by 2010/11, equivalent to 0.56% of GNI. This was consistent with the EU collective commitment for 2010 and Britain's share of the Gleneagles commitment to increase aid by $US50 billion. Within this total the Department's oda budget was planned to increase by an average of 11 per cent per annum to reach £7.9 billion, equivalent to 0.49 per cent of GNI. The balance was largely made up of anticipated debt relief which does not fall on the Department's own budget. While at the time of writing Britain remains committed to these increases, it is already apparent that a number of major EU donors have not provided aid budgets consistent with their commitments.

Table 10.1 also shows Britain's performance against the UN targets since 1970 compared to the average for all DAC member countries. For total net flows to developing countries Britain exceeded the DAC average in all but five years, reflecting in large measure the strength of Britain's financial sector. As regards the 0.7 per cent aid target, Britain exceeded the DAC average in the 1970s but gradually fell behind it in the 1980s and early 1990s. The fact that Britain has exceeded the DAC average since 1993 (except in 1999 when it equalled it) is due to

Table 10.2 UN aid target: Britain's ranking among DAC donors as % of GNP

|  | Britain | DAC members meeting target | Highest performer | Lowest of all current members[a] | Lowest of original members[a] |
|---|---|---|---|---|---|
| 1975 | 11th/17 | 2 | Sweden | Italy | Italy |
| 1980 | 10th/17 | 4 | Netherlands | Italy | Italy |
| 1985 | 13th/18 | 3 | Denmark | Ireland | US |
| 1990 | 14th/20 | 5 | Norway | Ireland | US |
| 1995 | 14th/21 | 5 | Norway | Ireland | US |
| 2000 | 8th/22 | 5 | Denmark | US | US |
| 2005 | 7th/22 | 5 | Norway | Portugal | US |
| 2010 | 7th/22 | 5 | Norway | Korea | Japan |

[a] Originally the DAC had 17 members. Subsequently Ireland joined the DAC in 1985, Spain and Portugal in 1991, Luxembourg in 1992 and Greece in 1997.

Britain's eventual recovery in its own performance but importantly to the decline in the DAC average only marginally reversed since 2003. This decline is due to a number of factors including the political response of donors to the emergence of the Countries in Transition to a market economy and the fall in the aid budgets of the US. Germany became preoccupied with the needs of East Germany following unification and EU member states provided growing bilateral aid programmes and financed expanding EC budget aid programmes to the transition countries, little of which has counted as oda. The recent global financial crisis has put aid budgets of other donors under tight constraints. Thus the so-called peace dividend for developing countries following the end of the Cold War proved illusory.

Table 10.2 shows Britain's ranking among the DAC countries since 1970 in relation to the UN aid target for developing countries. This is relevant because of the wide difference in DAC countries' performance and in particular the heavy weighting of the US in the DAC average. A number of the smaller DAC countries have met or exceeded the UN aid target, such as the Netherlands, Denmark, Norway and Sweden, while the larger G7 countries (now the G8 including Russia) have generally performed well below it even before the end of the Cold War.

It can be seen from Table 10.2 that Britain gradually slipped down the DAC rankings until 1995 when in terms of GNI its oda percentage was only 14th out of 21 DAC members. By 2006 it had risen to seventh out of 22 DAC members. During the period 1970–2005 the number of DAC countries meeting the UN aid target reached five (Denmark, Luxembourg, the Netherlands, Norway and Sweden). After 1980 the new members had, not surprisingly, the lowest ranking, though of the original members of the DAC the US has been the lowest since 1985.

## The Department's aid budget

Apart from the ex-post publication of Britain's performance against the UN aid target, the annual announcement to Parliament of the Department's aid budget for the next three years is what attracts most attention, particularly by the House of Commons' Select Committee on International Development.

The Department's aid budget comprises:

i. bilateral development assistance to countries on what was both Parts I and II of the DAC List, including activities funded from two 'conflict pools';

ii. multilateral development assistance including global environmental assistance under the Montreal Protocol, and that part of Britain's assessed contribution to the European Commission (EC) budget allocated for development programmes; and
iii. administrative costs.

Aid budget expenditure is the sum of funds voted by Parliament and Britain's share of that part of the EC budget used for development assistance, which is paid for directly by the Treasury, but 'attributed' to the Department's aid budget. EC budget aid expenditure is separate from the European Development Fund which, as explained in Chapter Seven, is replenished every five years by the member states, Britain's share of which is voted annually by Parliament.

The Department's out-turn expenditure may differ from the aid budget set at the beginning of the year for four main reasons:

i. additional resources provided to the aid budget in-year from the Central Reserve for major humanitarian aid operations and other purposes which could not have been foreseen and which it is accepted could or should not be met within the existing budget. In recent years examples include Montserrat, Kosovo, Afghanistan, Iraq and the Tsunami disaster;
ii. the attributed figure in relation to EC budget expenditure set at the beginning of the year being different from outturn expenditure;
iii. an underspend on the cash limit collectively by the Department's expenditure divisions, though generally this would be very small given the flexibility the Department has in the timing of certain payments between different financial years; and
iv. the government, for overall public expenditure reasons, imposes a cut in the aid budget in-year, but this happened only once when in 1979/80 the incoming Thatcher government cut the aid budget during that year by 6 per cent in real terms.

## Britain's gross public expenditure on aid

Gross Public Expenditure on Aid (GPEX) is now reported on a financial year basis in the Department's statistical publication. It seeks to bring together all the government's expenditure on overseas development. It is shown gross of any repayments of past loans because it is the gross amount which it is at the discretion of the government to provide.

It encompasses the bulk of the Department's aid budget; any flows from other government departments (for example, that proportion of WHO expenditure that, as assessed by the DAC, counts for development purposes but which is paid for by the Department of Health), less that part of the Department's contribution to other UN Specialized Agencies for which it is responsible but which is not for development purposes (such as the worldwide regulatory and other functions of UNESCO and the FAO); investments made by the CDC less any advances to the CDC which are made from the aid budget; and debt relief by the ECGD.

GPEX on Development meets one of the DAC criteria for oda (that is, it is for development purposes) but otherwise goes wider. It embraces all official flows for development purposes regardless of the degree of concessionality and thus includes all CDC investments. It does not include oof such as the ECGD's substantial expenditure in earlier years on interest rate subsidies for export credit. On an annual basis it differs from oda in that unrecallable promissory notes desposited at the Bank of England in respect of the IFIs only count for GPEX when they are encashed and expenditure is incurred by the Department. However, like oda, stock of debt reductions are shown in the year in which they are granted. GPEX includes development expenditure for all non-OECD countries, not just those that count for oda purposes.

Table 10.3 shows total GPEX on Development from 1970 to 2010/11 in current (that is, cash) prices and its constituent parts. It also provides a constant price index (1970:100) for total GPEX on Development and total gross development expenditure by the Department including CDC investments. For the period 1970–87 figures are available only on a calendar-year basis as a by-product of reporting to the DAC. Since 1988/89 figures have been compiled on a financial-year basis. The former are more liable to fluctuations caused by factors other than changes in policy.

In cash terms the series in Table 10.3 reflects a number of factors, including the relatively high rates of domestic inflation in the 1970s, the public expenditure constraints, particularly on the aid budget in the 1980s and much of the 1990s, and the substantial increase in expenditure on debt relief in the 1990s and even more so in the last few years as a result of international initiatives to relieve the debt burden primarily of the poorest countries. Now that relief of the stock of debt of poorer countries counts as GPEX in the year in which it is forgiven, these have become very substantial indeed as the figures for recent years demonstrate. Constant price indices for GPEX and the Department's programmes are shown in columns (7) and (8) of Table 10.3. Until

Table 10.3  UK gross public expenditure on development 1970–2011 (£ million)

| | Total GPEX on development | Aid programme[a] | CDC investments | Total DFID programmes | Other govt programmes | (of which debt relief) |
|---|---|---|---|---|---|---|
| | (1) | (2) | (3) | (4) | (5) | (6) |
| 1970 | 218 | 205 | 13 | 218 | – | – |
| 1971 | 288 | 265 | 23 | 285 | – | – |
| 1972 | 298 | 276 | 20 | 296 | 2 | – |
| 1973 | 299 | 275 | 21 | 296 | 3 | – |
| 1974 | 379 | 340 | 35 | 375 | 4 | – |
| 1975 | 452 | 422 | 27 | 499 | 3 | – |
| 1976 | 513 | 483 | 26 | 509 | 4 | – |
| 1977 | 589 | 549 | 36 | 584 | 4 | – |
| 1978 | 726 | 690 | 32 | 722 | 4 | – |
| 1979 | 890 | 841 | 44 | 885 | 5 | – |
| 1980 | 966 | 911 | 45 | 956 | 10 | – |
| 1981 | 1151 | 1071 | 68 | 1139 | 12 | – |
| 1982 | 1085 | 1013 | 51 | 1064 | 21 | – |
| 1983 | 1173 | 1087 | 56 | 1143 | 30 | – |
| 1984 | 1316 | 1177 | 108 | 1285 | 31 | – |
| 1985 | 1324 | 1206 | 79 | 1285 | 39 | – |
| 1986 | 1350 | 1237 | 64 | 1301 | 49 | – |
| 1987 | 1298 | 1201 | 66 | 1267 | 31 | – |
| 1988/89 | 1616 | 1414 | 117 | 1531 | 85 | (33) |
| 1989/90 | 1736 | 1499 | 150 | 1649 | 87 | (27) |
| 1990/91 | 1893 | 1610 | 159 | 1769 | 124 | (59) |
| 1991/92 | 2132 | 1882 | 124 | 2006 | 126 | (39) |
| 1992/93 | 2389 | 2034 | 223 | 2257 | 132 | (80) |

| | | | | | |
|---|---|---|---|---|---|
| 1993/94 | 2390 | 2112 | 183 | 2295 | 96 | (45) |
| 1994/95 | 2603 | 2259 | 235 | 2494 | 109 | (58) |
| 1995/96 | 2609 | 2219 | 282 | 2501 | 108 | (58) |
| 1996/97 | 2415 | 2128 | 189 | 2317 | 98 | (34) |
| 1997/98 | 2530 | 2039 | 249 | 2288 | 242 | (170) |
| 1998/99 | 2568 | 2326 | 167 | 2493 | 165 | (87) |
| 1999/2000 | 2986 | 2541 | 269 | 2810 | 176 | (101) |
| 2000/01 | 3231 | 2799 | 201 | 3000 | 231 | (82) |
| 2001/02 | 3447 | 2918 | 159 | 3077 | 400 | (252) |
| 2002/03 | 4159 | 3352 | 237 | 3589 | 533 | (399) |
| 2003/04 | 4658 | 3956 | 350 | 4306 | 352 | (163) |
| 2004/05 | 5422 | 3846 | 238 | 4084 | 1338 | (627) |
| 2005/06 | 6914 | 4526 | 173 | 4699 | 2215 | (1588) |
| 2006/07 | 7591 | 5023 | 279 | 5302 | 2553 | (1867) |
| 2007/08 | 6027 | 5196 | 361 | 5547 | 831 | (4) |
| 2008/09 | 7183 | 5799 | 436 | 6235 | 1384 | (280) |
| 2009/10 | 7767 | 6629 | 354 | 6983 | 1137 | (7) |
| 2010/11 | 9007 | 7689 | 416 | 8105 | 1318 | (54) |

[a] Excludes Aid Programme advances to the CDC.

debt relief became significant these two indices moved together. Since the early 1990s they have significantly diverged. The increase in the Department's index reflects first the increase in gross (though not net) investments by the CDC and more recently the size of the aid programme itself in real terms. In real terms, in 2010/11 GPEX was about three times its 1970 level, and the Department's gross expenditure, including that of the CDC, rather more than double.

# 11
# The Department: Managing Itself

## Introduction

This chapter sets out the series of organisational and management changes that have taken place within the Department over its life. It seeks to show how the Department adjusted to the changing demands on it as development policies and practices evolved within the context of wider civil service reform.

## The early years

The Northcote-Trevelyan reforms in the 19th century had established the principle of a politically neutral career civil service serving ministers who were answerable to Parliament and to the public for the government's policies of the day. The Plowden Committee Report of 1961 recommended an annual five-year real resource (public expenditure in constant price) planning exercise, the Treasury taking a stronger interest in management efficiency and more civil service time devoted to management, using more quantified techniques. The first two recommendations were accepted and implemented; the third had to await further initiatives and a gradual change in culture.

Harold Wilson, himself a former civil servant, had a strong regard for the civil service but wanted to see reform that would make it better placed to carry out the future role he saw for it. As Prime Minister, he appointed the Fulton Committee to make recommendations on the future of the civil service. Fulton criticised as amateur the generalised administrative cadre of senior civil servants, typically, though not exclusively, recruited after private schooling and an arts degree from Oxbridge; poorly trained subsequently in-service, and subject to frequent changes of job. They lacked in-depth knowledge of particular issues and were not equipped for a new managerial role. Fulton recom mended a broader intake of staff with a 'preference for relevance' in their degrees (particularly the social sciences), more in-service training, and the creation of a classless uniformally graded structure from the top to the bottom of the civil service. Fulton also proposed the hiving off of executive functions to separate bodies.

The Fulton Report (Cmnd 3638) was published in June 1968 and Wilson immediately announced that he broadly accepted the recommendations. But Fulton's recommendations were implemented only in part. They came up against the vested interests of the more powerful parts of the civil service and the bigger civil service unions. A number felt, with some justification, that Fulton failed to fully appreciate that senior administrators became professional in their ability to formulate policy options and present advice to ministers in a way that facilitated political decision-making. It was an art not quickly learnt by others moving horizontally from other civil service careers. Few functions were hived off, largely on the grounds that they were either not self-financing or they were politically too sensitive. Judgement on Fulton might be that while civil service reform ran out of steam in the short term, it did provide a framework and insight for a more determined government to take forward after 1979.[103]

Thus when the Department was established its first Permanent Secretary, Sir Andrew Cohen, who came across from the Department of Technical Co-operation, was made essentially in the mould of his peers in Whitehall, as were the many others who came via the Department for Technical Co-operation (DTC) from the Colonial Office. The other early intake of administrative and professional staff came from the colonial service. What distinguished the Department from some, though not all, departments in Whitehall was its large and influential Economic Planning Staff (EPS) and the much larger number of scientists in the Scientific Units it inherited. But despite Fulton, and like the rest of Whitehall, the division between the civil service classes within the Department remained largely frozen for a long time. The partial exception to this was the economists: however, between about 1975 and 1985 only four economists were allowed to make the transition to the administrative cadre at below the Open Structure, including the author. Much later one young economist with field experience with the Botswana government joined the Department's economic staff, made the transfer to administration as Lynda Chalker's Private Secretary, and later became the Department's Permanent Secretary. Thus, by 1979 it can fairly be said that the Department, with the exceptions noted above, looked rather like any other government department and had like them yet to be visited materially by the spirit of Fulton. One advantage which the Department did enjoy, and would continue to do so, was its popularity among fast-stream entrants, second usually only to the Treasury, and many of those with a preference for coming to the Department had social science degrees, though a few more historians would not have gone amiss. Sir Gus (now Lord) O'Donnell, who became Cabinet Secretary, gave the Department as his first preference but had to make do with the Treasury. Another advantage was that complementing the fast-stream administrators were the 'late entry principals' coming in as administrators and professionals, including economists with field experience of developing countries.

There was another important distinguishing feature of the Department that was to become an important driver of change as advances in information technology were made. In 1964 the Department was located in London (Stag Place) with two exceptions. The Middle East Development Division, then based in Beirut, had started life as the Middle East Technical Assistance Office shortly after the Second World War and had become part of the DTC. In addition, it was seen as both politically and managerially necessary for much of the Department's relations with developing country governments to be conducted through a Development Section of the local British High Commission or Embassy, staffed by both the diplomatic service and the Department. However, in the first decade or so of the Department's life further regional Development divisions were created in the Caribbean (Bridgetown), East Africa (Nairobi), Southern Africa (Lilongwe, later transferred to Harare) and South East Asia (Bangkok). They were comprised of multi-disciplinary teams headed by a senior administrator. However, until the 1980s the Development Divisions (and the Development Sections in diplomatic missions) were there to implement the policies determined by the Department in London. The primary task of the Development Divisions was to help design and appraise individual projects for submission to London for approval.

The Department initiated a review of the senior management structure before the change of government in 1979. The Hudson Review focused on the open structure of the office (Under Secretary level and above). It recommended a streamlining of top management with only two Deputy Secretaries, with the Principal Finance Officer (today called a Finance Director) reporting directly to the Permanent Secretary. One Deputy Secretary (a career administrator) would be responsible primarily for the bilateral country and multilateral aid programmes and another, the Director General of the EPS, would become responsible for all the professional cadres and the Scientific Units. But further important structural change was recommended: in future each professional Chief Adviser would become managerially responsible for the relevant research and development programmes funded by the office, rather than acting as advisers to one or more administrative Under Secretaries. Amongst other things this meant the Chief Renewable Natural Resources Adviser becoming directly responsible for the Department's Scientific Units, an important change not without future consequences. The Hudson Report was completed in 1980 and implemented thereafter. It was to set the framework for further changes within the Department under the new government.

## The Thatcher/Major reforms

Margaret Thatcher became Prime Minister with a hitherto unseen zeal for fundamental change in the way the civil service operated. Furthermore, her success in achieving change, an agenda which her successors have largely continued to pursue, was due to the fact that, unlike her predecessors, she never lost interest in the subject. For her it was part of a wider agenda of political change in the role of the government that was central to her years in office, and which therefore could not be lost sight of. The essence of her reforms, not dissimilar to Fulton's ideas, was that the civil service should become more managerial and, literally, businesslike, and therefore more effective and efficient, and importantly for her, smaller and less costly. Like their peers in Whitehall, some in the Department initially saw all this as an unwelcome, and probably temporary, distraction from their more traditional role as policy advisers. Others welcomed the challenge and looked forward to the increase in the delegated authority the reforms would bring. The more recent generation of senior civil servants, including within the Department, can justifiably say that they have willingly taken forward the management change agenda for its own sake, but that it has become internalised within the civil service culture is down to Thatcher's persistence, and that of her successors.

In 1979 Sir Derek (later Lord) Raynor of Marks and Spencer was brought in to head a new Efficiency Unit reporting directly to the Prime Minister. He began with a series of Efficiency Scrutinies across Whitehall looking at particular areas of activity and conducted under his supervision by a member of the department concerned. The first scrutiny was of statistical services within departments and the author conducted the review for the Department. The statistics scrutiny for the Department recommended a change in focus and cost reductions of 35 per cent which were implemented over time. The second series of scrutinies were on scientific units in government. For the Department this resulted in more important recommendations for a number of organisational changes and cost savings which were put into effect, though only after being contested by the House of Commons Select Committee (see Chapter Eight).

In 1988 the Prime Minister launched her new wave of reforms set out in the Efficiency Unit's report entitled *Improving Management in Government: The Next Steps*.[104] The new focus was on the hiving off of executive functions into separate agencies with greater financial autonomy and management flexibility. It was a return to the ideas first put forward by Fulton but this time the Prime Minister was determined that it should impact on a large part of civil service functions and the initiative was continued under John Major when he became Prime Minister. Before establishing an agency, 'prior options' were looked at, including privatisation, but the agencies were designed to improve performance of those activities that should remain part of government. For the Department the obvious candidate for this was the Natural Resources Institute (NRI) which was being formed by the amalgamation of its Scientific Units into one body and relocated to Chatham naval dockyard (see Chapter Eight). As with all such Agencies a Framework Document was agreed, setting out the relationship between the Department and NRI, and a business plan was drawn up. The Director of NRI became its Accounting Officer, which raised questions about the responsibility of the Department's Accounting Officer (the Permanent Secretary) for the NRI which were never entirely resolved. By 1994 Next Steps Agencies accounted for 65 per cent of total civil service staff numbers across all departments, though for the Department NRI accounted for about one-third.

When Major succeeded Thatcher as Prime Minister he introduced the idea of market-testing work done by the civil service with a view to contracting out large amounts of work undertaken by departments and their agencies to the private sector: it emphasised the split between the purchaser and the provider of services. Market testing required departments to cost the work in-house against the cost of contracting out. The government set ambitious targets for market testing (covering first 25 per cent and then 50 per cent of staff) and each department was required to come up with a plan covering a substantial proportion of its functions. For some of the big battalions with large numbers of staff engaged in executive functions these targets were easier to meet than for the smaller policy departments.

The Department focused on its support and pension payment functions for market testing. The IT support function was considered and rejected. Within the Department market testing went ahead for two departments located in East Kilbride, the Department's other headquarters office (see below): the Pensions, and Overseas Consultancies and Recruitment departments. In preparation for market testing the in-house teams were allowed to come up with their own proposals for how they would manage their business in future and at what cost. Both teams came up with proposals involving a 20–25 per cent reduction in costs, which in part was the result of the more flexible use of staff of different grades. It should be said that the 'market testing' exercise in Abercrombie House in East Kilbride was overseen by someone who had the confidence of staff and the trade unions, both of whom co-operated positively to achieve the outcome. On this basis it was agreed that the Department should not proceed with market testing against private sector providers. There were other qualitative considerations against contracting out, particularly in the case of the pensions payment function given the fragility of the legislation which continued to throw up difficult and sensitive casework amongst what was sadly a, literally, dying number of customers. It might be added that when the Rt Hon Stephen Dorrell MP was Economic Secretary to the Treasury he also suggested that the Department should market test the CDC by creating a challenge fund which would be open to both the CDC and the private sector to bid for to invest in private sector businesses in the poorest countries. After some discussion this idea was not taken up, though given later developments some may think this was a missed opportunity.

A further review of the government's scientific research activities put the privatisation of NRI back on the agenda, dismissed in the earlier prior options exercised before making it a Next Steps Agency. NRI was not only doing business for others but the Department was also increasingly making it compete for the work it gave it, as there were others outside government, particularly in downstream consultancy services, that could undertake the same work. Thus, 1996 saw the privatisation of NRI by selling it to the university sector. Likewise, the Crown Agents provided services on a commercial basis to many overseas clients and most, if not all, the services provided to the Department could in principle be provided by the private sector. Thus, Crown Agents were a further candidate for privatisation in one form or another (see Chapter Eight). Finally, the Department examined the possibility of privatising the CDC, albeit with a minority shareholding by government to entrench its objective of developing ethical private sector business largely in the poorest countries, but in this it was only partially successful (again see Chapter Eight).

## The Blair/Brown years

The new Labour government of 1997 continued to pursue greater civil service efficiency. The 1999 White Paper[105] focused on five key areas: policymaking, responsive public services, quality public services, information age government, and public service staffing and organisation. The first of these was outlined in a 1999 Cabinet Office report 'Professional Policy Making for the Twenty First Century' which emphasised that policymaking should be strategic and outcome-focused, joined-up, evidence-based, and inclusive and participatory. The Department believed it had a good story to tell, and did so in Chapter 9 of its 2001 Departmental Report.

Amongst other things, on policymaking the Department pointed to the outcome-focused Millennium Development Goals and the two White Papers of 1997 and 2000; the more joined-up approach to development policy issues in Whitehall; its knowledge and research programmes and evaluation work to inform policymaking; and the increasingly inclusive and participatory nature of all its strategy papers. As regards responsive public services, the Department was able to cite the performance of its Overseas Pensions Department in providing payment to some 2,700 pensioners and dependents, which exceeded standards set out in its Service Level Agreement.

The Department was also able to say that it achieved Investors in People (IIP) accreditation in December 2000, though this was not without some difficulty. The Labour Party as an organisation had achieved IIP status by 1997 and the new government expected each Whitehall department to do likewise. Achieving IIP status for all civil service organisations, however, was first implicit in the 1994 White Paper on the civil service (*Continuity and Change*), and made more explicit in the 1996 White Paper (*Development and Training for Civil Servants: a Framework for Action*) by setting a target date of 2000 for all civil servants being employed in organisations recognised as Investors in People. This commitment was repeated in the 1999 White Paper on *Modernising Government*.[105] It only surfaced in the Department after the 1997 General

Election, with a Secretary of State committed to better management of people, and as 2000 was by then fast approaching. After many years when management initiatives appeared to be more about managing financial resources than concern for people this was welcomed by staff, though it was initially viewed cynically by junior staff as yet another centrally imposed initiative which senior management felt obliged to respond to. That said, IIP was not an end in itself: it was a means of running a better business.

The opening campaign was a stocktake by the Management Board and a minute to all staff from the Permanent Secretary, then Sir John Vereker, in October 1998. It set out what staff at all levels should expect from their managers in terms of induction, communication and team-building, and from the annual cycle of personal appraisal and reporting. A subsequent 'health check' by an external consultant gave the Department a serious assessment of ill-health. Staff were committed and well-motivated and generally well understood the aims of the Department. But communications were still regarded as poor and a reasonably good system of annual staff appraisal and reporting was given very low priority and poorly implemented. The paper to the Management Board concluded that the 'overall assessment was bad' and that 'drastic action was needed'. The issue was what short-term measures could be put in place while a long-term change in culture could be achieved. How did one incentivise staff to be better managers of people: more top management and central direction and monitoring; upward reporting and 360-degree appraisal; capping performance marks for poor managers; and financial incentives for good managers? All of these were given their role and by 2000 the Department did seek and achieve IIP, though some thought it was lucky to have achieved IIP status so quickly. But more attention to good management has been given in recent years and the Department retained its IIP status in each three-yearly review, which themselves have become more demanding.

In recent years the Department has had, on the one hand, the advantage of a clear vision and expanding resources, and on the other, the challenge of adapting itself to new ways of doing business both overseas and within Whitehall. The former has been good for staff morale and the latter has required staff to face up to considerable change. A Staffing Needs Review in 2001/2 articulated these changes in terms of a triangle of skills mix needed of all staff in varying degrees: interpersonal, management and influencing skills; professional expertise; and knowledge of development issues. It reflected a growing need to work across traditional specialist advisory and administrative disciplines to achieve development outcomes. It proposed training programmes to equip staff to meet these needs, and a managed market within the Department for recruitment, promotion and postings, giving a stronger role for a central Human Resources Division. It was in this context that a number of new Head of Country Office posts went to members of the professional cadres who were acquiring the broader range of skills required through the changing nature of their work.

The emphasis in the 1999 White Paper on joined-up government was essential for the success of the Department in carrying forward its wider development remit after 1997. That said, it has been slower to change its own culture than some would have liked. In the first 15 years after 1964 joined-up government was seen as largely irrelevant, and in the next two decades the Department had for the most part learned to keep its head down and plough the development furrow hopefully unnoticed. The Aid and Trade Provision was hardly a good example of joined-up government; it was more like guerrilla warfare. When the opportunity came in 1997 to join up with others in Whitehall many within the Department seized the opportunity but there was both an ingrained defensiveness and a belief that the Department knew best. It had become accustomed to working with the FCO, particularly in Africa where there was a common economic and political agenda and few commercial distractions, and parts of the office had worked closely with the Treasury, for example on debt, and with DEFRA on environment issues, but for a large part of the Department their eyes were turned firmly overseas rather than towards the rest of Whitehall. It has been an important management challenge to change this culture and embrace joined-up government, particularly with the focus on fragile states and the increasing range of non-aid issues with which the Department has become involved since 1997.

## Home-grown change

### Financial and project cycle management

The Department has always prided itself on having relatively strong financial management systems for the aid programme itself. Having secured aid resources for the following three years it set out a strategy for their use agreed by ministers and allocated the resources available to individual multilateral and bilateral programmes accordingly having regard first to what the Department was already committed to spending. In-year financial monitoring was designed to ensure that the aid budget was spent in full, as effectively as possible, except to the extent that there was an end-year flexibility agreed with the Treasury to roll over unspent resources into the next financial year. Individual aid commitments spending over a number of years approved at the appropriate level were the responsibility of budget holders to ensure they could be accommodated within their annual expenditure limits.

For bilateral aid activities a system of project cycle management has evolved over a long period. It began in the 1960s with particular emphasis on project identification, design and appraisal. Identification was in the context of a country's development plan and priorities and periodic discussions with the recipient government about the particular areas in which the Department could most appropriately assist. Project design was undertaken (more or less) jointly between the recipient government and the Department, using outside consultants wherever appropriate. While good design also embraced appraisal, the Department developed its own cost benefit appraisal methodology, and a formal appraisal was a key step before seeking approval for any new aid commitment. There has been a system of delegated authority for approvals, with larger commitments being approved until a few years ago by a Projects Committee of senior management including Chief Advisers. Levels of delegated authority have been increased considerably in the past decade and the role of the Projects Committee has been abolished. Proposed commitments above £20 million, or any 'novel or contentious proposals' (a well-established phrase in Whitehall) are now put to ministers directly by the Divisional Director.

In the early years of the Department the most effort was put into these early stages of the project cycle. The Department does not generally implement projects; that is the responsibility of the recipient government, reinforced as necessary by technical co-operation in the form of consultants and/or individual experts. The job of the Department was to monitor implementation and intervene and advise as necessary. This function was given greater emphasis in the 1980s. At the same time the Department pioneered the use of Logical Frameworks designed (preferably on no more than one or two sides of A4) to relate more directly individual inputs to outputs and then to specified outcomes. These were to be used at every stage of the project cycle and proved to be a good discipline in project design, monitoring and evaluation.

Ex-post evaluation of selected aid activities also began early in the life of the Department, but its effectiveness in either accounting better for the resources spent or learning lessons for the future has been more limited than hoped. In the past the number of evaluations were either too small to give meaningful accountability or too backward-looking to give helpful lessons for the future as the nature of the business changed. They were also frequently too detailed and took far too long to undertake, and focused too much on the process of decision-making rather than on impact. Most evaluations were carried out by external consultants, normally drawn from a panel of those familiar with the Department's work, supervised by staff in Evaluation Department, and whose reports were expected to be commented on by the relevant division in the Department and by the overseas government concerned.

The work of the Evaluation Department was the responsibility of the Principal Finance Officer, seen as independent of spending divisions. Whatever the deficiencies in the Department's ex-post evaluation system, it has not shied away from publishing the reports, warts and all. Some consultants may say that their comments were censored, but generally only to ensure that their findings were supported by the evidence. Ministers were alerted to each publication but never offered any objection. The comment that the projects concerned had seldom been agreed on their watch would be unfair, particularly in the case of Lynda Chalker whose watch it was for more than a decade.

In the late 1980s project cycle management (PCM) was completed by the introduction of Project Completion Reports (PCRs) designed to assess the success or otherwise of the project and draw lessons. These were also potentially an important element in demonstrating accountability. Their strength lay in the fact that those filling in PCRs often had little or nothing to do with the initial decision to finance the project and not necessarily much to do with its implementation. Their weakness, for the sake of administrative brevity, was that they were largely a box-ticking exercise. It was an important end part of PCM but provided little by way of lesson learning. It did, however, provide the basis for the Evaluation Department providing an annual synthesis of the findings of PCRs completed over the last year, and became the basis of judging performance against one of the PSA targets of improving the quality of the Department's bilateral aid portfolio (see Chapter Twelve).

The Department's efforts at ex-post evaluation have been mixed. Outsiders might reasonably say that too few resources were devoted to it, and it was overseen too closely by internal staff and procedures. the However, the charge that staff in the Evaluation Department might feel threatened in terms of their future career is unfounded. Long-term professional evaluators may be a good thing but the disadvantage is that they do not take their experience with them to their next job within the Department. The recently created Independent Commission for Aid

Impact is an overdue innovation and it will have to grapple with the above issues in finding the right way forward.

## PSAs and business plans

The Fundamental Expenditure Review of 1995 had offered a development paradigm within which the Department's activities could fit. It was translated into three broad aims related to conditions for growth, human development and sustainable economic activity. Its advantage was that it offered staff a clearer framework and rationale for what they were being asked to do. Its disadvantage was that it was capable of embracing everything they were already doing and did not provide a cutting edge for allocating resources. Clare Short, in 1997, provided the Department with a clear over-riding mission to reduce poverty. However, except for cutting out activities that had other or dual motives, it did not by itself provide a basis for allocating and managing an expanding aid budget, not least because Short, rightly, saw the breadth of the agenda that reducing poverty required. The CSR process had the advantage of making the Department bid for resources in terms of achieving outcomes, and the PSA targets provided a broad framework for measuring outcomes rather than outputs against inputs.

A pre-condition for a sharper management of the Department and its resources, both financial and human, was the change in the way top management organised itself. The traditional way that decisions were taken was through a vertical chain of command, going as necessary to the Minister. The only exception to this was the Projects Committee's oversight of large projects and, as necessary, meetings of senior management to agree resource allocations annually for the coming three years. The latter was often seen as a relatively large number of barons fighting their own corner, rather than a small group taking strategic corporate decisions in a collegiate manner. The use of collective senior management for wider aid policy issues depended upon the inclinations of the Permanent Secretary of the day. Some had an appetite for collective policy discussions; some thought decisions should be made more economically; and others, particularly in earlier times, were used to the traditional vertical command chain.

After about 1995 it was agreed that a somewhat more formal and smaller group should come together to take key decisions of concern to the office as a whole, in the form of a Management Board. This evolved from a still relatively large group of 13 senior managers to a smaller group of top management (the Permanent Secretary and three Directors General), and two non-executives from outside the Department, including one from the private sector (a total membership of six). However, it took time for the Management Board to set itself clear and more pro-active terms of reference for managing the Department, and with sub-committees of the Board also with clear remits. This clarity in the collective role of top management had emerged by about 2002/3. More recently the Coalition government's Secretrary of State, Andrew Mitchell, established a small Ministerial Board, including senior civil servants and two non-executive directors.

## Location, location, location

### Overseas

The Department was established in 1964 in Eland House, Stag Place, in central London with one regional overseas office in Beirut and a number of scientific units dispersed mainly around central London. Since then the London headquarters has moved twice, but never more than a few yards from where it started: the first two buildings were demolished as unfit for purpose long before the work of the Department was in sight of being completed. Even with the creation of further regional Development Divisions, the administrative front office was still the Development Section of the local High Commission/Embassy.

As explained earlier, the original concept of the regional Development Divisions were that they should be responsible for the design, appraisal and monitoring of projects, with identification and approval of projects being the responsibility of London. Policy responsibility (that is, being responsible for country aid strategies and therefore project identification) only shifted gradually to the overseas offices. It accelerated in the 1980s as policy dialogue on a range of macro-economic, governance and sectoral issues became more central to the work of the Department. It was realised that this required more continuous contact with ministers and senior officials locally rather than periodic visits from London. But as the policy dialogue deepened it also became apparent that the relationship, for example, between the regional Development Division based in Nairobi and the Kenyan authorities (and with the local donor community) was qualitatively different from its relations with the Ugandan and Tanzanian authorities. This led, in the late 1990s, to the creation of country rather than regional offices where the Department had significant bilateral aid programmes.

There were, however, some important regional variations. The South East Asia Development division was established early on in Bangkok because of regional communications, despite the Department not having a significant aid programme to Thailand. As the Bangladesh programme became larger and more complex a country office was established, though initially answerable to Bangkok. As the pattern of bilateral aid in the region changed a further country office was established in Vietnam, and the Bangkok regional office was closed. Despite the importance of India and Pakistan in the Department's bilateral aid programme a regional office for the Indian sub-continent was never established for political reasons. These programmes were run largely from London until the country offices were created. West Africa programmes were also managed from London until country offices were created because of poor regional communications and because of the volatility of countries such as Nigeria and Sierra Leone in the past meant that levels of future aid were uncertain. The creation of country offices has been an important development over the last decade or so, but it has also made the Department more vulnerable to changing circumstances in individual countries (such as Zimbabwe), and particularly with a greater emphasis on fragile states.

Despite the delegation of aid policy to the regional offices, even in the early 1990s there were departments in London 'shadowing' the same countries and remaining responsible for clearing issues within Whitehall, notably the FCO, and for servicing ministers in respect of MPs' letters and Parliamentary Questions. However, it became increasingly apparent that this was both costly and largely unnecessary. Those with the information were overseas, and with improving communications it was possible for these traditional civil service functions to be carried out from the field. This change was not without its critics: those in London were doubtful that it could be made to work, and those overseas complained that they had opted to get out of London to do some real development and escape these more routine civil service tasks. The FCO was particularly nervous because of the differences in culture. The FCO was in general structured in a way that missions provided intelligence and advice and London decided policy because they were close to ministers. They were resistant to the idea that the Department's overseas offices should clear policy issues with the Head of Mission rather than with London. Although this newer way of doing business has been sustained, the wider remit of the Department after 1997, and the increasing emphasis on joined-up government, has required the regional Directors to recreate some additional policy capacity in London to assist them.

The changes described above created broader tensions within the FCO about the respective roles of the Department's overseas units and the Development Sections in local missions. In the early days the latter was seen mainly as a postbox and chaser, though that is doing some injustice to the staff involved. As policy dialogue became more important it was not always easy to distinguish between their respective roles and much depended on the personalities involved. With the creation of country offices, and after 1997, the system was rationalised. But, at the same time, the local High Commissioners/Ambassadors had also become more important in the policy dialogue with recipient countries: they had become a crucial tool of development diplomacy and in some countries, particularly in Africa, aid and development were a large part of their work. It has been important in the last decade in particular that Heads of Country Offices and Heads of Mission work effectively together.

### Abercrombie House

In the late 1970s the government undertook a major review of the scope for dispersing civil service functions outside London for a mixture of cost and political considerations. The Harding Report included a recommendation that certain support functions within the Department (mainly Accounts and Procurement, with some 600 posts) should be relocated outside London, and East Kilbride just outside Glasgow was identified. There was little enthusiasm in the Department for such a move and some hoped that the new Thatcher government would not implement it. However her determination to cut civil service costs meant that she endorsed the recommendations and the Department was obliged to go ahead.

It was a time of both opportunity and challenge but the former was not then yet in sight while the latter definitely was. The first problem was that the number of posts in the support functions had already been reduced. To help make up the shortfall it was decided to take back inside the Department the pension payment functions hitherto contracted out to Crown Agents. The second problem was that few staff either filling the posts to be relocated or currently serving elsewhere within the Department were willing to go to Abercrombie House. While this offered an opportunity for employment in Scotland it created a challenge for the Department. It was required to export a large number of people into other Whitehall departments or achieve voluntary and/or compulsory redundancies. The change was achieved mainly by the former, but the main problem was that the unions insisted upon applying the 'last in first out' rule which meant that at Executive Officer (EO) level the last in were generally graduates recruited into the civil service at that grade. In the short term the loss of graduate EOs was a significant loss to the Department and set back Fulton's ideas of a more integrated administrative civil service structure. At Abercrombie House the challenge was rather the opposite: it recruited a large number of 'over-qualified' staff because of the lack of employment opportunities at that time: some of the most junior staff had postgraduate degrees but with limited career opportunities given the nature of the functions transferred.

But whatever the short-term trauma, the long-term challenge was to create a sense of a unified headquarters located on two sites hundreds of miles apart. Improving IT was only a small part of the answer. Interchange of staff between London and Abercrombie House was made particularly difficult by the differential housing market. However, it has to be said that some who did go north valued the quality of life and stayed. Similarly, in good Scottish tradition, some from Abercrombie House applied for, and got, jobs in overseas offices and were reluctant to return home because of the lack of equally fulfilling job opportunities.

This last point was the focus of much discontent among staff and the unions in Abercrombie House. Apart from the nature of much of the work, there were only two senior civil service posts in the early years, and these tended to be filled by staff from London, who were in one way or another induced to go. Periodically the Department has been obliged to consider putting more posts in Abercrombie House, mainly as a result of pressure on running costs, but still until more recently with no great enthusiasm. Although it managed to have large numbers increasingly involved in policy work overseas it was not convinced that policy departments could readily be located in Abercrombie House. However, with the move of the London Headquarters to Palace Street at a time when the numbers employed centrally were increasing, there was a need to think further about putting more posts in Abercrombie House. In recent years the Evaluation Department, one multilateral aid policy department and parts of the central research and corporate performance departments have moved there as part of meeting the 'Lyons' target of moving a further 85 posts to Abercrombie House. The future of Abercrombie House was secured by the Department taking ownership of the building and extending it a few years ago. Meanwhile, with the current headcount reductions required of the Department and pressure on running costs generally, there will be a continuing incentive to move further posts to Abercrombie House and release sufficient space in London to sublet part of Palace Street.

### Diversity

The Department began, like most Whitehall departments, heavily concentrated in London with the administrative fast stream and professionals drawn from a national graduate market and executive and clerical staff from a regional market. The senior staff were almost exclusively white males and most were educated at public school and Oxbridge. This is much less true today but even in 2000 focus groups on diversity within the Department still perceived them in that way. The fact that the then Permanent Secretary, Sir John Vereker, was the product of a grammar school and Keele University understandably did not change that basic perception. The junior grades were ethnically more diverse and contained more women.

The initial corporate approach to diversity was typical of the day: it would look after itself with normal competitive, non-discriminatory recruitment and promotion procedures and it was for the education system and society to ensure equality of opportunity.

In terms of ethnic diversity it can be fairly said that in addition to legislation and decency of behaviour by an organisation committed to reducing poverty overseas, the Department has had the opportunity for diversity thrust upon it. As it located more of its work overseas it had both the opportunity, and increasingly the incentive, to employ more local staff. It traditionally employed local staff only in very junior support positions and like the FCO did not regard such staff as an integral part of the Department, even though many were long-serving officers. One of the many obstacles to seeing local staff differently has been security of classified information: they were not allowed to see restricted material, not on the basis of the usual Whitehall vetting system but because they were nationals of the country concerned. This sense of 'them and us' was exacerbated by employing British nationals locally (usually white females) on more favourable terms, which by the 1990s the Department increasingly found discriminatory and unacceptable.

As the overseas offices changed from being operational outposts to just another part of the Department that happened to be located overseas, the perception and role of local staff changed. This was reinforced by the shift in the role of the Department itself, with a much greater emphasis on policy dialogue and the need to understand local circumstances. Local staff became valued not just as a source of cheap labour but for the contribution they could make through their understanding of local political, economic and social issues. It is also true to say that with increasing pressures on running costs the Department also had a financial incentive wherever possible to use local staff in somewhat more senior positions, though this had implications for the career prospects and job interest of junior staff in London.

The changes described above led to a major review of what were then known as locally engaged staff, a term which itself was thought to be divisive – though the term adopted by the review, 'staff appointed in country', is only a modest improvement and has the unattractive acronym, SAIC. The conclusion of the review was that staff appointed in-country should so far as possible within the constraints set by the Department being a British government organisation, be treated like all other staff and have the same expectations in terms of the way they were managed. If there had to remain a glass ceiling on promotion it should be a lot higher. More professional staff could be expected to be appointed in-country. There were aspirations that some local staff could spend time in headquarters and in other overseas offices, though there were nationality constraints on this.

In 2007 a further review of SAIC staff was undertaken. It showed that nearly all (94 per cent) of 132 B2/EO posts overseas were filled by local staff, as were almost two-thirds of B1/HEO posts. At A2/Principal level the figure was less than 20 per cent, and there were only a few third-country postings of SAIC staff. The sense of 'them and us' had diminished as local knowledge had become more valued, but the scope for attachments in Headquarters remained limited. This represented a substantial change over the last decade, albeit driven in part by cost pressures.

Within the home civil service considerable progress has been made in terms of civil service-wide targets. The target for April 2008 for the senior civil service was 37 per cent of women and 4 per cent of ethnic minority staff. As of December 2007 the Department had met the former target and exceeded the latter threefold. For disabled staff in the SCS the Department recorded a figure of 2.1 per cent against a civil service-wide target of 3 per cent.

## The role of Chief Advisers

The office had operated a system of matrix management since its creation. For the most part administrators administrated and professional advisers advised. The latter were attached to administrative divisions which set their work priorities, but they were professionally managed by the relevant Chief Adviser who also advised on career development and decided on postings. As part of senior management Chief Advisers were responsible for professional advice to ministers and participated in corporate decision-making.

By the early 1990s the demands of the Department for professional advice was changing. Economists no longer did much cost benefit analysis and were more concerned with macro-economic and budgetary management issues. Capacity-building in the form of institutional change rather than just technical inputs was back on the agenda and needed different skills. There was a growing understanding of the need for stronger political skills as part of a growing governance agenda. By 2008 there were some 150 governance advisers embracing a wide variety of skills, and many social development advisers. A broader sectoral focus also required a more multi-disciplinary approach to identifying problems and achieving outcomes. Some of the Chief Advisers responded to this by adapting the skill mix within their cadres and adopted more inter-disciplinary working within their groups at Headquarters. But bilateral aid divisions wanted more freedom to recruit staff, both internally and externally if necessary, to meet their changing requirements.

These issues came to a head in 2001 when management finally decided that there needed to be a fundamental review of what was now known as Policy Division, essentially comprising the nine Chief Advisers and their central staff in 14 departments, and who now had larger financial resources to operate on their own account. The Report, in April 2002, which involved wide consultation within the Department, noted a number of strengths, including the provision of valuable policy insights and quality papers, and having considerable influence within the international community. Chief Advisers would be relieved of their current management responsibilities (including for their financial resources) and given more time to provide specialist advice and lead their respective professions. It was without doubt the most ambitious structural change the Department ever attempted, and was deeply resented by Chief Advisers and others. However, a further reorganisation took effect in April 2004 which created five permanent groups covering all key policy areas: development effectiveness, governance and social development, growth and investment, human resources, and sustainable development. Chief Adviser posts were abolished (except the Chief Economist post) but Heads of Profession would instead continue to provide cereer advice for staff, policy advice and support to the new Heads of the policy groups.

The House of Commons Science and Technology Committee undertook a review of the Department's use of science.[106] While acknowledging that the Department had 'earned worldwide respect for the quality of its work' the report concluded that the Department suffered 'from a fundamental lack of scientific culture' no doubt in part because it had abolished Chief Adviser posts and only during the course of its enquiry did the Department announce that in common with other Whitehall departments it was to appoint a Chief Scientific Adviser, which the report described as long overdue. The Committee went on to say that they were concerned that 'the quality of policy making may, on occasion, have been compromised by a lack of recognition of the value of research and evaluation'. This judgement was regarded as harsh by many in the Department who valued evidence-based policy analysis. But over the years, partly as a result of running cost pressures, changing priorities and the demise of the Department's Scientific Units, the in-house science and research capacity had been eroded.

## Capability Review

As part of the Capability Review Programme under the auspices of the Cabinet Office the Department was subject to its first review in 2007 carried out by an external review team with a mix of private and public sector experience. The Department came out of it well compared with other government departments. The positive messages were:

i.  it had a clear mission and attracts and inspires passionate and commited people; the Board provides strong and purposeful leadership;
ii.  it has clear objectives and targets connected to actions on the ground; is a world leader in research and analysis and policy development;
iii.  DFID has a sound business model that has served it well and is good at managing performance and delivery.

But the Review also identified certain areas of weakness, including:

i.  the Department 'needs to embed a culture of challenge and change and to strengthen people management and communications'. Surprisingly the Review noted that only 42 per cent of senior civil servants 'feel that it is safe to speak up and challenge the way things are done . . .';
ii.  working with other government departments 'remains a big challenge'; and
iii.  it needs to strengthen its accountability to the UK public'.

The Department, as required, produced an action plan for remedying these areas of weakness. This was absorbed into the agenda of the then new Permanent Secretary, Minouche Shafik, 'Making It Happen', emphasising delivery, focus and impact (including 'communicating our mission and successes to the UK public').

## Comment

The Department has come a long way in the last two decades in managing itself as distinct from the aid programme. It has become a more diverse organisation and one which is better equipped to manage itself across a large number of locations. However, in strengthening leadership it appears to have discouraged a culture of challenge at senior levels. It may also have diluted its scientific base too far in making important and necessary changes in recent years, and become less well equipped to manage a growing research budget. The wider agenda since 1997 remains a major challenge which probably requires greater interchange of staff within Whitehall. In terms of explaining to the public what the Department is achieving the greatest challenge will be to account for general budgetary support rather than the impact of individual projects, particularly as much media coverage of developing countries continues to be about poor governance, including corruption. This is something the Coalition government is trying to address.

# 12
# Development Impact

## Introduction

The stated mission of the Department has been summarised as reducing poverty in the poorer developing countries and it is against this that it should primarily be judged. In the early years this was largely about the use of aid and, later, the policy dialogue that went with it. More recently the Department has had a remit beyond aid to influence a wider range of development issues which government as a whole seeks to address. In exploring impact, one is immediately confronted with the fact that the Department is just one player among many: aid-recipient developing countries, other donors, and more recently other Whitehall departments. This makes it difficult to assess the development impact of the Department itself but does not, of course, reduce the importance of accountability for the resources it is provided with. It is not possible here to provide a detailed and comprehensive assessment of the Department's impact on development over nearly half a century, but rather to offer some guide as to how the subject might be approached. Nor is the author best placed to offer an objective assessment. For a fuller study of the impact of foreign aid more generally the reader is referred to the recent work by Roger Riddell.[107]

The original rationale for aid was that poor countries could expect to achieve lower domestic savings rates as a proportion of national income than richer countries (the poverty trap) and inherently had limited access to international capital markets with which to supplement them. The role of official aid was to make good these deficiencies and provide the investment resources by which poor countries could grow more quickly than would otherwise be the case. Even if economic theory is thought not to support either of these two earlier propositions (savings rates are no longer thought to be a function of income levels, and international capital, other things being equal, tends to gravitate towards countries with capital scarcity), this does not undermine the moral or economic case for official aid that can still help poor countries grow and reduce poverty at a faster rate than might otherwise be possible if it is used effectively.

There is a vast amount of literature on aid effectiveness but there are two pieces of work, very different in time and approach, that deserve particular attention here. The first are the writings of Professor P. T. Bauer in the 1960s and 1970s which were concerned with the political economy of development and aid, and the second is the more technical econometric work undertaken by the World Bank's Development Research Group in the late 1990s. Professor Bauer was a free market economist who believed passionately that aid generally did more harm than good. The World Bank's work was driven by criticisms on both the right and left: the former convinced that aid was not effective and the latter that the structural adjustment policies espoused by the Bank over the last two decades and more were wrong.

One of the harshest critics of official aid was Bauer.[108] He often wrote that at its best the value of aid was the lower debt servicing it involved compared to private capital, and at its worst it propped up corrupt and incompetent governments, allowing them to follow misguided macro-economic policies that retarded growth, and micro-economic policies that exploited the poor and undermined enterprise. He was heavily influenced by his work on West African small-scale entrepreneurship and the policies of Nkrumah in Ghana. By the protagonists of aid he was dismissed as a polemicist but in some important respects he was ahead of his time and his criticisms need addressing if one is to look seriously at the development impact of aid, including that provided by the Department.

The World Bank published a book in 1998 called *Assessing Aid*[109] which was based upon econometric work done by Dollar and Burnside and by Collier and Dollar, though the latter did further work subsequently.[110] An excellent critique of this work was provided by Jonathon Benyon in 1999 as a member of the Department's Economic Service.[111] The key findings of 'Assessing Aid' were:

i. countries with better economic management grew faster;
ii. the single relationship between aid and growth was weak;
iii. aid contributes towards growth in well-managed economies but not in badly managed economies;

iv. the contribution of aid to growth was stronger in well-managed low-income economies, where it concluded that additional aid equivalent to 1 per cent of GDP increased growth by 0.5 per cent, though with diminishing marginal returns;

v. there was a good correlation between growth and poverty reduction, though the nature of that relationship depended upon starting conditions and policies.

The policy conclusions were that more aid should be targeted at low-income countries with sound economic management; too much went to middle-income countries which needed it less and to low-income countries with poor policies where it was relatively ineffective. Related to this last point, the studies also concluded that aid could not buy good policies, or put another way ownership of good policies by the country concerned was essential. Whether Professor Bauer would have agreed with this analysis one cannot know but it does support his own views that too much aid in the past, however unintentionally, financed bad policies.

The definition of good economic management remains controversial, but for the purposes of the above analysis it was based primarily on the World Bank's own Country Policy and Institutional Assessment scores which covered macro-economic management, structural policies (including trade, foreign exchange regimes, property rights and rules-based governance), policies for reducing inequalities, and public sector management (including equity of public expenditures and accountability of the public service).

## Aid for the poorest countries

It has been a basic tenet of the Department that the bulk of the aid budget should go to the poorest countries. The main deviations from this as regards bilateral aid has been Britain's special responsibility for its remaining overseas territories, relatively modest technical co-operation programmes in the middle-income countries of Latin America and to a lesser extent South East Asia, the Aid and Trade Provision, focused on creditworthy middle- as well as low-income countries (1977–97), the technical co-operation programmes to the Transition Countries of Central and Eastern Europe and the former Soviet Union after 1990, and some humanitarian assistance, which since 1990 has been provided to European countries (formerly part of Yugoslavia) and more recently Iraq. Most multilateral aid over which the Department had a policy choice has gone to the soft windows of the International Financial Institutions for low-income countries, and to the European Development Fund for the mainly low-income ACP countries.

In recent years the Department had a formal target for bilateral aid to low-income countries as one of its PSA targets (90 per cent). The table below shows the proportion of bilateral aid allocable by country going to low-income countries at five-yearly intervals since 1965. Partly because of the policies it inherited in 1964 the proportion of bilateral aid going to low-income countries was only about 60 per cent in the first decade but then increased steadily to reach a peak of 90 per cent prior to the end of the Cold War. The reduction thereafter was the result of increased aid to Europe, either to assist in the transition to market economies or in response to humanitarian crises. In recent years the proportion going to low-income countries has increased again, reaching over 80 per cent. With the increase in bilateral aid resources the 90 per cent target should be readily achievable except for the need to help reconstruct Iraq.

The Collier and Dollar studies referred to earlier (note 110) developed a poverty-reducing efficient model of aid distribution based, among other things, on the number of poor people and good policies. It concluded that if the sole objective of aid was to reduce poverty it should be better distributed. Indeed, it estimated that an optimal distribution of aid would do as much for reducing poverty as a tripling of aid budgets with the existing (1990s) geographical distribution of aid. Jonathon Benyon (see above, note 111) examined the Department's bilateral aid distribution against the Collier and Dollar model. He concluded that on

*Table 12.1*   Proportion (percentage) of bilateral aid to low-income countries[a]

|          | Total | of which India |
|----------|-------|----------------|
| 1965     | 59    | 16             |
| 1970     | 62    | 23             |
| 1975     | 56    | 31             |
| 1980     | 71    | 14             |
| 1985     | 79    | 16             |
| 1990/91  | 91    | 11             |
| 1995/96  | 69    | 18             |
| 2000/01  | 75    | 10             |
| 2005/06  | 84    | 13             |
| 2010/11  | 82    | 7              |

[a] Proportion of country-specific aid, including humanitarian aid.

this basis alone the Department should be providing less aid to Central and Eastern Europe, Latin America and the Caribbean and more to the larger Asian countries (notably India). However, he recognised that other factors were also important, including the Department's comparative advantage. The fact is that the distribution of global aid has for political reasons always disproportionately benefited small countries, and the relative decline in aid to India in the 1990s also accounts significantly for the Collier and Dollar finding that donors collectively appeared to buy out of countries with good policies. The Department, partly for historical reasons, has nevertheless provided a larger proportion of its bilateral aid to the Indian sub-continent than most other bilateral donors. However, with better economic management over the last 20 years, India has benefited from rapid overall growth in GDP and the Department now anticipates scaling down its aid to India despite its having a very large number of very poor people.

## Support for good policies

In the early life of the Department it is not obvious that commitment by developing countries to poverty reduction per se and the policies that were required for growth was a significant factor in allocating resources, though it provided little aid to those countries whose governments were wilfully incompetent or more corrupt than might otherwise have been expected by its historical links (such as Sierra Leone and Burma). It relied instead on financing projects that were thought to be economically beneficial either to the country as a whole (such as infrastructure investments) or directly beneficial to the poor (such as rural development projects). It believed that its own approach to cost benefit analysis would have a wider demonstration effect on the governments with which it engaged. While this may have had some limited impact on officials there is little evidence to suggest that it had much impact upon governments as a whole. Perhaps the one area where the Department did have some modest effect even in the early years, together usually with the World Bank, was to engage governments on sector policies in relation to pricing and the financial sustainability of public sector institutions providing services to the public. Support for rural development seldom led it to tackle basic policy failures related to incentives.

But with the poor overall economic performance of many low-income countries, and their increasing indebtedness, the Department realised by the 1980s that financing good projects in bad environments was not enough, neither for achieving its objectives nor accounting sufficiently for the funds it spent. Finding ideal projects which were unlikely to be sustainable in economies, particularly in Africa, that were collapsing about them became a thing of the past. However controversial the Washington Consensus, the Department joined it in the belief that supporting economic reform with new aid instruments and debt relief was the only way forward if it was to achieve its mission.

There is no doubt that the Department, like other donors, must plead guilty to attempting to buy good policies, particularly in Africa, and largely failing to do so in the 1980s and early 1990s. Against falling resources available for bilateral aid it continued to provide project aid including technical co-operation at modest levels and put more resources into programme/budgetary aid. The latter was required to help governments struggling with a fiscal crisis and having to cut public investment in an often vain attempt to maintain public consumption, and find a way out of administered foreign exchange regimes where demand vastly exceeded supply. In the early period it was a policy of stop-go in countries which lacked ownership and failed to deliver on promised reforms. Whether many countries in Africa would have achieved the per capita income growth and poverty reduction experienced in recent years without the difficult period of reward and punishment will have to be left to future historians and econometricians to debate. But Professor Bauer and *Assessing Aid* would appear to say it would have occurred, and maybe sooner had aid been less forthcoming. The NGO community may continue to believe that had aid been more forthcoming more poverty reduction in difficult policy environments would have been possible: what is less clear is whether it believes that the current growth and poverty reduction now being experienced would have been possible with the same poor policies.

In moving on to an era of global MDGs and country-level poverty-reduction strategies that everyone can unite around, the Department provided some important value-added. Having been more willing than others to provide programme/budgetary aid to countries in crisis it argued that while this helped countries to graduate to a more market-determined foreign exchange regime it was importantly providing support to a government's budget. This legitimised donors' interest in the overall balance of government expenditure that was crucial in reducing poverty and making progress towards the MDGs. For the first time it also emboldened donors, including the World Bank, to discuss the amount of the budget allocated to defence expenditure, and more generally to engage in a dialogue about stronger financial management of public expenditure.

In Asia, particularly India and China, donors including the Department knew that politically they could not buy good policies even if they were prepared to find the resources that might have been necessary to do so. It was therefore with considerable relief that India found its own way towards adopting new policies in the 1990s that have led to its remarkable growth in recent years. Some analysts would argue that if the key MDG of reducing poverty by half globally is achieved it will be because of the economic policies in China and India rather than aid. In a presentation at the Overseas Development Institute, Professor Danny Quah of the LSE pointed out that since 1981 the number of people living on less than $1 a day had fallen from 1.5 billion to 1 billion, wholly accounted for by China. On the other hand if substantial progress is made towards the MDGs in a range of low-income countries, particularly in Africa, then aid will continue to be an important element in support of better policies. The external evaluation of the Department's work in 2003[112] found that the Department 'is, overall, managing both to increase the proportion of its bilateral country aid to poorer countries, and to increase the proportion going to countries with a favourable policy environment'.

## The transformational impact of aid

The Department has been flexible, particularly in recent years, in the way it has been willing to provide aid, and this has contributed to its effectiveness, particularly in countries heavily dependent upon aid to finance their budgets. However, financial aid is highly fungible: that is to say if donors provide aid for one particular purpose such as primary education it does not follow that the recipient country necessarily allocates more resources overall to primary education; it may shift its own domestic resources into other sectors, including military expenditure – or it may reduce its domestic resource mobilisation effort. The econometric work reflected in the World Bank's *Assessing Aid* concluded that, in general, aid was highly fungible, reinforcing the argument that aid was more effective in promoting growth and poverty reduction in countries with good policies. Ironically, if one accepts that aid is fungible then to the extent that the Aid and Trade Provision went to creditworthy low-income countries (indicating at least moderately reasonable policies such as in China, India and Indonesia with large numbers of poor people) it may not have been so damaging to the Department's mission as its critics believed.

Thus, the impact of financial aid cannot be judged simply by looking at the sectors to which it was targeted. The value of project aid lies not so much in its sectoral distribution but whether or not it is a mechanism for creating and transmitting knowledge and building institutional capacity: in short, ideas matter as much as money. For example, the Department might finance the construction of a power station which was designed and built to time and budget and commissioned at its rated capacity. But what was the value of this compared to writing a cheque on the budget? Was the recipient institution involved in its design and construction so it was better equipped in future; did it involve new technology effectively introduced; were staff trained in operation and maintenance; was there a dialogue about financial sustainability and pricing structure for the power system as a whole? If the answers are no, one may just as well have written a cheque, except that this one project was built successfully possibly because of supervision by the Department and its consultants. It could be argued that adopting a sector-wide approach in education, health and water enabled the Department to have a more transformational effect on sectoral policies and financial management which would not have been achieved by financing discrete projects.[113] Likewise, the provision of general budget support sought to achieve important changes in macro-economic management and sought to influence, with technical co-operation, the overall management of public finances. The key issue in recent years has been whether through increasing general budget support one can achieve policy and institutional change at a sectoral level.

Technical co-operation is generally less fungible and potentially more transformational. Growth (and poverty reduction) is a function of increases in productivity requiring the transmission and adoption of new ways of doing things. Just as private foreign direct investment brings new management and technologies so aid is capable of doing likewise. Much technical co-operation in the early days was about providing people, but this was often more about filling gaps than institutional capacity-building and institutional change. In recent years the Department has focused much more on the latter. In the last decade or more the Department has contributed towards substantial institutional change in a number of areas, including for example in the management of public finances and in Customs and Revenue authorities in several African countries. The Department increased support for civil society organisations in recent years, particularly when combining empowerment and advocacy with community service delivery, and is also likely to prove transformational in strengthening governance in developing countries. The National Audit Office (NAO) Report of July 2006[114] concluded that civil society organisations 'can help to hold developing countries' governments accountable for poverty reduction, give voice to the concerns of poor people, and secure access to government services for marginalised groups'. A scrutiny of the Department's ex-post evaluation studies over the last 30 years would no doubt yield many other examples where aid has, with varying degrees of success, achieved transformational change.

When the Department was able to provide local costs in India in the 1980s as a result of a deal over aid debt relief it was able to undertake innovative work with the government in areas of rural development such as forestry management. In the late 1990s the Department persuaded the Indian government to allow it to work more directly at state level. It focused on four of the poorest and more reform-minded states (Andhra Pradesh, Madhya Pradesh, Orissa and West Bengal) to help bring about a transformation in public finances and delivery of public services. The Indian government in recent years has been less open to this approach. In its Report on the Department's bilateral programme to India the International Development Committee of the House of Commons[115] concluded that the Department 'adds most value in India through its innovation, research, technical advice and demonstration projects and should be concentrating on developing capacity in India within the civil service and elsewhere to enable India to deliver such [poverty-reducing] programmes'.

The research and development work carried out by the Natural Research Institute and its predecessors provided the basis for substantial increases in agricultural productivity (something noted in the 1997 DAC Peer Review of UK aid), and the Department's now larger research programme across a range of sectors has the potential for spreading new ideas and increasing productivity provided it can re-establish its own capacity for managing it. Although no longer fashionable, the early country training programmes funded by the Department provided the basis for long-term capacity-building and it could have done more in this regard by greater support for the education sector in recipient countries, including at secondary and tertiary level. Roger Riddell, in his recent work, concludes that much technical co-operation has been effective, but it comes at a high cost; hence the importance that it is sufficiently transformational in its impact to be cost-effective.

The National Audit Office is empowered under its 1983 Act to undertake value-for-money studies of expenditure incurred by government departments. Since then it has undertaken many studies related to the Department's activities. The early studies were focused on individual projects, bilateral country aid programmes (India and Indonesia) or particular sector studies (water and the environment, and health and population). They were concerned primarily with process and outputs; though they also addressed sustainability and increasingly recognised, particularly in the social sectors, that this depended on continued capacity-building and a dialogue over recipient government budgetary allocations. More recent sector studies (water and HIV/AIDS) show a stronger understanding of the importance of aid interventions being transformational. For example, in its January 2003 Report on the water sector[116] the NAO recognised the importance of policy dialogue and the Department having the necessary professional expertise to engage in this, including as more resources were provided as general budget support. It highlighted the case of Uganda which had ambitious targets in the water sector; the Department complemented its budget support with a technical co-operation project to help address longer-term capacity and policy issues. Likewise in its June 2004 Report[117] the NAO highlighted the importance of policy dialogue in the Poverty Reduction Strategy context to ensure HIV/AIDS is properly addressed and the need for programmes to reflect up to date research and knowledge on the subject. In its 2011 Report on Bilateral Support to Primary Education the NAO estimated that the Department was financing some five million children in primary schools but criticised the lack of emphasis on improving quality and education outcomes.[118]

## Project portfolio performance

One of the targets in previous PSAs was to increase the proportion of the Department's bilateral projects evaluated as successful. The index covers projects and programmes with a value over £1 million which have been in operation for at least two years and which are scored annually. Success is defined as a project being likely to completely, or largely, achieve its intended objectives. It is therefore a health check on a living portfolio of projects rather than ex-post judgement on actual achievements, and the scoring is done by current project managers. Against a baseline for the last quarter of 2002/3 when less than 60 per cent were judged as successful, the index had moved up to 75 per cent by number, and 77 per cent by value of projects by the end of 2006/7, but whether they were transformational is another matter.

Projects are classified by the degree of risk attached to meeting their objectives. Although the proportion by value and number varies, broadly about 20 per cent of the portfolio has been classified as high risk, 60 per cent as medium risk and 20 per cent as low risk. The end-2002/3 baseline for success for these three risk categories by value was 24 per cent, 61 per cent and 75 per cent respectively. By the end of 2006/7 there had been a notable improvement with success ratings by value being 64 per cent, 77 per cent and 94 per cent respectively. This reflects the Department's strategy for improving its project portfolio, though some might wish to invoke Charles (now Lord) Goodhart's law on monetary targets.

Project Completion Reports (PCRs) have been part of the Department's project cycle management since the latter half of the 1980s and also provide a guide to project-level impact, though methodologies have changed over the past 20 years making it difficult to assess trends. Two studies of PCRs were produced by the Department's Evaluation Department (EV 637, November 2001 and EV 664, February 2006) providing data for the period 1986–2005 by date of project approval, using broadly the same measure of success as above. The first, covering the period to 1999, shows a generally rising trend in the proportion of projects judged successful from just over 60 per cent in the 1980s to 77 per cent in the period 1994–99. This study showed greater likelihood of success in sectors such as energy and transport, and a lower success rate in RNR and water and sanitation. It also showed considerable regional variation, with projects in Africa doing less well and those in middle-income countries doing better. The second study covering the period 2000–05 shows a success rating of between 65 per cent and 70 per cent, with better than average performance in health and lower performance for human rights and governance projects. In this period there was significantly less regional variation.

## Performance management

The focus on the MDGs by the international community coincided with the introduction of PSA targets for the Department. The latter were relatively short-term (three years) but were based on making progress against the longer-term MDGs. Both represented a shift from measuring project outputs to development outcomes and made attribution of the efforts of any one donor or recipient even more difficult. The NAO's 2002 report[119] recognised and supported the outcome-based approach to performance management. It noted that 'targeting outputs might solve attribution problems. But they can introduce other problems, such as putting more emphasis on activity rather than achievement . . .'

It supported the Department's approach to PSA targets of focusing on outcomes in those countries where it provided most aid and could be influential.

This NAO report was particularly important as the Department moved from a period of short-term programme aid to helping countries in crisis to longer-term budgetary aid in support of poverty-reduction strategies focused on making progress towards the MDGs at a country level. The 2008 NAO report on budget support[120] was generally positive in its findings. It concluded, importantly, that through support for poverty-reduction strategies, budget support had enabled partner governments to increase expenditure on priority sectors (such as health and education); increase their capacity to plan and deliver services effectively; and strengthen their financial management systems. However, the NAO noted that 'service expansion has often been at the expense of quality' and 'progress in strengthening financial management systems has been slower than expected'. The report additionally found that 'budget support can also improve domestic accountability by increasing the proportion of development expenditure reflected in government accounts and therefore increasing the potential for scrutiny by domestic stakeholders'.

In addition to its Annual Report to Parliament, the Department produces an annual Autumn Performance Report, outlining progress against its PSAs. The December 2007 report (Cmd 7274), emphasised that the PSAs are based on the MDGs and 'are used as a tool to manage and improve performance, providing a high-level framework against which policy decisions and financial commitments can be assessed, and successes and underperformance measured'.

The International Development Committee of the House of Commons has scrutinised the work of the Department more intensively since 1997 than its Select Committee predecessors. In its First Special Report, Session 2000–01, the Committee stated that it 'had seen our work both as ensuring that DFID maintains and improved its standards of development assistance, but also as an advocate, alongside DFID, of the needs of the poor'. Apart from its specific enquiries into individual activities of the Department it also examines progress against the PSAs. The Committee has noted the problems of attributing to the Department its individual contributions towards progress, or lack of it, against PSA targets, which it accepts. However, it has asked that the Department 'provides evidence of corrective or remedial action it is taking in instances where PSA targets are not going to be met'.[120]

The Department responded to this criticism in its 2006 and 2007 Reports, which the Committee has acknowledged. For example, in its 2007 Annual

Review,[121] the Department recorded under-achievement on its PSA target for under-five mortality in a number of African countries and set out what specific actions it was undertaking, such as helping Sierra Leone formulate a new long-term Child Survival and Maternal Health Programme.

## The Paris Declaration on Aid Effectiveness

The Paris Declaration[122] in March 2005 was agreed by over 100 donor countries and organisations and developing countries, and was based on the belief that more effective aid would have a greater 'impact on reducing poverty and inequality, increasing growth, building capacity and accelerating achievement of the MDGs'. It is based on five principles: ownership by developing countries; alignment of donor support with national development strategies, institutions and procedures; harmonisation of donors' actions; managing for results; and mutual accountability. Each of these has one or more indicators (12 in all) with targets for 2010. The international community reinforced their commitment to these targets in 2008 with the Accra Agenda for Action.

A baseline survey of performance was carried out in 2006 by the DAC. Based on this survey and the Department's own analysis (which was somewhat more critical) the conclusions were as follows (see DFID Annual Report 2007[123]):

| Targets largely met | Good progress | Limited progress |
|---|---|---|
| Joint missions with others. Co-ordinated technical co-operation. Use of national financial management and procurement systems. | Aid reported on countries' budgets. Reduction in parallel implementation units. | In-year aid predictability. Use of programme-based approaches. Joint analytical work. |

The Department published a medium-term action plan on aid effectiveness in 2006 to comply with the targets set out in the Paris Declaration. However its actions were primarily qualitative in nature except for two specific targets: all aid to governments should be reported in national budgets (not a major innovation for the Department unless it embraced technical co-operation) and no new parallel project implementation units (again not something the Department was often guilty of in recent years). That said, the Department has shown greater commitment than most donors to meet the aspirations of the Paris Declaration, particularly in terms of joint working with other donors. It is reflected in the fact that the Department published an 'Action Plan to Promote Harmonisation' in February 2003 following the work of the DAC Task Force on Donor Practices and prior to the High Level Forum held in Rome in 2003, which paved the way for the Paris Declaration two years later. The Department strongly supported the 2008 Accra Agenda for Action, which agreed stronger commitments to implement the Paris Declaration.

The 2006 DAC Peer Review[124] noted that the Department 'is currently seen by many aid practitioners and donors as one of the bilateral models for today's evolving world of development co-operation'. However, it commented that the Department's enthusiasm for certain initiatives is not always 'shared by other partners . . . (such as general budget support) . . . broader donor receptivity and collaboration could be possible in a more inclusive and empirical environment for partnership . . . [the Department] should seek to strike a balance between its interests in promoting aid reform and in leading donor harmonisation efforts'. In short the Department should listen more. A 2008 article[125] by Easterley and Pfutze examined the aid practices of bilateral and multilateral aid agencies. With regard to transparency and overall best practices the Department came second only to the World Bank. However, one can question some of the authors' criteria for best practice, particularly their assumption that technical co-operation, alongside food aid, is an ineffective form of aid.

It is perhaps too early to judge definitively on the Department's impact on broader development issues beyond aid since its remit was formally widened only in 1997. However, Chapter Five indicates the Department has influenced the government's international policies on debt and the environment over the past 25 years and more recently on international trade. The key to this has been the previous government's more joined-up approach and commitment to international development,[126] and the Department's own technical capacity and field-based understanding of development issues. However, as the 2007 Capability Review noted, whilst the Department has had some successes in working with the rest of Whitehall on strategic policy issues '. . . [it] needs to strengthen these relationships . . . working with other government departments . . . remains a big challenge'.

## Comment

Early efforts to projectise every aid activity and wishing to see a stated developing-country demand (including training and research) probably did more harm than good in terms of achieving long-term development impact. In recent years the Department has embraced both the concept of fungibility and the potential for aid to be transformational. It has provided a larger proportion of its bilateral aid for programme funding (general budget or sector-wide programmes) in support of agreed poverty-reduction strategies and budgetary priorities, and complemented it with more effective technical co-operation activities which have the potential for far-reaching change. In terms of development impact and aid effectiveness it is likely to prove a winning combination, not just another fad. Likewise, a renewed emphasis on research and development to correct for market failure (and in some cases to create a market) has the potential to be transformational, including in helping developing countries address important issues such as agricultural productivity and climate change. Finally, it has had an impact beyond its own bilateral aid programme by its influence on the practices and impact of the wider international aid system.

The public debate on aid, such as it has been, has focused on two issues. The first in the 1980s, conducted largely by the NGOs, was on the government's meanness and misguided self-interest in a time of 'plenty'. More recently it has been conducted by the critics of aid in a time of austerity. The former were arguably too forgiving of corrupt and incompetent regimes and the latter too ready to write off all developing countries suffering from the failures in economic and political governance that some in developed countries have endured. Both groups need to be hard-headed in deciding where and when British aid can be effective in reducing poverty in an imperfect world.

# Notes and References

1. D. J. Morgan, *The Official History of Colonial Development*, 5 vols (Basingstoke: Palgrave Macmillan), 1980.
2. Harold Macmillan's 3 February 1960 'Wind of Change' speech. Available online at: www.africanhistory.about.com.
3. Anthony Nutting, *No End of a Lesson – The Story of Suez* (London: Constable and Company), 1967. Nutting was a former Minister of State at the Foreign and Commonwealth Office.
4. Sir Lawrence Freedman, *The Official History of the Falklands* (Cabinet Office Series of Official Histories) (London: Taylor & Francis), 2005.
5. White Paper 1931 (Cmd 3952): Measures to Secure Reductions in National Expenditure.
6. White Paper 1940 (Cmnd 6175): Statement of Policy on Colonial Development and Welfare.
7. House of Commons debate Vol 361 Col 76, 21 May 1940.
8. House of Lords debate Vol 116 Col 724, 2 July 1940.
9. Colonial Paper, Col (No 306), 1954: Re-organisation of the Colonial Service.
10. White Paper 1960 (Cmnd 1193): Service with Overseas Governments.
11. Cmnd 786: Report of the Committee of Enquiry into the Financial Structure of the Colonial Development Corporation 1958–59.
12. White Paper 1971 (Cmnd 4677): Colonial Development and Welfare Acts 1929–1970: A Brief Review.
13. Association for World Peace: *War on Want: A Plan for World Development*, 1952.
14. UN Experts Committee Report: *Measures for the Economic Development of Under-developed Countries*, 1951.
15. Harold Wilson, *The War on World Poverty* (London: Victor Gollancz Ltd), 1953.
16. White Paper 1957 (Cmnd 237): The Role of the United Kingdom in Commonwealth Development.
17. White Paper 1960 (Cmnd 774): Assistance from the United Kingdom for Overseas Development.
18. White Paper 1963 (Cmnd 2147): Aid to Developing Countries.
19. Select Committee on Estimates: Fourth Report, July 1960.
20. White Paper 1962 (Cmnd 1698): A Progress Report by the New Department of Technical Co-operation.
21. *Daily Herald*, 22 January 1964.
22. Hansard, 28 February 1964.
23. Fabian Society Working Papers, May and July 1964.
24. Anne Perkins, *Red Queen: the Authorised Biography of Barbara Castle* (London: Macmillan), 2003.
25. Ben Pimlott, *Harold Wilson* (London: Harper Collins), 1992.

26. White Paper 1965 (Cmnd 2736): Overseas Development: The Work of the New Ministry.
27. Barbara Castle, *Fighting All the Way* (London: Macmillan), 1993.
28. Lisa Martineau, *Politics and Power. Barbara Castle: a Biography* (London: Andre Deutsch), 2000.
29. White Paper 1975 (Cmnd 6270): The Changing Emphasis in British Aid Policies: More Help to the Poorest.
30. Judith Hart, *Aid and Liberation: A Socialist Study of Aid Policies* (London: Victor Gollancz), 1973.
31. White Paper 1997 (Cmnd 3789): Eliminating World Poverty: A Challenge for the 21st Century.
32. Clare Short, *An Honourable Deception? New Labour, Iraq, and the Misuse of Power* (London: The Free Press), 2004.
33. OECD/DAC Paris, 'Shaping the 21st Century: Contribution of Development Co-operation', May 1996.
34. White Paper 2000 (Cmnd 5006): Eliminating World Poverty, Making Globalisation Work for the Poor.
35. White Paper 2006 (Cmnd 6876): Eliminating World Poverty: Making Governance Work for the Poor.
36. White Paper 2009 (Cmnd 7656): Eliminating World Poverty: Building our Common Future.
37. PSA Delivery Agreement 29: Reduce Poverty in Poorer Countries through Quicker Progress towards the Millennium Development Goals, October 2007.
38. The Coalition: Our Programme for Government. Cabinet Office ref 401238/0510, May 2010.
39. DFID, Draft Structural Reform Plan, 27 July 2010.
40. DFID, UK Aid: Changing Lives, Delivering Results, March 2011.
41. Harry G. Johnson, *Economic Policies towards Less Developed Countries* (London: George Allen & Unwin Ltd), 1967, Chapter III.
42. Robert Bates, *Markets and States in Tropical Africa: The Political Basis of Agricultural Policies* (Berkeley: University of California Press), 2005, first published 1981.
43. Evsey Domar, 'Expansion and Employment', *American Economic Review*, vol. 37, March 1957, pp. 34–55; Roy Harrod, 'An Essay in Dynamic Theory', *Economic Journal*, vol. 39, March 1939, pp. 14–33.
44. W. W. Rostow, *The Stages of Economic Growth* (Cambridge: Cambridge University Press), 1956.
45. W. A. Lewis, *The Theory of Economic Growth* (Homewood: Irwin), 1955; 'Economic Development with Unlimited Supplies of Labour', *The Manchester School*, vol. 22, no. 2, May 1954, pp. 139–191.
46. P. Rosenstein-Rodan, 'Problems of the Indistrialisation of Eastern and South Eastern Europe', *Economic Journal*, vol. 53, no. 210/11, 1943, pp. 201–211.
47. H. B. Chenery, M. S. Ahlawalia, C. L. G. Bell, J. H. Duloy and R. Jolly, *Redistribution with Growth* (London: Oxford University Press), 1974.
48. Frances Stewart, *Basic Needs in Developing Countries* (Baltimore: Johns Hopkins University Press), 1985.
49. A. K. Sen, *Commodities and Capabilities* (Oxford: Oxford University Press), 1985; *Development as Freedom* (Oxford: Oxford University Press), 1999.

50  A. K. Sen, Paper presented to the IAB Conference on Development Thinking and Practice and the Beginning of the Twenty First Century, 1999.

51. Robert Chambers, 'The Origins and Practice of Participatory Rural Appraisal', *World Development*, vol. 21, no. 7, 1994; PRA Challenges: Potentials and Paradigms: *World Development*, vol. 22, no. 7, 1995; *Whose Reality Counts? Putting the First Last* (London: Intermediate Technology Publications), 1997.

52. Frances Stewart, Ruhi Saith and Barbara Harriss-White (eds), *Defining Poverty in the Developing World* (Basingstoke: Palgrave Macmillan), 2007.

53. World Commission on Environment and Development, *Our Common Future* (Oxford: Oxford University Press), 1987.

54. Robert Chambers and Gordon Conway, 'Sustainable Rural Livelihoods: Practical Concepts for the 21st Century', February 1992.

55. A. K. Sen, *Poverty and Famines: an Essay on Entitlement and Deprivation* (Oxford: Clarendon Press),1981; *Resources, Values and Development* (Oxford: Basil Blackwell (1984); *The Standard of Living* (Cambridge: Cambridge University Press), 1987.

56. John Williamson, *The Political Economy of Reform* (Washington, DC: Institute of International Economics), 1994.

57. Readers interested in critiques of early IMF programmes may refer to the following: Tony Killick (ed.), *The IMF and Stabilisation: Developing Country Experiences* (London: Heinemann Educational Books), 1984; Tony Killick (ed.), *The Adaptive Economy*, (Washington, DC: Economic Development Institution, World Bank), 1993; Tony Killick, *IMF Programmes in Developing Countries* (London: Routledge), 1995.

58. *DAC Peer Review of UK Aid* (Paris: OECD), 1997.

59. Goran Hyden, Julius Court and Kenneth Mease, *Making Sense of Governance* (Boulder: Lynne Rienner), 2004.

60. John Farrington, Rachel Slater and Rebecca Holmes, 'Drivers of Change Analysis: Purpose, Limits and Relevance to the Study', ODI Background Paper, January 2006.

61. *Report of the Commission for Africa*, 2005, published in short version by Penguin Books under the title *Our Common Interest: The Commission for Africa*.

62. Speech by Rt Hon Douglas Alexander, Secretary of State for International Development 'Growth at the Heart of Development', March 2008, at the Institute of Directors, London.

63. DFID, 'A Guide to Social Analysis of Projects in Developing Countries' (1995).

64. Review of Poverty Environment Partnership's work on 'Environment for the MDGs', World Summit 2005.

65. DFID, 'Poverty and the Environment', 2006.

66. DFID, 'Climate Change and Poverty', 2004.

67. *The Economics of Climate Change, The Stern Review*, Nicholas Stern, Cabinet Office, HM Treasury (Cambridge: Cambridge University Press), 2006.

68. David Pedley, *Change in Strategic Influence: DFID's Contribution to Trade Policy*, Evaluation Report EV6, September 2003, available at: www.gov.uk/government/uploads/system/uploads/attachment_data/file/67939/ev644.pdf

69. 'Trade Matters in the Fight against World Poverty' in conjunction with the DTI (www.ubuntu.ie/media/Trade-Matters-DFID.pdf); 'DFID's Work on Trade

and Development 2005–7' (www.eldis.org/vfile/upload/1/document/0708/ DOC19887.pdf).

70. B. K. Gray, *A History of British Philanthropy from the Dissolution of the Monasteries to the Taking of the First Census* (London, 1905; repr. London: Frank Cass, 1967).

71. Dr M. G. Marshall, 'Conflict Trends in Africa, 1946–94: A Macro-comparative Perspective', Centre for Systemic Peace, George Mason University, US, prepared for the British Government. Available at: www.systemicpeace.org/africa/AfricaConflictTrendsMGM2005us.pdf

72. DFID, *Reducing Conflict in Africa: Progress and Challenges*, Africa Conflict Pool Prevention Report, 2001–05 (2006). Available at: www.humansecuritygate-way.com/documents/DFID_ReducingConflict_Africa.pdf

73. For a readable account of events on the island during this time see Phil Davidson's *Volcano in Paradise* (London: Methuen), 2003.

74. DFID, *Saving Lives, Relieving Suffering, Protecting Dignity: DFID's Humanitarian Policy*, 2006, available at: http://webarchive.nationalarchives.gov.uk/+/http:/www.dfid.gov.uk/Documents/publications/humanitarian-policy.pdf

75. DFID, Lord (Paddy) Ashdown, Humanitarian Emergency Response Review (2011), available at: www.gov.uk/government/uploads/system/uploads/attachment_data/file/67579/HERR.pdf; DFID, Humanitarian Emergency Response Review: Government Response (2011), available at: www.gov.uk/government/uploads/system/uploads/attachment_data/file/67489/hum-emer-resp-rev-uk-gvmt-resp.pdf

76. The 1999 and 2000 papers are: DFID Institutional Strategy Paper: 'Working with the United Nations for International Development', 1999. DFID Institutional Strategy Paper, 'Working in Partnership with the United Nations Development Programme', 2000.

77. Speech delivered at the Inaugural Meeting of the British Council at St James's Palace, 2 July 1935, BW 2/61, F243, GB/4/43.

78. Cmnd 9138 (1954): Report of the Independent Committee of Enquiry into the Overseas Information Services.

79. Report of the Official Committee on the Teaching of English Overseas, Ministry of Education, March 1956.

80. White Paper 1957 (Cmnd 225): The Hill Report on Overseas Information Services.

81. *Overseas Posts: An Examination of Their Role as Export Promoters*, Central Policy Review Staff, Review of Overseas Representation 1977 (The Berrill Report). Available at National Archives (www.nationalarchives.gov.uk), piece FV 75/25.

82. White Paper 1978 (Cmnd 7308): The United Kingdom's Overseas Representation.

83. Report on Non-Department Public Bodies (Cmnd 7797), January 1980.

84. Review of the British Council by Lord Seebohm, Lord Chorley and Mr Richard Auty (The Seebohm Report), March 1981.

85. Government's Response to Select Committee 1982/83 Session Report (Cmnd 8857), April 1983.

86. CDC High Level Business Plan 2011–15, March 2011.

87. For a fuller account of the early history of the Crown Agents, see A. W. Abbott CMG CBE, *A Short History of the Crown Agents and Their Office* (London: Chiswick Press), 1959.

88. *Report of the Stevenson Committee* (1972), published 1 December 1977 (London: HMSO).
89. *Report of the Faye Committee of Inquiry into Crown Agents* (1975), published 1 December 1977 (London: HMSO).
90. White Paper 1976 (Cmnd 6445): Future of Crown Agents.
91. *Report of Tribunal of Enquiry into Crown Agents*, published 26 May 1982 (London: HMSO).
92. B. P. Uvarov, *Grasshoppers and Locusts*, Volume 1 (Cambridge: Cambridge University Press), 1966.
93. W. Thesiger, *Arabian Sands* (London: Longmans, Green and Co), 1959.
94. Cmnd 9003, July 1983.
95. C. J. Jepma, *The Tying of Aid* (Paris: OECD), 1991.
96. Aid and Trade Provisions, HL Deb 17 June 1993 vol 546 cc82-3WA. Available at: http://hansard.millbanksystems.com/written_answers/1993/jun/17/aid-and-trade-provisions
97. PAC 17th Report, Session 1993–94 (HC 155): Pergau Hydro-electric Project.
98. FAC 3rd Report, Session 1993–94 (HC 271-I).
99. T. Lankester, *The Politics and Economics of Britain's Foreign Aid Policy: The Pergau Dam Affair* (London: Routledge), 2012.
100. Commission on International Development, *Partners in Development: Report of the Commission on International Development* (The Pearson Report), 1969.
101. H. B. Chenery and A. M. Stout, 'Foreign Assistance and Economic Development', *American Economic Review*, vol. 56, no. 4, 1966, pp. 679–733.
102. M. A. Clemens and T. J. Moss, 'Ghost of 0.7%: Origins and Relevance of the International Aid Target', Centre for Global Development Working Paper 68, September 2005.
103. For a fuller account of civil service reform in recent decades see: Peter Hennessy, *Whitehall* (London: Secker and Warburg), 1989; Kevin Theakson, *The Civil Service since 1945* (Oxford: Blackwell), 1995; Michael Barber, *Instructions to Deliver* (London: Methuen), 2007.
104. *Improving Management in Government: the Next Steps: Report to the Prime Minister* (London HMSO), 1988.
105. White Paper, 1994 (Cm 2627): Continuity and Change; White Paper, 1996 (Cm 3331): Development and Training for Civil Servants: a Framework for Action; White Paper 1999 (Cmnd 4310): Modernising Government.
106. 'The Use of Science in UK International Development Policy', 2004 (HC 133–1).
107. Roger Riddell, *Does Foreign Aid Really Work?* (Oxford: Oxford University Press), 2007.
108. P. T. Bauer, *Dissent on Development* (Cambridge, MA: Harvard University Press), 1972.
109. World Bank, *Assessing Aid: What Works, What Doesn't, and Why* (New York: Oxford University Press), 1998.
110. D. Dollar and A. C. Burnside, 'Aid, the Incentive Regime and Poverty Reduction', World Bank Policy Research Paper No. 1937 (1998); P. Collier and D. Dollar: 'Aid Allocation and Poverty Reduction', World Bank Policy Research Paper No. 2041 (1999); P. Collier and D. Dollar, 'Aid Allocation and Poverty Reduction', World Bank Policy Research Mimeo, April 1999.

111. DFID, 'Assessing Aid and the Collier/Dollar Poverty Efficient Aid Allocations: A Critique', by Jonathon Benyon, December 1999.
112. DFID, 'How Effective is DFID?', November 2003.
113. DFID, 'An Evaluation of British Aid to Primary Schooling', Evaluation Report 639, September 2002.
114. NAO Report (HC 1311) Session 2005–06: DFID Working with Non-Governmental and other Civil Society Organisations, HC 1311 Session 2005–06.
115. NAO Report (HC 124–1): Third Report of Session 2004–05.
116. NAO Report (HC 351): Maximising Impact in the Water Sector.
117. NAO Report (HC 664): Responding to HIV/AIDS.
118. NAO Report (HC 69): Bilateral Support to Primary Education.
119. NAO Report (HC 739): Performance Management – Helping to Reduce World Poverty, April 2002.
120. NAO Report (HC 6): Providing Budget Support to Developing Countries, February 2008.
121. Third Report of Session 2006–07, HC 228.
122. OECD, *Declaration on Aid Effectiveness* (Paris: OECD), 2005.
123. DFID, *Independent Evaluation in DFID: Annual Report 2007/8* (EV695). Available at: www.gov.uk/government/publications/independent-evaluation-in-dfid-annual-report-2007-08-ev695
124. *DAC Peer Review of UK Aid* (Paris: OECD), 2006.
125. William Easterly and Tobias Pfutze, 'Where Does the Money Go? Best and Worst Practices in Foreign Aid', *Journal of Economic Perspectives*, vol. 22, no. 2, 2008, pp. 29–52.
126. A. Seldon (ed.), *Blair's Britain* (Cambridge: Cambridge University Press), 2007, especially Chapter 25, 'Development', by Richard Manning, former Director General DFID and Chairman of the DAC; Owen Barder, *Reforming Development Assistance: Lessons from the UK Experience* (London: Centre for Global Development), 2005.

# Index

Printed and bound by CPI Group (UK) Ltd, Croydon, CR0 4YY